**Teaching *Hamlet*
as My Father Died**

Published by Lisa Hagan Books 2020

Powered by

SHADOW
TEAMS

Copyright © Erica W. Cantley 2020

ISBN: 978-1-945962-31-8

Interior layout by Simon Hartshorne

Teaching *Hamlet* as My Father Died

Erica W. Cantley

More Advance Praise for *Teaching HAMLET as My Father Died*

In *Teaching Hamlet as My Father Died*, Erica Cantley seamlessly interweaves a profound personal loss with the literary themes and archetypal insights of Shakespeare's *Hamlet*. Through her artful yet vulnerable storytelling, she communicates both the ephemeral nature of life and the mysterious timelessness of love.

— Lisa Oz, author *US: Transforming Ourselves
and the Relationships that Matter Most*

Anyone who performs, or teaches, or speaks for a living is all too familiar with the implication that "the show must go on". Cleverly structured and gently written, [*Teaching Hamlet*] is a terrific read. I found myself jealous of the lucky students in her class, and immediately wanted to share it with my own father. A very special book indeed.

— Conor Hanratty, host of *The Hamlet Podcast*

A *Dead Poets Society* for a new age, Erica Cantley's *Teaching Hamlet as My Father Died* is an illumination of grief as commensurate with love, the reading of Shakespeare, and the art of teaching. To enter Cantley's high-school classroom is to glimpse the skill and heroism of our greatest teachers whose stages face more audiences a week than Broadway, and whose patrons require more than diversion for the price of their ticket. Cantley's students form an inspiring cast of characters whose existences celebrate the very condition criticized by Hamlet while her own dying father demonstrates that a good life can be even better than a great one. As page-turning as it is profound, to read this book is to experience an increase of love for our mortal coil and the opportunities for meaning that may be life's only guarantee.

— Cassandra Csencsitz, New York-based arts and commercial writer, publisher of *Alcoholite at the Altar: The Writer and Addiction*

This is partly a book about life lessons —perhaps the most obvious of which is, "being human is complicated" —revealed through the framework of Cantley's classroom curriculum and "this play obsessed with death." But at its core, *Teaching Hamlet as My Father Died* is a love story. One that celebrates the affection of a dynamic teacher for her subject and students, and the ever-deepening appreciation of a free-spirited daughter for her father, "a bird of quiet nobility, if you paid attention." Maybe most importantly, it's a story honoring "the magic between love and loss," an idea that contains all the bittersweet beauty of our human legacy.

— Karen Bussen, CEO Farewelling, Celebrating a Beautiful Life Beautifully

Contents

Even in our sleep, pain which cannot forget falls drop by drop upon the heart until, in our despair, against our will, comes wisdom through the awful grace of God.

~ Aeschylus

The book of life is brief
And once a page is read
All but love is dead
That is my belief

~ Don McLean

Life moves pretty fast.
If you don't stop and look around once in a while, you could miss it.

~ Ferris Bueller

For Esther Yardumian-Smyth,
Who gave me *Hamlet*
&
Emily Finkeldey Ballard,
Who gave me my father

ON QUOTING SHAKESPEARE

All citations from *Hamlet* come from the Folger Shakespeare Library edition of *Hamlet*, edited by Barbara A. Mowat and Paul Werstine, which is the edition I use to teach high school students. Folger Shakespeare Library print editions feature detailed notes from the world's leading center for Shakespeare studies, and use a variety of punctuation signals to distinguish between the First Folio and Second Quarto version of *Hamlet*. For ease of reading, I have eliminated these punctuation signals. The text of the play appears here in italics, and I have enclosed stage directions in brackets. Line number references from *Hamlet* and Shakespeare's other plays come from the Folger print and Folger Digital Texts online version of the texts, which are identical. Folger Digital Texts are free and a wonderful way to quickly access meticulously accurate texts from the Folger Shakespeare Library editions. Any inconsistencies or inaccuracies are mine alone.

AUTHOR'S NOTE

I have endeavored to re-create classroom experiences and student interactions from my memories of them. The students featured here are pastiche characters based on hundreds of students I've taught over the years. I have changed their names, and changed and combined identifying characteristics and details such as physical properties, places of residence, and life experiences. Any resemblance to actual persons, living or dead, is purely coincidental.

EWC

PROLOGUE

All the world's a stage

All the world's a stage,
And all the men and women merely players.
They have their exits and their entrances,
And one man in his time plays many parts,
His acts being seven ages. At first the infant,
Mewling and puking in the nurse's arms.
Then the whining schoolboy with his satchel
And shining morning face, creeping like snail
Unwillingly to school.

(As You Like It 2.7.146-54)

It was a dreary March morning and I was waiting for my father to die.

Decades of dread and mental preparation had led to this moment. I always assumed my dad would die young, like his father did. But he was 77, and still with us.

I shrunk down in my office chair, my salt-stained suede snow boots up on my desk and my big black sleeping bag coat still on. I stared down into the turquoise Ball jar of lukewarm coffee I was cupping with both hands. I was cold. And tired. Not in the mood to teach. Or breathe, for that matter.

Early that morning a heavy foreboding settled atop my down comforter and made it harder than usual to get out of bed. How was I going to stand up and teach about dead dads, bones, and graves, when my own Dad had been told "There's nothing else we can do for you"? He might hang on for weeks or even months, but my father's time was running out. He was due to *shuffle off this mortal coil* anon.

> —*aye, there's the rub,*
> *For in that sleep of death, what dreams may come,*
> *When we have shuffled off this mortal coil,*
> *Must give us pause.*
>   (3.1.73-76)

"*Give us pause* means make us stop and think," I explain every time I teach *To be or not to be*. "Think about what we're doing, and whether it might cause us regret later. And in Hamlet's case, also think about what he's *not* doing."

Hamlet. *Hamlet.*

Teaching *Hamlet* to high school Seniors in their spring term is such a privilege; I've got to be on top of my game. For most of the students, this is their first exposure to *Hamlet*. For some it's their first Shakespeare play ever. My teaching can't be flat. It has to be inspirational: evangelical, even.

But I was not in the mood to be onstage.

Stage.

All the world's a stage…. Yep, yep, and I must play my part. Excitable English teacher. Shakespeare fanatic. *Hamlet* obsessive. For me, teaching Shakespeare is both indulgence and responsibility. Most days teaching *Hamlet* I feel like I'm on Mr. Toad's Wild Ride. There is so much to squeeze in and never enough time. I keep thinking, they have to get this! They can't walk away from my class thinking Shakespeare is boring or inaccessible. I want them to fall for Shakespeare the way I did.

"We can't possibly get to it all," I tell them every year before we start. How can we? I've been teaching *Hamlet* for years and I have still barely begun to unravel all the play has to offer. Kind of like how I've been anticipating my dad's death for years….

Now that my father's death was imminent, I leapfrogged over acceptance and into a quagmire of questioning. I spent my whole life knowing my beloved father was going to die and wondering when it would happen. Why didn't I just spend more time with him while he was alive? Why hadn't I gone to Costa Rica once a year instead of every other year? Why didn't I fight harder against death? Make him take herbal remedies or do cleanses? Why hadn't I been more like his wife Maureen and refuse to even think about life without him?

Maureen and my sister Paige always seemed in denial of my father's inevitable death. But I was realistic. My cancer-ridden Dad, whose bones were crumbling, and who still smoked almost a pack of unfiltered cigarettes a day, was going to die. What was the point of being pissed at the disease? We had him longer than many people have their parents. As Gertrude, Hamlet's mother, tells him:

> *'tis common; all that lives must die, passing*
> *through nature to eternity*
>   (1.2.74-75).

My office clock said it was time to get ready, but I felt paralyzed. I still had my feet up and my coat on and I was getting sweaty. Hey, that's a *Hamlet* word—*sweaty.*

> *What might be toward that this sweaty haste*
> *Doth make the night joint-laborer with the day?*
>   (1.1.88-89)

Act 1: scene 1, on the platform with the guards and Horatio. *Sweaty haste.* What great imagery. I never noticed that before. I was in sweaty non-haste. I walked across the wall-to-wall carpeted hallway to my classroom, opened the *Hamlet* Day One file I had left on the podium, scrawled a quick "sweaty haste" at the top of the first page of light blue printer paper, and circled it.

I loved those moments before school starts. The halls were still quiet, desks were nice and straight, and the yellow words I chalked up there yesterday looked crisp against the clean mint-colored surface. I'm one of the last teachers who has a real chalkboard.

At the center of the chalkboard was written in big block letters:

Who's there?

The enigmatic first line of Shakespeare's most esteemed play.

On my big wooden desk was a collection of swords and a blue plastic trash bag with the ingredients for a ghost costume. Everything was in order. I had come in the night before to get it all set up. I don't do well first thing in the morning. Especially these days.

I stood behind the podium and looked across the empty classroom out the windows. The sun was streaming in politely right now, but by the time class started it would be shining right in my eyes, so I lowered the shades to leave only about 18 inches of back campus visible. This was a good classroom. And a good stage.

I don't think my father ever saw this classroom. Or if he did, he's never seen me teach. How odd. He's with me all the time. We've had so many phone conversations in this room, or in my office across the hall. Making plans, sharing updates. Hanging up and wondering when he was going to turn that corner you don't come back from. At some point, probably not too long from now, I'm going to be standing here in my classroom or office on a Monday morning getting ready to teach, and he will be dead. And then he'll be dead every other Monday after that for the rest of my life.

Everyone at school knew my dad was dying. Hamlet was away at school when his dad died, too. But I'd gotten far more sympathy and attention from my colleagues and students than Hamlet ever gets, and my dad hadn't even died yet!

What if I find out when I'm at school? I imagined myself walking like a stunned accident victim down to the principal's office and saying: "I have to go. My dad just died. My students are doing silent reading. Someone take over."

"Miss Erica," said a voice from my classroom doorway. "Are you okay?" It was one of the teachers from down the hall. I shrugged my shoulders and looked away.

"Why didn't you just stay down in Costa Rica with your dad?" she asked. "Someone would sub for you." She was not the first person who asked me this question since I got back from visiting my father. I knew they meant to be sympathetic, but these friends were sowing unwanted seeds in my conscience. Would I feel better about my father dying if I were there to watch it? Was I a horrible person not to be there? Or to not want to be there? Who says goodbye to their dying father, gets on a bus, then into a cab, then onto a plane, another plane, then a train, and finally a car ride back home? Who does that?

> *Who calls me villain? Breaks my pate across?*
> (2.2.599)

No, that's not until Act 2.2.

The kind of person who has to get back to work, that's who. My sister, uncle and I had to get back to our jobs. Was I wrong to be back in Pennsylvania, working, going to grad school, making salads for my husband, opening the back door for the dog, living my life?

Two weeks ago my sister, uncle and I had set up camp at my father's hilltop retirement paradise in Costa Rica for a week. Despite the uncomfortable beds, disappointing coffee, and specter of death, we had a great visit. His wife Maureen said it was Dad's "last good week." We got to say goodbye. Some people, like Hamlet, don't even get to say goodbye. And then we left. And then my dad got much worse. And now I was here, in suburban Philadelphia, wondering when I was going to get the call. How far into teaching *Hamlet* would I be when it was time to send out group texts to my friends with the message "My father has *shuffled off this mortal coil*"? (Yes, that was my plan.) Would he be in the grave long before the graveyard scene?

What happens if I start crying in front of the students?

Okay, stop thinking about Dad.

Dad, Dad, Dad....

I had to get my head straight. Focus on the text. Think about Hamlet. Teaching *Hamlet*.

It was 7:30 and I needed to go down to the teachers' lounge to reheat my oatmeal and coffee. Chapel was in half an hour. The precious twenty minutes I spent at my desk having breakfast, checking my lists, and looking at emails was what I'd been looking forward to since I slouched out of bed and crept unwillingly the 800 steps uphill to school.

ACT ONE

Thou know'st 'tis common; all that lives must die
Passing through nature to eternity

(1.2.74-75)

1:1

Who's there?

(1.1.1)

The four-minute warning bell rang and students trickled in.

"Miss Erica," called out Catherine, a tall bespectacled blonde with a reliably cheerful personality, as she crossed the threshold. "It's *Hamlet* today—are you psyched?"

Hamlet.

Psyched.

I should be. I usually am.

But not today. Not this week, or even this month. I wanted to curl up in a fetal position and have someone else take over. I gave her a weak smile and said, "You know it." As Catherine passed the podium she leaned in conspiratorially and said, "The boys are scared."

"Really? Even after last week?"

"Just a few, I guess. I heard some complaining the reading was hard and they already didn't understand what's going on."

That made me smile for real. My job was to help them understand. Time to forget about my dying Dad and do my job.

My classroom had a variety of desk/chair combinations to choose from: six stand-up desks with stools (three in each of the back corners by the windows), two right-handed chair desks, and eight traditional table-style desks; there were three hard red plastic-covered metal rocking chairs, one cushy, low-rider, royal blue rolling office chair (a popular power seat), two red rubber exercise balls, and the rest of the chairs were retro industrial metal with thin black Naugahyde covered seats. The desks were set up in a three-sided rectangle along the sides and back wall of the classroom.

The U-formation of desks created an 8 x 10' "stage" where we stood up, paced, recited soliloquies, acted out scenes, and—one day, at the end of Act 4—sent each of the characters to therapy. The setup was perfect for those activities, but to see all the students I had to swing my gaze from side to side, and when I looked at students on one side of the room I couldn't see the other side at all.

This was our fifth class together. Last week we warmed up to Shakespeare's language with an overview of the sonnets and iambic pentameter. I had been teaching the girls all year, and many of them Sophomore year as well. Spring term Senior year we mix the Boys and Girls English classes together. The boys and I were still getting to know each other, and the new classroom dynamic was starting to gel.

The bell rang and the students stood up.

"Good morning everyone," I said in my usual cheerful refrain, minus about 75 percent of the energy and enthusiasm.

"Good morning Miss Erica," they responded dutifully.

"Okay, please be seated," I nodded.

Feona (who was a shoo-in for the English Award, unless she completely crumbled between now and the end of the year) sat in the far-left corner in one of the high desks. She was the only girl whose level of contribution to class had remained consistent all year long. She seemed to remember everything she ever read or learned, and her personality was as confident and buoyant as her dark auburn mane of curls.

Two other candidates for the English Award were Catherine and Meredith: local girls who had been besties since before kindergarten and were always academically neck-and-neck for the top overall GPA in their class. They sat along the back row at about one o'clock and tended to hold off raising their hands until I was desperate for someone to answer, but they each always had something on point—and often insightful—to say.

Jerome, a dorm boy and basketball player from Jamaica, Queens, had chosen the desk on my right by the door, and chances were, like everyone else, he would stay in that seat for the rest of our time together. He had a wide, warm smile that went all the way to his dark eyes, and he did a very nice job on his sonnet presentation—their initial assignment for the class. It was too soon to tell how he would take to *Hamlet*.

"Where in Queens are you from?" I had asked him on the first day.

"I'm actually from Fort Greene, where Spike Lee's from," he said. "Except we moved to Queens."

"I love Spike Lee!"

He lit up. "I saw him in Primo's diner on Lafayette once."

"No way!"

"Yep. He was just picking up takeout."

"Cool. Where in Queens are you?" I asked, trying to keep the NYC bonding going. "My cousins live in Long Island City, right next to the Pepsi sign."

"Oh yeah, I know where that is," he said. "It's nice there."

Back on the far-left side of the room, directly across from Jerome, was Albert, who gave off a quirky, mad scientist vibe. He had almost white Justin Bieber-ish hair going all over the place and was prone to throwing his long arm way out and up in front of him to answer a question. He had already been quoting lines from the play.

Along that row, between the intellectual lynch pins of Albert and Feona, sat Mei-Mei, Sage, and Diane, who were good English students doing solid work, but so far this term I had to call on them: they weren't raising their hands. Not sure if they had Senioritis or were just hesitant to speak up now that boys were in the room.

To the right of Jerome were two Canadians, Duncan and Vincent. So far both were somewhat taciturn. Duncan had a huge, deep voice, a full beard, and had been described to me by Mr. Reuter, the Senior Boys English teacher, as someone who "could live as a wood cutter in the great white north and be so happy just helping a deer with a broken hoof, nursing it back to health." Doug Reuter and I met before the beginning of spring term every year to tell each other what to expect from the students we'd be sending each other. "Duncan's a gentle giant. And it's impossible not to love that voice."

Vincent had thick dark bangs that sliced just over the edge of his black framed glasses. The top of Vincent's head reached Duncan's shoulder. By the time I met the boys I usually forgot what Doug had told me about them, but I remember he pegged Vincent as "quietly hilarious. His presentation is so subtle that it's easy to forget he's even around."

Wedged into the far-right corner at a high desk between Vincent and Jimmy Wong was Gino, a lighthearted, shiny-faced linebacker with a Greek last name and a terrific Italian accent. Ciao, Gino! Che fai, bello? Like my predecessor, Mrs. Esther, I spoke Italian in class whenever possible.

Jimmy Wong was a short, bespeckled dorm boy from Korea: very funny and obviously a cult figure among his classmates. He had gotten grandiose reciting John Keats' "Bright Star" last week, but he also frequently nodded off, so I was going to have to keep an eye on him. I had two other sleepers: Mei-Mei and Coleman. Mei-Mei was a hard-working, energetic little girl from Beijing. She had thick chin-length black hair, and I was pretty sure the only reason her eyes kept drooping was because she was the yearbook editor, took all AP classes, and stayed up way past midnight every night. Coleman was a lacrosse player who looked like Michael J. Fox. I'm not sure he would even know who that is, and I doubt he'd appreciate the implication about his height if he did, but he was a cute kid who sat low in his chair and whose head had already bobbed once or twice last week.

In the middle of the back row, between Coleman and Catherine, was Bradley, the Jimmy Stewart-esque son of one of my best friends; and Luis, whose soft-spoken demeanor, and bright, wide smile made him a pleasure to have front and center. Next to Luis sat Imani Ingram who, bless her heart and big brown doe eyes, had done more to make me a better teacher this year than any of the intimidating intellectuals I've taught in the last fifteen years. Imani was usually behind and frequently missed the point, but since we had our big talk last fall, "Double I" and I had a connection. Bradley was a hard worker and conscientious citizen in and out of the classroom. He did the mulching at my house in the spring, paid close attention to what was said in class, and was about as upright and respectful as they come.

Luis reacted to everything I said with an encouraging nod and smile and made great eye contact with his almost-black eyes. I wasn't sure yet whether this was a survival strategy so he wouldn't be called on, or if he was trying to make me feel good about myself. Either way, it was working. Luis had missed the first two days of class and came after school to catch up.

"So, the main thing you missed was iambic pentameter. Have you spent any time with iambic pentameter?"

"I've heard of it," he smiled as one smiles when they hope you'll change the subject. I grappled for a starting place.

"Do you do anything with music? Didn't I see you in Telegrams?" He nodded. "Do you play an instrument?"

"No," he said, "that won't help, I'm a drummer." Ha!

"A drummer, are you serious? Okay then, you're all set," I

said and explained that iambic pentameter is all about rhythm and keeping time. "Ba BUM ba BUM ba BUM ba BUM ba BUM."

Last night they read Act 1: scene 1. In addition to the assigned text, they write five reading responses. Reading responses work well and function on several levels. My students know I want each of them to contribute to our discussion at least once a day, and this way they always have something to say or ask, written down right in front of them. The reading responses also allow me to conduct individual conversations and give me a gauge on what still needs to be addressed the next day in class. I use the reading responses, and the "everyone say something" rule to guide what we talk about each day.

"I have a list of things I want to get to," I told them within the first few days, "and I will make sure that we get to them. Eventually. But I want to know what your questions and interests are. I want your questions to guide what we talk about, since we can only cover so much in twenty days."

As they settled into their chairs, I stood behind my wooden podium on wheels.

"So, how did the first reading go?" I asked, after they were settled.

"Hard." "Weird." "Creepy."

"Good, good. Did anyone watch it on YouTube?" Rumble, grumble, no distinct response. "Did anyone watch a clip of Act 1: scene 1 on YouTube? Anyone?"

Meredith said, "I did."

"So did I," said Feona.

"What version did you watch?" Blank stares. "Kenneth Branagh? David Tennant?"

"Hmm, I'm not sure…"

I pointed to the laminated picture of Tennant playing Hamlet in the BBC movie from 2009. "Was it this one?"

"Yes, that's it," said Meredith.

"Wait, is that the 'Doctor Who' guy?" asked Vincent, perking up. "I love him."

"Yes, exactly!"

"Me, too," said Albert to Vincent, across the room, and they exchanged some enigmatic gesticulation.

"Listen folks, let me tell you my philosophy on reading and studying Shakespeare." I took my book out and opened it. "When we sit down and read a Shakespeare play, we are engaged in an unnatural act." A few heads perked up. "Do you know why?"

"Because it's so old?" asked Gino.

"Ha, ha, no, although you're right, the language is not what we're used to. Anyone else? Why is it unnatural to be reading a Shakespeare play? Girls? Remember?"

"Because it's a play and you're supposed to watch it?"

"Yes, Meredith, exactly. Thank you. These plays were written to be performed and watched, not read. In fact, Shakespeare didn't even publish his plays in his lifetime. Four hundred years later, there's much for us to get out of reading these plays, but we can't enjoy the complexity of Shakespeare's words if we have no idea what's happening. My philosophy is, do whatever you can to help yourself understand the basic plot and who's who. Watch scenes on YouTube—I think for your purposes probably the Branagh version is the best. If you watch the scene first and then read it, you will have a much better idea of what is going on, and then you can get more out of the language."

I saw a couple of heads tilt together here and there: otherwise silence.

"Any specific questions before we take the quiz?"

Typically, the first thing we do every day is take a quiz on the previous night's reading. Once all the quizzes are turned in and I have checked their reading responses, I begin.

"Okay, a few things on the docket before we start talking about last night's reading. We need to say a few words about the Elizabethan theater. The Elizabethan era was when who was on the throne?"

"Queen Elizabeth," boomed Duncan.

"Exact-a-mo. Which is most of Shakespeare's artistic life. During the reign of Queen Elizabeth, Shakespeare was a member of the Lord Chamberlain's Men, the premier acting troupe that played to, and was patronized by Queen Elizabeth. When she died, she was replaced by King James and the troupe became the King's Men. We are going to talk about the difference between theater in Shakespeare's time and today. What do you already know was different about the theater-going experience 400 years ago?" The girls covered this in the fall with *The Taming of the Shrew*, and Sophomore year with *Much Ado About Nothing*.

"No women actors," called out Double I. I encouraged them to raise their hands and be called on, but I also wanted them to feel they could blurt something out when it occurs to them.

"Right, what else?"

"No electricity," said Sage.

"Yes, and so, guys, you get in on this too" I encouraged. "If there is no electricity, what else don't they have that is a big part of the theater today?"

"Lights!" said Coleman, "heh, heh."

"Don't laugh. You're right, and no lights is a big deal. Ladies, what did they have to do since they had no lights? Feona?"

"That's why The Globe theater had no ceiling," she explained. "To let the light in. And they had their plays at 2PM, before it got dark."

"Good memory, thank you!" We went on to talk a little bit more about how the groundlings had to stand (those were the cheapest spots and closest to the stage), and how there was no sound amplification, and minimal props. Now that they were warmed up, I went on.

"Why Shakespeare?" I always ask on Day One of the play. "Anyone? Why do you read Shakespeare?"

"Because we have to," someone said with a sigh.

"Because it's classic," said Bradley.

"Because it's school," said my Michael J. Fox look alike.

"Ahh!" I pointed my finger to the ceiling, "I think you may be onto something there, Coleman." He gave me a single nod of the head. I try to use their names as many times as possible during the first few days to help me memorize them. "Coleman said we read Shakespeare because it's school, and we all know that school is where you read stuff that you wouldn't read otherwise. Do you think there's a method to that madness?" I use that phrase once or twice—not more though—before we get to where Polonius says *Though this is madness, yet there is method in 't*, so the contemporary version of the saying is fresh in their minds (2.2.13-14).

I continued, "the main reason we should read the classics is that all of history's great storytellers knew these stories. The people who are busy creating the culture you consume today—TV, movies, books, graphic novels—know the *Odyssey*, and *Hamlet*, and clearly today's storytellers know their mythology and fairy tales. If you're interested in telling stories for a living —or writing about any aspect of our culture, including sports, food, travel, art, dance—you need to have a basic knowledge of classic literature." It was looking like I had already lost them, so I started reciting:

To be, or not to be: that is the question:
Whether 'tis nobler in the mind to suffer
The slings and arrows of outrageous fortune,
Or to take arms against a sea of troubles,
And by opposing end them? To die: to sleep…
NO MORE—
  (3.1.64-69)

Around the third line I started to see eyes opening and a few bodies sitting forward in their chairs. Ha—it worked. Students don't need me explaining stuff to them. They just need to hear and speak Shakespeare's words.

I raised my arms in the air. "It's fun to know things! Memorize some great lines of Shakespeare. It's the furniture of the soul. It's for your own private museum, right in here," I said, tapping the side of my head. Furniture of the soul; your own private museum: I stole those from Mrs. Esther. "Hey!" I added, feeling generous, "I'll give you extra credit if you memorize those first five lines."

"Really?" a chorus of three or four voices sang out.

"Sure."

"Umm, can we go over the quiz questions?" asked Mei-Mei, who always wanted to know whether she'd gotten it right.

"Absolutely. What is the first line of the play and what did you say you thought it meant?" Nothing, nothing…I scanned the desks and bodies: nothing. The play's first line *Who's there?* is spoken by an anxious watchman at the gate and captures the tension that surrounds Denmark at the play's opening.

"Nobody got that?" I asked. "What's the first line of the play?"

"*Who's there*," a few muttered.

"Right. Gino, what do you think? What's the significance of *Who's there?*"

"He's trying to find out who's there?" his voice wasn't as booming as Duncan's, but it was still deep.

"Yes, yes," I said, "but it's Shakespeare so let's dig for a deeper meaning than that. For example, the line could be interpreted existentially: Who's there for us? Who's out there in the universe paying attention? Who's in charge? Or as suggested by critic Harold Bloom, Who's there for Hamlet?"

I didn't want to get too far ahead of myself since they hadn't even met Hamlet yet. I was tempted to talk about how, as far as the text tells us, the only warm relationship Hamlet remembers from his childhood was with Yorick, the king's jester. Hamlet reflects on how his queen-mother and his Herculean king-father doted on each other, but never mentions any memories of playing or living with them. Or Claudius for that matter.

"We can imagine a young prince might spend more time with a nanny, or the court clown, than with his royal parents. There is much backstory left out of *Hamlet*, and the text poses many unanswered questions. As in any good story, what is omitted can be as significant as what is included."

"What did you say about why the Ghost stalked off—did you get that?"

"It said the *cock crew*," Albert blurted out.

"Yes, good. So what does that mean? What's the point?"

"The sun is coming up," he added, bouncing in his seat.

"So," Vincent asked from across the room, "is the ghost a vampire or something?"

"I don't know," I sort of lied, "what do you guys think?" No answer. "Does that make sense? Based on what we know about ghosts?"

"Yeah," said Jerome slowly. Light bulb: "In movies you pretty much only see ghosts at night!"

"Exactly," I confirmed.

"Listen, here's what you need to do when you're reading this play," I told them, turning to write the points I was about to make on the rolling white board easel behind me.

"Three things. You have to look at what is said, what isn't said," (I wrote "significant omissions" in parentheses) "and what you can infer based on what you know about the characters and about human nature. Since they say the Ghost stalked away when the cock crew, that suggests that, at least in the superstition of Shakespeare's world, ghosts could only come out at night."

"Okay," I continued, "look at your reading responses. Let's hear something from everyone."

"Yes, Feona?"

"I noticed the echoing of 'speak' and 'spoke' throughout the scene and I'm wondering if maybe voice is a theme or motif?"

"Good, what else? Vincent?" Vincent sat next to Gino in the far-right corner, wearing a dark blue hoodie, a thick mop of black hair, and glasses that distorted his eyes. He spoke in a squeaky voice with a slight Canadian accent. He began slowly and with a smirk:

"I'm seeer-i-ously starting to doubt the intelligence of Marcellus," he said, and finished with a self-satisfied smile.

"Interesting...why so?"

"Because he asked if he should strike the ghost," he said, like it was obvious.

"And why does that make him unintelligent?" I prodded.

"Uh, because, it's a ghost," said Vincent.

"So?" He looked at me as if I had asked why you can't punch the sky.

"You can't touch it."

"Why?" I asked. "Because it'll just go right through him?" I suggested.

"Basically."

I set up for our first acting exercise.

"Okay, speaking of ghosts, every production of *Hamlet* tries to make the opening scene as gripping as possible. What will be the first thing the audience sees? What kind of mood must the actors create? What words does Shakespeare use to create the impression of night, darkness, and cold? How will Barnardo deliver his opening lines? How will the audience know it's cold and dark?" No reaction. Nary a hand or a glance my way.

"Forget for a minute whatever deeper significance the words *Who's there?* might hold," I continued. "Why does Barnardo say *Who's there?* Literally, why?"

"He wants to know who's there?" Luis said. Umm, yeah.

"He doesn't know the person," added Bradley.

"Good thinking," I confirmed, "but in a moment it turns out that he does know the person; it's Francisco, and in fact Barnardo was expecting to find Francisco. Why?"

"Because it was midnight?" said Luis.

"Yes. What about midnight?"

"End of his shift," he said.

"EXACTLY, thank you." Like an innate understanding of rhythm, practical logic is very useful in the Shakespeare classroom.

"Okay, so back to the first line," I continued. "Why does Barnardo need to ask *Who's there*? It's midnight…it's cold…what else did you say about the weather in this scene?"

"It's dark!" said Albert.

"He can't see!" said Jerome.

"Yes, exactly. It's dark and he can't see. Here's what we are going to do. We need four people to act out this scene where the Ghost appears."

Hands popped up all around. I picked the first ones I saw— Albert, Coleman (that was a surprise), Gino, and even though he didn't raise his hand, Jimmy Wong because he hadn't said anything

yet today and I wasn't sure how much he was tracking. I told
him to be the Ghost and gave him the blue trash bag containing
a dollar store crown and a bunch of clear trash bags to make a
ghost costume. I gave Gino the swords, and I told Albert to be
Horatio, "You're a scholar." He reached for a sword. "Sorry no
sword. Swords are only for watchmen."

"Aww." He got over his disappointment by borrowing
Vincent's glasses for the role and periodically stroking his chin.

I sent the four actors out into the empty classroom next door
and gave the rest of the class a drawing project illustrating some
of the more obscure passages from the scene.

When I checked on the actors a few minutes later Jimmy
was wrapping himself in plastic bags and already had the crown
on. They were talking and making plans: good sign.

"Okay guys, just make sure that you seem really cold, and
scared, and like you can't see." I turned to Albert. "Horatio, you
are Hamlet's trusted friend. The watchmen have asked you to
be there because you are a scholar, and you have direct access
to Prince Hamlet." He nodded. "Two more minutes then come
back, okay?"

It's Horatio who decides they should tell Hamlet about seeing
the ghost of Hamlet's dead father. Horatio is a good friend. I'm
trying to think, who is my Horatio? My husband Tom is a trusted
advisor. But as far as an analogue to Hamlet's situation, my step-
mother Maureen is the one who has played Horatio for me. For
us. A different type of woman might have kept us in the dark:
kept him to herself. I've heard some devastating stories about
stepmonsters who make it hard or uncomfortable for children
to see their fathers. Not Maureen.

Well, that's not entirely true. She did take him down a Third
World rabbit hole that made it essentially impossible to visit for a

weekend. The upside of the trips he had to make to Florida for his cancer treatments was we got to see him on a regular basis. In retrospect, I wish Maureen had made a bigger deal about how much it would mean to my dad if I had come to visit more often. But at least when the time came, she didn't mince words.

A few days after the doctors said, "there's nothing more we can do," my father went into a decline visible via Skype. Maureen's calls evinced that even she was semi-accepting the end was near. Dad wouldn't be making any more trips to the States for treatments. I was glad I had gone down to Florida to see him in December, and I wished I had gone down in February, too. Stupid.

Now there was no time to wait. Maureen told me to come as soon as possible. I got the message and went down a few days later to Costa Rica. After all these years of preparing myself for my dad to die, the last thing I wanted was to miss saying goodbye to him. I was going to get the timing right on this one.

I told my principal that I'd be taking a week off. At the time I happened to be teaching books with two of literature's greatest fathers: *To Kill a Mockingbird* and *Captain Corelli's Mandolin*. My dad always told me life is better than the best movie, and he was right. You can't make this stuff up. Life paralleling literature. When I returned from Costa Rica it was winter term exam week, then spring break, and my dad was still hanging on. Sometimes he could talk on Skype and sometimes he couldn't. It was undeniable he was deteriorating quickly. He was smoking some of the pot we got him when we were down there, and even taking morphine at night, which he had refused up until now.

Several times a day impending doom washed over me. My father was dying. I called him almost every day, which seemed obvious and awkward; there was not much to say, and he couldn't stay on the phone long. And yet I couldn't believe there was ever a day in my life—much less a week—in which I didn't call him. What a waste.

Jimmy was a hilarious ghost. He stalked around our little stage waving his arms and going "Wooo, wooo…" like a Saturday morning cartoon phantom. He tried to keep a serious face while we were laughing. So far so good. I forgot myself for a while, but soon something reminded me that my dad was dying. I nudged reality away and paid attention to the scene that will outlive me and a million fathers by centuries.

"You don't look that cold, guys," I heckled, and they started hugging their arms and stomping their feet.

The bell rang just as they finished the scene to applause and cheers. Mission accomplished.

1: 2

Your father lost a father,
that father lost, lost his

(1.2.92-93)

The following day I was getting ready to teach Act 1:2. I needed my students to understand what was going on at Elsinore (that Hamlet's father died, and his mother has married her brother-in-law, Hamlet's uncle). It's essential for them to understand the general set up before they move on to read the rest of Act 1.

"Raise your hand if you have an uncle," I said. Hands went up around the room. Almost everyone had an uncle. "Picture your uncle." I paused for a full five seconds. "What kind of uncle is he? Is he the funny uncle? The weird uncle? The black sheep uncle?" I saw their eyes rolling and smiles lifting all 16 faces in the room. "Do you know the word 'avuncular'?" I wrote AVUNCULAR on the board and underlined the UNC. "See the "UNC" in there?" I pointed out. "Someone who is avuncular is uncle-like. An uncle is the person who, God forbid something happens to your dad, would be there for you. Now, imagine your dad dies and a few months later, your mom marries that uncle."

A chorus of "Ewwww!" rang out and I smiled with satisfaction. "Now you know how Hamlet feels."

Besides the big "ewwwww" and a few other bright spots, the morning section felt flat. That always makes me feel like the most boring teacher. I decided next time I would try opening with improv exercises featuring college students whose parents are forbidding their kids to do something they really want to do. I jotted it down on a sticky note and put it on the lesson plan.

From what little I remember of my own high school experience, it was the teachers who were willing to act weird, excited, and overly dramatic who caught my attention. Even if I wasn't really interested in the material, those teachers planted the seed that "This is good stuff—you should know this." So, while I didn't necessarily get why *The Great Gatsby*, or Clytemnestra, or "The Cask of Amontillado" were so great or important, I knew they were worth knowing. In retrospect, I did leave high school with the vague idea books were interesting and important and could help you understand life.

My first year or two here I was shocked to learn that even after a decade teaching the same subject, teachers would still tweak their lesson plans. Why reinvent the wheel once you've got it all set, I thought? They said because the students change and your own interests change. I didn't understand until I had taught for a few years and realized there is no such thing as a perfect lesson plan and each group of students has its own personality. Then new layers in the texts revealed themselves as my circumstances changed. For example, teaching *The Taming of the Shrew* when I was thirty-something and single was much different than as a married woman in my forties.

"What's your impression of Claudius?" I asked.

"Don't like him," said Feona.

"He's a jerk," said Albert.

"Why does he like Laertes better than Hamlet?" piped up Coleman from his slouched down position.

"Ha!" *Ding, ding*, I rang the green buzzer on my podium. "You guys hear that? 'Why does Claudius like Laertes more than Hamlet?' What makes you say that, Coleman?"

"Well, he lets Laertes go back to school but he doesn't let Hamlet." I like this guy. The back-left corner is looking like the logic zone in this class.

"Yes, good noticing. But let's look. Where does Laertes say he wants to go?" I directed the question to the whole class. Someone called out:

"France!"

"Yes, exactly, France. And just to be clear, he doesn't say anything about going to school there. As we will find out in Act 2, there's no indication Laertes is interested in scholarly pursuits. But anyway, back to the question, which is a good one. If you pay attention, this play is full of kids doing their duty and obeying their parental figures. Why does Claudius let Laertes do what he wants, yet doesn't let Hamlet go back to school in Wittenberg?" Wait, wait, I told myself. Let the question hang out there for at least five seconds, which feels like a long time. I saw Diane examining her book.

"Diane, what do you think?"

"I think he's very controlling. And he just cares what it looks like." Nice.

"Hmmm...what do you guys think, does that make sense? Why might it look good for Claudius if Hamlet stays in Denmark? Prince Hamlet wasn't living there before. He was away at school. Yes Feona?"

"Well, first off, Hamlet's mother wants him to stay, so he's trying to make it look like they are one big happy family," said Feona.

I was trying to think if I have any Claudiuses in my life. I'd have to say, thank God, no. I do have stepparents. But my stepfather, Ray, is no Claudius. He's always been supportive without trying too hard. Here Claudius, on the day he is marrying Hamlet's mother, a mere two months after Hamlet's father died, is calling Hamlet "son," and asking Hamlet to look upon him as a father.

"Okay, everybody. Let's take a close look at Claudius's speech to Hamlet, starting at 1.2.90. Let's go around and read it—each of you take a line. Pay close attention to what Claudius says to Hamlet. Remember, Hamlet is depressed, he's dressed all in black at his mother's wedding."

> *'Tis sweet and commendable in your nature, Hamlet,*
> *To give these mourning duties to your father:*
> *But, you must know, your father lost a father;*
> *That father lost, lost his, and the survivor bound*
> *In filial obligation for some term*
> *To do obsequious sorrow: but to persever*
> *In obstinate condolement is a course*
> *Of impious stubbornness. 'Tis unmanly grief.*
>   (1.2.90-98)

And as far as my uncles go, there were no Claudiuses there either. Obviously neither of my father's brothers killed him for his birthright, and neither of them have ever tried to tell me what to do and what not to do. My uncles were there for me as my father's life was winding down. Far from telling me *'tis unmanly grief*, they were sharing the gravity of the impending loss with me. They swooped in like we lived around the corner: like we saw each other once a month instead of once a year at best. Like family. They too, had my father with them all their lives. It had been 54 years since their father died, *your father lost a father*, and sometimes I got the impression that part of each of these brothers had been suspended in time and space since then.

When I decided I was going down to Costa Rica, Uncle Larry said he wanted to come, too. We met at the airport in Charlotte and together made the rest of the trip (comprised of a five-hour flight to San Jose, about two hours to rent a car, and four harrowing hours driving along the highroads) to Casa Cantley. Uncle Larry and I have always had a connection, but we really bonded for life on this trip. We got there on a Tuesday night, and by Thursday, my third night of seven, I'd already had a few moments when I thought, jeez, this is a long time to be in someone else's house in the middle of nowhere. On one hand I wanted to be with my dad forever. On the other, sitting there watching my father's life trickle away was exhausting. The hours he spent with us were ephemeral, and each night when I folded myself into bed I felt like the pointy red hands of a giant clock were stabbing into my gut and throat. Time was in charge. Time was all we had left and not much of it. Why does it seem like knowing how and when something bad is going to happen will somehow make it easier?

The landscape at my father's Third World paradise was steep hills and narrow winding roads surrounded by the deep tropical greens of coffee, cacao, and bananas. Larry and I walked their red-clay dirt road along the mountain ridge every day, trying to get steps, clear our heads, and pass the time while Dad slept. So close to my own father's death, I kept thinking about how it must have been for them.

"It must have been hard to lose your dad at such a young age and never be able to say goodbye."

Your father lost a father, that father lost, lost his.

"You have no idea," Larry said.

After a long pause he added, "Your dad's the closest person to me in the whole world." My throat tightened. "Losing him is going to leave a big hole."

I noticed the way Larry segued from talking about his dad to talking about mine. There has always been a palpable, deep-rooted sorrow and sense of incompletion in their family from losing their father so young.

My grandfather found and ran a successful structural steel company in the 1940s and 50s and died in the back of a cab on the way home from a Philadelphia labor union meeting in 1960. Even though this happened six years before I was born, it was the formative snatch death of my life. My dad was 23 years old, away at the National Guard at Fort Knox, and like Hamlet, had to be called home for his father's funeral. Apparently, the Red Cross had a plane waiting for him. My uncle Larry had been at the movies at the Highway Theater in Jenkintown, and when he got back to his friend's house after the show he was told only "Your Mother called, she wants you to come home." My uncle Walter was at a Phillies game and his name was called over the PA system to come to the information booth. He turned to the woman he was with and said, "It's my father."

I knew it was going to be horrible to lose my father. But to lose such a revered, accomplished, patriarch out of the blue like that in your early twenties without being able to say goodbye. *O horrible, O horrible, most horrible!*

"So, what do you think?" I asked after they finished reading Claudius' lecture to Hamlet.

"Claudius is a jerk," Imani piped up.

"Pretty much," Catherine nodded.

"True," said Meredith.

"Worst stepfather ever," said Bradley.

"Okay," I said, "how long do you think you're going to mourn when your father dies?" This, too, is right out of Mrs. Esther's repertoire. They never look happy when I pose this question.

"A month? Two? Six?" No responses. "Come on. Think about it. How long do you think you're going to be upset about your father dying?" I asked.

"Forever," said Gino, somberly.

"Yeah," said Bradley.

"Definitely," said Feona.

I used to be afraid to mention someone's loss at the wrong moment. Now I appreciate any acknowledgement of what I'm going through like a cool glass of water after a hard workout. I noticed this similar dynamic in Act 1:2, the first time Horatio sees his friend Hamlet since Hamlet's father died. Horatio jokes that the reason he's at Elsinore and not back at University is because he has a *truant disposition*. Sometimes friends think it's better not to bring up the obvious. Maybe Hamlet's not thinking about his dead father this very minute, so why should I say *I came for your father's funeral* and remind him? But when, a few lines later, Hamlet speaks to the subject: *My father! —methinks I see my father,* Horatio responds *I saw him once, he was a goodly king. Goodly king* might sound generic. But every time someone said my father "was such a nice man," I felt like they saw him and understood.

In Hamlet's case, we must remember he is a prince and no doubt used to being surrounded by sycophants telling him how great his royal parents are. When Horatio tells Hamlet his father *was a goodly king*, Hamlet's response seems to downplay his father's greatness: *He was a man, take him for all and all, I shall not look upon his like again.* Every time I speak that line I choke up.

Hamlet, the son of a celebrated warrior king, is obsessed with how death is a great equalizer.

He was a man.

There are great men, famous men; men of means and men of consequence. There are rich, successful fathers; fathers who build fortunes; fathers who are pillars of the community; fathers who are kings; fathers with connections and influence. But in the end, no matter who they were, they all go back into the dirt. When your father dies, most of the time you don't care how accomplished, or average, he was in the eyes of the world; what matters is your own personal loss.

He was a man.

He was my father.

That's Hamlet's way of saying he had his good and his bad parts. He was human. Sadly, only as you get older do you gain some insight into how exhausting being human can be. Why is criticizing and condemning our parents such an essential part of growing up? We can't see ourselves clearly enough yet to know that everything that disappoints us about our parents is part of our own hardwiring. When Hamlet says his Dad, the King, *was a man,* it may seem like Hamlet is telling Horatio, oh my father wasn't that great. But I think Hamlet is lending a certain dignity to the job of being human. And being a parent.

He was a man. And a father. King or not, being human is complicated.

The phenomenon is an all-too-natural cycle: when you're a kid your dad is a hero, an icon, superhuman. Then you get into your twenties and start to see your father's human frailties. You're horrified, maybe even a little disgusted. You thought he was better than that. Then, as you get into your thirties and forties, or start to have your own kids, your perspective shifts again. I think the impact of losing a parent really depends on what stage of the relationship you're in when they die – or disappear. My dad said he had never really talked to his father about life.

"I never really saw him as a man," my father remarked wistfully. "He was always Daddy."

As *a man.* Come to think of it, that is probably a big part of why our grandfather was immortalized as a larger-than-life entity: because they never knew him as anything but "Daddy".

"I was 28 when my dad died," Tom said. "The difference between 24 and 28.... I started to see the human side of my dad when I was around 24. Not the superdad who can do everything, who's invincible, who's got all the answers, who's always there for you." He faded off a bit, as people do when they talk about their dead parents. "Now my dad was just another man," Tom said with wonder.

"You don't know what you don't know."

That is another one of Mrs. Esther's many well-worn phrases. It's one of those magical truisms that opens layers of profound meaning the longer you live and the more you experience. I quote it often and write it on the board as least once a year because (as she also used to say), "We teach best what we most need to learn." But how can I teach these kids to be humble, and to not take their parents for granted? In other words, to not have regrets? I can't, of course. And I guess the point is that most parents are pretty darned forgiving of their children's trespasses. Probably because they remember having committed similar offenses themselves. But it's still gotta hurt.

"He was a man, take him for all and all. I shall not look upon his like again." I banged on the chalkboard with my silver-painted wooden Sword of Truth to call their attention to the line. "What does that mean?" I asked the class. Niente. "Hello….is anybody home?" I raised my voice. "Wake up," I crooned. Still nothing. I was surrounded by an army of droopy eyes and heavy skulls.

"By the way, every time I call your attention to a passage in the text, you should be highlighting it. Increase the resale value of your book! How else are you going to be able to study for the quote identification part of the test?"

"What?" said Gino. "Quote identification? Are you serious?"

"Yes, I'm serious," I said with a smile. "And guess what, you're going to be able to do it. But, let's not get ahead of ourselves. It's only Act 1: scene 2. Everyone needs to get in the habit of looking in the book. My question is, what do you think Hamlet is saying when Horatio says his dead dad was a good king, and Hamlet says in response, yeah *he was a man, take him for all and all,*" and I raised my voice here to repeat the phrase with additional meaning, "*I shall not look upon his like again?*"

Imani raised her hand. "Double I?"

"He won't see anyone like him again?

Meh.

"Yes," I said, encouragingly, "and what does that suggest?"

Niente. Pause, pause, pause...give them a chance.

"What's Hamlet really saying here?" I opened my arms wide in front of my body and turned from one side of the room to the other. Pause, pause, pause.... "Anyone?" I droned.

"No one is like your dad."

"Yes! That's right! Who said that?"

"Me," he said.

"Bradley," Catherine said.

I turned back towards the left side of the three-sided rectangle of desks to the tall, long-limbed blonde, Bradley. You'd think I'd recognize his voice from all the time he has spent working in our backyard. In student mode he seemed laidback and comfortable with the guys but a little less at ease with the girls.

"Yes, Bradley! You got it!" Then I turned my head back and forth again to scan the room. I reached inside the podium, got out my stack of gold star stickers, peeled off one and presented it to him. "Listen, no matter how flawed he may be, you've only got one dad. Once he's gone, he's gone. You won't find anyone else quite like him. And that, of course, can be said about every person who dies." Bradley looked proudly at his star then stuck it to his book.

"The point is, as we saw in Sonnet 73 last week, *This thou perceiv'st that makes thy love more strong / To love that well which thou must leave 'ere long.*"

What I'd really like them to understand is that we can't comprehend the depth behind the philosophical wisdom of these deceptively simple lines until we, too, are about to lose the irreplaceable.

I shall not look upon his like again.

Something squeezed my heart. Then my face. My eyes. My God. I'm never—.

"*I shall not look upon his like again,*" I repeated, for the fifth or sixth time today. "Doesn't that sum it up? Suddenly, when you know you're going to lose something, it becomes more precious to you." I kept pushing away images of my own father and tried to focus on Hamlet and his father.

"Listen up. You can get too big for your britches. You can be more successful, make better business decisions, be more famous, healthier, more popular than your parents, but at the end of the day, you only have one father, and one mother. What makes them special—what makes any individual human being on the planet special—is quite simply a collection of attributes we will not see again once they are gone."

"Amen," said Jerome.

"Amen, brother," I smiled back, and nodded. "What else? Yes Diane?"

"You asked us for favorite lines?" she said, consulting her page of handwritten reading responses.

"Yes!"

"I thought *Thrift, thrift, Horatio. The funeral baked meats did furnish forth the marriage table* was funny. I heard that line before and now I finally know what it means."

"Yes, fabulous! I love that line."

The idea of *funeral baked meats* made me think of cooking for my dad. Both of my parents were good cooks and took food seriously.

Dad was enthusiastic and appreciative about anything he loved. I wish I could have cooked for him more, like every Sunday night if we had ever lived in the same town as adults. Less than a week ago in Costa Rica I had made him a big pot of split pea soup. "My fav-or-ite soup of life!" he'd say. Some he ate while we were there, and a lot of it I packaged up into serving-size containers in the freezer. Maureen later told me he ate it all before he died, "That soup was one of the last things he could eat."

I remember standing above their stove stirring that soup, first the finely chopped onions, then the pea-sized cubes of celery and carrots. Stirring, stirring, looking down into the pot and saying to myself—while they were in the living room watching TV or Dad was taking a nap—this is the last split pea soup I will ever make for my father. What a strange feeling to make soup that will work its way through a body that was going to stop digesting food soon. The familiar aromas of sautéing mirepoix, then the earthy green of the dried peas blending with the salty sweetness of the ham, swathed me in a moment of comfort. Then my eyes looked deep into the pot and dragged my stomach down into a bottomless pit of darkness. Last soup. His fav-or-ite. At least favorite homemade. He loved "pasta fazoul," but I suspect he liked saying it as much as eating it. Not everyone likes split pea soup, but its rustic smell feels so Dad-ly to me.

I heard him clear his voice. Twice.

"Erica," my father announced, sitting at the table bent over the bowl with a spoon in his hand, "you are an excellent split pea soup maker." He sounded exactly like himself: his voice strong and clear. He said it like it was any other day. Like he might have the chance to say it again. My throat tightened.

"Really?" I said from the other side of the counter, my eyes heating up. "Well that's good. I'm...I'm glad you like it, Dad," I managed to say.

"Don't like it. Love it. It's the best split pea soup I've ever had."

That's good, Dad, that's good. I walked around the kitchen counter bar to the dinner table, came up alongside him, and gave him a hug around the shoulders. He leaned into it, putting his arm around my waist, while never letting go of the spoon in his other hand.

The bell rang. I survived another class. There were minutes at a time when I hadn't thought about my dad. Delving into micro details of the plot and mincing the meanings behind Shakespeare's language is nepenthe itself. It's like deseeding a pomegranate. When I go into the text, it demands such attention that within seconds I'm miles away, deep inside the fruit, carefully extracting each shiny seed.

When the room emptied out of students, I walked across the hall to my office and checked my phone. There was a message from Larry. Oh no. I was scared to listen. Maybe I should wait until I was done for the day. Of course I didn't. His message said that Dad had gone to the emergency room that morning in terrible pain. He told me Maureen had made a point of saying that her cell phone wouldn't work for international calls, so there would be no way for her to contact us, or vice versa, until she got back to the house. And she had no intention of going home until she brought Dad with her. This message was a few hours old—for all I knew he had already died. Oh God. I rifled through papers on my desk, checked emails, and finished grading the reading responses for the afternoon section.

Then, in the middle of lunch I had a harrowing experience. It felt like a wave of thick electricity crashed through my torso. Like I had been struck by lightning. It was as if part of me had flown out the window and was, at that very moment, circling above front campus. I was sure he was gone. I literally wailed, my voice sounding like something I never heard before. I grappled towards the window, leaned up against it, searched the gray sky for some great bird or other sign, then watched myself sink slowly down to the ground.

O, O, O, O....

I always thought those seemed anemic last words, especially for one as eloquent as Hamlet, but that's what really comes out sometimes. *O, O, O, O.* I felt for sure my Dad was dead. That my Dad's spirit had just passed through my office, my heart, and my soul on his way out of this world. He came to say goodbye. I always knew it would be like that; or at least I had hoped. That I would know. That I would have "a feeling." I would somehow instinctively know he was on his way.

My heart slid slowly down to my gut. Oh God. I managed to grapple my way to the door, push it closed, and turn off the office light so no one would think I was there.

O, O, O, O, I howled. I felt a prickly sensation on my skin. I was gasping for breath. Was my father dead?

I called their house, just in case. No answer. That could be good. If he were already dead she might be home by now. Though I doubted it. I thought about calling Larry back. He might have heard. She would have called him. And he wouldn't have called me back and left me another message. Especially not the message, "Your dad's dead." I was scared to call him back, but eventually I did. Larry hadn't heard anything. He said he would let me know as soon as he did.

"Okay," said. "Listen, when it happens, I want you to tell me, okay?"

He made a noise. "Okay."

"Maureen can call you, you call me, and I'll call Paige, okay?" I did not want Maureen to tell me. I did not want to listen to her sobbing when I found out.

Shortly after talking to Larry I had to go back to teach. I had harnessed my breath, but my body was covered in freeze-dried sweat. After class I saw a text from my high school friend Laura saying, "I'm so sorry to hear about Matt."

What?

What about Matt? Matt my old boyfriend. The one before Tom. Or before the one before Tom. It was beyond surreal. I simply couldn't believe it. Don't tell me that my old boyfriend and my dad were going to die on the same day. Matt must have died. Why else do people say, "I'm so sorry about so-and-so"? I was sweating and panting. I took my phone and fast walked downstairs and out the front of the building. I called Laura and just paced around the circle in front of the school talking to her for about 20 minutes with no coat on. I had been freezing all winter, but now the cold didn't touch me.

She had seen it on Facebook; I hadn't.

Matt was gone.

My dad, on the other hand, came home from the hospital later that night. They thought maybe he had a kidney stone that was causing all that pain. Okay, he wasn't dead yet, which was a relief. And yet living with the knowledge that he could die any hour strangled my body with constant fear. The suspense kept building and I kept wondering how and when his story was going to end.

1: 3

You speak like a green girl

(1.3.110)

After dinner on Wednesday I went back to school to get ready for Day 3 of *Hamlet.* I used to be able to prep at home, but these days I can't be anywhere near a bed or a couch. Tomorrow was Act 1: 3-5 and based on the reading quizzes, we needed to review who's who and what's going on. The first two scenes of the play build the platform for all the action to come. I couldn't remember which bits I already soliloquized on, and which I glossed over. My mind would seize on a theme in the play, then dart to a thought about my dad. How many more days, how many more hours—or minutes—did he have left? Will he come back as a ghost?

I found eerie solace in the immortality of the text and the questions it raised. How many fathers have died in the four hundred years since this play was written? Millions? How many hearts have erupted in sorrow? Millions more. Maybe billions. Everyone alive today will die—some will die young, some old—but Hamlet and his story will outlive us all. This kind of thinking reduced my measly life and my father's inevitable departure to mere blips on the timeline of humanity.

Which is probably why I felt incapable of delivering the essential plot information without getting off track. At the beginning of the year, when we were doing *The Canterbury Tales,* Imani told me that a teacher should focus on just a few things every day.

"Be blunt and don't talk about a whole bunch of things at once," she told me. I gave too many examples too fast and she couldn't tell what was important. "Only add the extras later if we don't understand," she explained. "And make it fun. Something we can relate to. Put it in my language." The third week of school she stopped by after school.

"Umm, Miss Erica, how am I doing in your class?" she asked.

"Oh, I don't know, I think you're doing fine so far," I said. She was quiet and when she did speak I felt like I was going deaf. Her reading quizzes weren't very good either, but she didn't need me to tell her that. "Why do you ask?"

Her big brown eyes opened wide and rolled back halfway. "Because I don't understand most of what you're saying in there. I mean, the words you're using. Do you always talk like that?"

She had enrolled as a junior last year, and had difficulty adjusting to the rigors of private school.

"I don't know what's an analogy, or allusion, or whatever it is you keep talking about. I feel like I'm so far behind I'll never catch up," she said. She tried to put it in a way I'd understand: "It's like you're Harvard and I'm Lincoln."

She was referring to Lincoln University in Chester, PA.

"Well, you might not know what an allusion or an analogy is, but you sure know how to make them."

"Huh? What do you mean?"

That day began a special bond between us. She had a knack for cutting through all the BS. She was the first student who ever asked me to teach in a different way and explained exactly what she needed. I wasn't sure I could give it to her, but I tried.

Remembering Imani's advice, I decided to focus on three things in today's lesson: indications that Hamlet hates his life, the morality of women, and the alcoholic subtext. Those motifs would become touchstones that we kept coming back to.

You would think that twenty class hours would be more than enough time to teach *Hamlet*, but when you factor in reading quizzes (which are essential motivation for students to do the reading) and some sort of "get up and speak the language" activity, it's pretty tough to get through all the material.

This year, with my father dying, I felt like I'd run a marathon just getting myself to class on time, with brushed hair and quizzes and reading responses graded. I kept wishing I could stay in bed. Yet, digging into the text was the only emotional relief I found from the horrible waiting and wondering. Would he die today? Tomorrow? Was he already dead and I just hadn't gotten the call yet? With my brain smashed full of different bits of the play I had less head space to think about my dad. Shakespeare, and work in general, was really helping me deal with—or at least not think about—what was happening.

"What kind of dad did you say Polonius is?" I asked in class the next day, after they handed in their quizzes.

"Good," said one of the boys.

"Loving," said Diane.

"Gives good advice," said Feona.

It makes me smile that this is their first reaction to Polonius. Later their opinion changes when they see how controlling and sneaky he is.

"You think he's giving Laertes sound advice?" I asked them.

"Yes!" said Albert, launching about six inches off his stool.

"It is good advice. But let's remember something—it's Laertes' second time leaving. Do you think when you head back to college after Thanksgiving your dad's going to give you the same lecture all over again?"

I heard a few voices go hmmm.

"Wait, what—oh, that's what this means here, *second leaving?*" asked Catherine.

"Yes, exactly," I said. "Remember how yesterday we talked about Laertes asking Claudius' permission to go back to France?

Well, this is where you have to do what I told you," I pointed to the board where my three points were still numbered out. "You have to not only notice what is said, but what is *not* said. Make inferences. If Laertes was already away before, we can pretty well assume his father gave him the going-away talk."

"Yeah, good point," Jerome said.

"Jerome, you're in the dorm, right?"

"Yeah."

"Did your parents give you any advice before you left to come here to school?"

"Oh, ho, yeah," he nodded, smiling. "Oh yeah."

"Okay everybody, let's look at the specific advice Polonius gave to Laertes and see if you think it might apply today. Everyone take one line, we'll start at Coleman. Okay Coleman?" He sat up a little in his chair and asked for the page number. Reciting one line each forces them to follow along, so we do it once in a while as the first approach to a larger speech.

> *Yet here, Laertes! aboard, aboard, for shame!*
> *The wind sits in the shoulder of your sail,*
> *And you are stay'd for. There; my blessing with thee!*
> *And these few precepts in thy memory*
> *See thou character. Give thy thoughts no tongue,*
> *Nor any unproportioned thought his act.*
> *Be thou familiar, but by no means vulgar.*
> *Those friends thou hast, and their adoption tried,*
> *Grapple them to thy soul with hoops of steel;*
> *But do not dull thy palm with entertainment*
> *Of each new-hatch'd, unfledged comrade. Beware*
> *Of entrance to a quarrel, but being in,*
> *Bear't that the opposed may beware of thee.*
> *Give every man thy ear, but few thy voice;*

Take each man's censure, but reserve thy judgment.
Costly thy habit as thy purse can buy,
But not express'd in fancy; rich, not gaudy;
For the apparel oft proclaims the man,
And they in France of the best rank and station
Are of a most select and generous chief in that.
Neither a borrower nor a lender be;
For loan oft loses both itself and friend,
And borrowing dulls the edge of husbandry.
This above all: to thine own self be true,
And it must follow, as the night the day,
Thou canst not then be false to any man.
Farewell: my blessing season this in thee!
                    (1.3.60-87)

What kind of a dad was my father? Well, he was no Polonius, that is for sure. He was not controlling and not much of a disciplinarian. He was a good storyteller, but not a pontificator. He gave good advice, short and simple. Some of my fondest memories are of sitting on the wide front car seat with him, driving the hour and half from Bryn Athyn, PA, to South Jersey when I would come home from ANC for the weekend. I can't remember any specific conversations, but the Atlantic City Expressway always reminds me of Dad listening to whatever friend or mom or sister drama I was going through.

"Well, sweetie, so-and-so has been a good friend. Just be honest and don't talk behind her back." "Maybe you should just tell her how you feel." "Sweetheart, your mom loves you very much. I can't stand it when you're so rude to her." "You're the big sister; you should be nice to your little sister." "I'm sorry you're going through a hard time, sweetie. Just remember, the only thing that really matters is what kind of a person you are."

Dad. My brain pushed against the back of my eyes and forced them to squeeze shut. It was is the strangest feeling, knowing he was still alive, but irreversibly on his way out. In Costa Rica he told Larry that he was at peace. He had a good life. He still didn't want to talk about dying, but we did get to talk a lot that last week. Mostly about the past, remembering our shared history.

"Remember the first time I hit you?" Dad asked, somberly one afternoon when we were playing cards. One afternoon exactly three weeks ago tomorrow. Twenty days ago we were together. "The only time I hit you," he amended.

"No," I said, curious to access that scene. I started reeling back through possible time frames, settings and scenarios and I couldn't find it.

An unfamiliar expression crossed his face and he said, "You don't remember? In Northfield?" "What, did I hit you back or something?"

"No...."

He told me how we were at the breakfast table and I was being particularly horrible to Mom, he couldn't take it and he walked outside. How I kept at it and how he finally hauled off and hit me.

"On her head?" Paige asked.

"On her face," he said, indicating the left side of my face. "You were just like—" and he made an O-face, to illustrate. "Everything stopped. You couldn't believe it."

"I'm sure." It was coming back to me, a foggy vision. Yet another confirmation of what I have suspected for a long time now: I was such a jerk back then. I yelled all the time, I was mean to my little sister, and horrible to my Mom.

"And you were never wrong!" Paige chimed in. Boy, I've heard that before and not long ago from Tom.

"Yeah," I admitted. "I remember that." I was hoping we'd move off the subject. It was so painful to go back in my mind to that house, to any and all of our houses; to see what could have been done differently, what was squandered, why (pardon the cliché) we always hurt the ones we love. How can our parents ever forgive us for how shittily we treated them? For how ungrateful we were? For the fact that there was always something we'd rather do than be with them? It's as if parents don't have a choice but to forgive us. Family comes with some sort of contract: we move through and hopefully past the bad stuff. But, in that moment at the card table in Costa Rica, more than thirty years since we had lived in that house in Northfield, the last one we all lived in together as a family, I could understand how it might be easier for some people to walk away and never look back on the pain, the embarrassment, and the regret of youth.

So much of who I am today developed in reaction to the inconsiderate, thoughtless, selfish teenager I had been. My friends were my life back then, and I treated my family like spectators. Maybe I could do that because I was so secure in their love, who knows? But now our precious family of four was dying, closing up shop. Only the memories remained. And soon there would be one fewer person on Earth to remember. Oh God…my chest, my heart, hurt. It was hard to breathe. And I was saying "Oh God" all the time, which I try to avoid.

"It was all downhill from there," Dad said, continuing the story it seemed he really wanted to get off his chest.

"You mean I got *worse*?" I said.

"No, no, it's like you started to realize what you were doing, and it got better," he explained. "Oh!" he said. "Now I remember what it was. I heard you yell FU to your mother and that was just too much. When you came to the door—"

"Into the breezeway?" I asked, still trying to locate the scene in my mind.

"No, out the kitchen stairs to the sidewalk, that's where I slapped you," he said. I could see him replaying the scene in his head. "When I said it was all downhill from there that was the wrong way to put it. It all got better. It seemed like it was good for you."

"I'm sure it was."

"But it sure was hard on me," he said, gazing out the window to the deep green expanse beyond.

We never got to talk about how Polonius tells Ophelia in 1:3 that she is a *green girl* and doesn't realize her duty to be virtuous and not bring dishonor to her father. Diane wrote a great reading response about it:

> *I like the extended metaphor on money and "tender"— reminded me of* The Taming of the Shrew *and how women were seen as commodities to their father. But I don't like that Polonius seems more worried about how she reflects on him than on how she feels about how Hamlet is acting.*

"Yes, you got it!" I wrote back. "You are absolutely right!"

This is why I loved the reading responses. I sat there for a minute and pondered the idea of what duty a daughter owes her father. The other day I was going through a book of old letters and cards from Dad and found a printed-out email that I had totally forgotten about.

Subj: CHINKS
Date: Wed, 7 Nov 2001 9:24:03
From: DKC1444
To: EW Cantley

Erica dear,
Got your sweet note with the enclosures on Monday but have been trying to find the right way to respond ever since. First of all NOT upset. Very touched and thankful again for having such a kid as you. Now how do I refuse your way generous gift without upsetting you? The only way you can "afford" it is because you have worked so hard and been so independent for so long. That's worth millions to your proud Dad. If you keep the chinks I know that they will be put to much better use than if they are mixed up with my funds, most of which I don't know where they go anyhow. :)

Put the money aside. Another chance of a lifetime might be right around the corner. You know they give me as much joy as they do you. Or designate the funds to an extra couple of days with your Dad. The two days you spent with us recently were priceless. Nothing gives me more pure joy than time with you.

Erica, you have already given me back tenfold all that I have ever been able to do for you. You are way ahead already. I am sending back the checks and I hope that rather than being upset you will understand the double joy for me. Getting the fabulous gift from you and then having the joy of being able to give it back to you to be put to better use.

I love you with all my heart. I miss you. I hope you can squeeze out the maximum days for us to be together over the holidays.

Love,
Dad

1: 4

To the manner born

(1.4.17)

"Hey Miss Erica," Coleman called as he, Luis and Bradley lumbered down the hall towards the classroom. The bell had rung, so officially they were late. "Hey, can I go to the bathroom?"

"Hey—" I imitated, "I don't know, can you?" Before he could answer I said "—and no, you may not. You're late late late for a very important date and I don't want to wait wait wait for you before we start." I resisted the temptation to point out that he was always gone for at least ten minutes when he went to the bathroom. "You can go later," I added. "I don't want you to miss this."

From the beginning of my exposure to Shakespeare I heard there is always something new to find in the text, and always a new way to interpret it. Harold Bloom says we don't read Shakespeare, Shakespeare reads us, and how we interpret what we find tells us more about ourselves than about the plays.

In other words, when the student is ready the teacher will appear; and Shakespeare is a brilliant teacher. The first year I taught *Hamlet* without Mrs. Esther, the first great love of my life was in the hospital terribly ill due to the effects of alcoholism. Suddenly I started to see more and more references to drinking and addiction in *Hamlet*. The extent of alcoholic subtext in the play struck and surprised me.

As 1:4 opens, Hamlet has joined Horatio and the watchmen to see if the Ghost will stalk again. While waiting in the cold dark, Horatio is startled by trumpets and a loud explosion.

HORATIO: What does this mean, my lord?
HAMLET: The King doth wake to-night and takes his rouse,
Keeps wassail, and the swaggering up-spring reels;
And, as he drains his draughts of Rhenish down,
The kettle-drum and trumpet thus bray out
The triumph of his pledge.
HORATIO: Is it a custom?
HAMLET: Ay, marry, is 't:
But to my mind, though I am native here
And to the manner born, it is a custom
More honour'd in the breach than the observance.
This heavy-headed revel east and west
Makes us traduced and tax'd of other nations:
They clepe us drunkards, and with swinish phrase
Soil our addition; and indeed it takes
From our achievements, though perform'd at height,
The pith and marrow of our attribute.
                (1.4.8-25)

If there is anything that falls under the heading of *either good or bad* it would be alcohol consumption. I particularly latched on to Hamlet's philosophical tangent in 1:4 where he explains to Horatio that some folks are predisposed to being addicts, and others aren't.

So, oft it chances in particular men,
That for some vicious mole of nature in them,
As, in their birth—wherein they are not guilty,
Since nature cannot choose his origin—
By the o'ergrowth of some complexion,
Oft breaking down the pales and forts of reason,
Or by some habit that too much o'er-leavens

The form of plausive manners, that these men,
Carrying, I say, the stamp of one defect,
Being nature's livery, or fortune's star,—
Their virtues else—be they as pure as grace,
As infinite as man may undergo—
Shall in the general censure take corruption
From that particular fault: the dram of eale
Doth all the noble substance of a doubt
To his own scandal.

(1.4.26-41)

This is a life lesson I really want my students to get. We probably don't have more big drinkers here than in any other community, but in small town life it's easier to trace the traits and tendencies through the generations.

On my lesson plan for today I have center justified and highlighted:

PAY ATTENTION TO YOUR RELATIONSHIP WITH ALCOHOL & other mind-altering drugs!!!!

"Okay, look at the back of the green handout, the section on Act One motifs. Would someone please read the heading for this section?" Coleman raised his hand—he was trying to get back on my good side.

"Yes, Coleman, go ahead."

"Another thing that Hamlet disdains about the grown-up world," he read from the handout, "is the excessive drinking that goes on at Elsinore and in Denmark. Was Hamlet's father a big drinker, too?"

"This is a good question," I said to the class, "and one that is not definitively answered in the text, though there are some bits where Hamlet indicates to Horatio that 'drinking deep' is the Danish way, and he does not specify 'since my uncle Claudius took over the throne.'"

I continued. "Take a look in the mirror and ask yourself: Do you have to drink to have fun? Do you embarrass yourself when you drink? Do you forget what happened the night before?" I looked around and paused for effect. "Do you wish you could?" I usually get a few laughs there.

"Do you lay in your bed cringing the next morning, afraid to look at your phone to see who you drunk texted? Is it hard to get up, even though you really have to pee?" A few more chuckles.

"Did you make out with more than one person?" Full out laughs now, some sounds of disbelief that their teacher just suggested such a thing.

I continued, glad to have their attention. "Because that only happens when you're intoxicated." I let the idea hang in the air with a few quieting giggles. "You only make out with multiple people in the same night when you're *wasted*." I heard heh, heh, heh, and saw a few buddies exchanging knowing glances and elbow pokes.

On the lesson plan it says:

The concept of FREEDOM.

I launched the next part of my message.

"Maybe right now, freedom looks like doing what you want when you want and not getting in trouble for it. Believe me..." pause, pause, pause, "nothing is less free than addiction. You can't stop eating sugar even though it makes you feel terrible. You get kicked off the team because you failed a drug test. You're out of the play because you got caught at a college party. You can't not drink, even though you're losing respect, friends, maybe even jobs." In the far-right corner, Jimmy, Gino and Vincent were nodding. The sleepy corner of the room was waking up. Sometimes it's like the Bermuda Triangle back there: things get lost. But not this time. They were right with me.

"Take a look in the mirror," I continued. "Your habits are going to shape your life." Nods.

"Some people can drink or smoke pot regularly, or even somewhat excessively, and live normal, healthy, productive lives. Others can't. And here's the rub. You don't usually know which one YOU are," I gesture to each one of them with an open palm (it's rude to point, I tell them several times a year) "until it's too late. By now you are old enough to know whether you have addiction issues in your family. If you do, you should pay even closer attention."

I looked around the room. They were riveted. Or comatose. A few heads were bobbing here and there; Luis was nodding and smiling, but he always does that; a couple sets of eyes grew wide at certain points. Then they started stretching and shifting in their seats. It was warm and they were restless. Or uncomfortable. Who could blame them? I had been thinking about my family and about my two dead boyfriends. Who knows what they were each thinking about? My dad was not an alcoholic but now that I'm starting to hear memories and stories from old friends of his, it does keep coming up that he was a big partier when he was younger. And he never did stop smoking cigarettes.

At that moment I realized it was four minutes until the bell. I had done it again. Exactly what I was trying to avoid. I had so much to say, so well planned, that I didn't get them up and speaking.

Everyone had said something, and a few students read passages, but they never got up. We never got to the Polonius-Laertes intention activity. They had been sitting the entire class. For forty-five minutes straight. [*This*] *is not nor it cannot come to good.*

I needed to get them up. And I needed to let Coleman go to the restroom. I gestured to him that now was a good time.

"Stand up everyone. Wow. Lots of advice being given!!! I'm kind of like Polonius, huh?" I sort of laughed. "Long winded, like to hear myself talk? Doesn't let anyone get a word in edgewise?"

I got a few smiles and huh, huh laughs. Okay, phewsh, teachable moment. I did that on purpose! Trying to illustrate the whole parent/child relationship dynamic. All part of the plan to focus less on the dead dad stuff and more on the depressed college student under the parents' thumb stuff. Yeah, yeah.

"Okay, so I'm going to set you guys up for an acting activity that we will do tomorrow." I turned around the whiteboard easel to reveal a list of possible attitudes and motivations for father and son.

"What kind of a dad am I?" I walk up to Mei-Mei, took her tenderly by the shoulders and, looking warmly down into her eyes said, *"This above all, to thine own self be true."*

(Or as my dad used say, "The only thing that really matters is what kind of a person you are.")

I gave each of them a partner and cards that indicated if they should be a down-to-earth, pompous, or genuinely concerned father, or an impatient, bored, or obsequious son. They spent the last few minutes of class conferring with their partners.

Thank goodness it was lunch next.

The first thing I did differently for the section after lunch was to get them to all stand up about 8-10 minutes into the period and read Hamlet's first soliloquy.

"Okay," I said, having brought their attention to the page, "we referred to several bits in this soliloquy yesterday, but we didn't read the whole thing. Everybody up." Literally no one moved. "Stand up, you can stay there at your desks." They lumbered to their feet. "Okay, I'll start," I said, "and we'll just go around, each person taking two lines. Be sure to speak up!"

O, that this too too solid flesh would melt
Thaw and resolve itself into a dew!
Or that the Everlasting had not fix'd
His canon 'gainst self-slaughter! O God! God!
How weary, stale, flat and unprofitable,
Seem to me all the uses of this world!
Fie on't! ah fie! 'tis an unweeded garden,
That grows to seed; things rank and gross in nature
Possess it merely. That it should come to this!
But two months dead: nay, not so much, not two:
So excellent a king; that was, to this,
Hyperion to a satyr; so loving to my mother
That he might not beteem the winds of heaven
Visit her face too roughly. Heaven and Earth!
Must I remember? why, she would hang on him,
As if increase of appetite had grown
By what it fed on: and yet, within a month—
Let me not think on't—Frailty, thy name is woman!—
A little month, or ere those shoes were old
With which she follow'd my poor father's body,
Like Niobe, all tears:—why she, even she—
O, God! a beast, that wants discourse of reason,
Would have mourn'd longer—married with my uncle,
My father's brother, but no more like my father
Than I to Hercules: within a month:
Ere yet the salt of most unrighteous tears
Had left the flushing in her galled eyes,
She married. O, most wicked speed, to post
With such dexterity to incestuous sheets!
It is not nor it cannot come to good:
But break, my heart; for I must hold my tongue.

(1.2.133-164)

That went well, so I started class the same way the next day. I got a laugh when Luis read the lines *Heaven and earth, must I remember?* as flat as a pancake, and I stepped out from behind the podium and into our "stage," raised my hands and arms up to the heavens and shouted to the ceiling: *"Heaven and earth, must I remember?"* That felt good.

"Do it again," I implored him, "and think of something awful."

This time he was louder and imitated my gestures.

"Yes!" I said, with cheering fists. "Keep going!" They laugh when I cheer them, and they chuckle when I give them gold star stickers for saying something particularly insightful. But I think they like my combination of irony and enthusiasm. Either that or they think I'm some weird middle-aged woman. Strange to reach the point in life where I'm the weird middle-aged woman. And to realize that every middle-aged woman out there is also someone's daughter. If she isn't mourning her dead parents yet, she will be soon.

"Yesterday we left off with an adult authority figure—me—giving you a ton of advice. You had probably already heard a lot of that before," I smiled scanning the semi-circle of faces. A few wan smiles returned.

"Just like Laertes!" said Bradley, who was crisply pressed into a different colorful dress shirt every day.

"Why does Laertes need to at least listen to his father's parting words that he has probably heard before?" Nothing. "Anyone?" Blank stares. "Anyone...?" I droned, in my best *Ferris Bueller's Day Off* imitation.

My dad loved *Ferris Bueller's Day Off*. He always laughed so hard when I'd say, "Anyone...?" like the teacher in the movie, and then he'd say "Bueller...Bueller," and laugh again. My dad's laugh was the best. Is. Is the best. The way he looked at me when I made him laugh…smiling in his eyes…the way his head tilted back….

Heaven and Earth, must I remember?!

I tried rephrasing the question.

"Why do you need to stay on your parents' good side?" Nothing. "What do you need from your parents?" Nothing. Seriously?

"What comes in mighty handy when you're traveling around Europe?" Coleman over on my left rubbed the fingertips of his right hand together. Albert, Feona and Meredith all shouted "Money!"

"Yes! That's it," I said. Finally.

We acted out Polonius' *To thine own self be true* speech to Laertes, with each of them playing either the son or the father, embodying whatever intention I gave them on the index card before they started. Then we all guessed from the body language if Laertes was bored, or impatient, or obsequious; and from the tone and gestures if Polonius was a pompous blowhard, a down-to-earth dad, or a concerned father whose son has already been in trouble several times. It worked out fine, but it's been better.

All this time with Polonius made me wonder who is the Polonius in my life? If not my father, there must have been someone. I vaguely remember my Mom being known for lecturing me—but I felt like I couldn't trust my mind lately. I wasn't sure what was a real memory and what was conflated impression, or completely imagined. I couldn't hold a train of thought for more than a minute; or at least that's how it seemed. The only time I didn't get distracted by thoughts of my dad, or my past, or my family was when I got on a roll in class. And yet, multiple times a day I caught myself zoning out when something reminded me of him, or my family, or our short, accelerated montage of a life together. Yes, Polonius likes to hear himself talk. Sounds familiar. And not just because I've taught this play for years.

In all fairness I must admit that the biggest Polonius I know is me.

1: 5

Adieu, adieu, adieu. Remember me.

(1.5.98)

The next morning before homeroom I saw Imani in the stairwell. She looked awful.

"What?" I asked. "What happened, Double I?"

"My grandmother died," she looked down to the floor.

"Oh noooo…. Were you close?"

She nodded.

"Oh, I'm so sorry. You want a hug?"

"No, not right now," which was notable because she was a big hugger. Somedays after school she would bear hug me and crack my back at the same time.

Teaching in the twenty-first century is not like "the olden days when I was in school." I surely wasn't hugging any of my teachers back then. Let alone cracking their backs. There seems to be much less of a formal barrier between kids and grown-ups these days. You can't just perch high above them and lecture anymore. Teachers today need to create interactive environments, fielding random comments and riffing off whatever free associations come our way. When we are analyzing literature for meaning, I try to find something of value in what every student sees or interprets in the text.

After the daily quiz I usually open the discussion with some slightly personal question that might not seem to have anything directly to do with the text. A question they can answer whether they've done the homework or not. Something to draw them in.

"How many of you have had someone close to you die?"

Imani met my eyes and I responded with a tiny nod. A few students raised their hands. She did not.

"Have they ever visited you in a dream?"

Nothing. Try standing through ten seconds of silence in front of a bunch of teenagers. Thank goodness for my podium.

"What do you mean by visit?" asked Victor.

"Hmmm.... Good question. I mean has someone who's died ever showed up in your dreams?"

"I don't remember my dreams," said Catherine.

"Me neither," said Jimmy Wong.

"I do," said Diane.

My lesson plan said: What was that like? / How would that be, if your dead grandmother visited you in a dream?

"Okay, let's see. Can you imagine what it would be like if someone who died showed up in one of your dreams?" Pause. Let them try to picture it.

"We aren't sure if what we see in dreams are spirits, or dislodged memories, or unfulfilled wishes. But here's the thing: Hamlet wasn't sleeping! He saw his father's ghost. And he had witnesses who saw it, too. What do you think of that?"

No response.

"What do you think of Hamlet, and the watchmen, and even Horatio the scholar, the intellectual, the professional doubter, seeing the ghost? Is that even possible?"

"That's weird, man," Jerome said.

"Yeah, that would freak me out," Catherine nodded enthusiastically.

"Yeah really," said Luis.

"Good, good. That would freak you out. I agree. That would freak me out, too. So, do you see what I mean by it's kind of silly for the Ghost to tell Hamlet *Remember me!?*"

"Yeah...."

"What's he really telling Hamlet to remember?

"To get revenge!"

"Yes! That's it! To remember his words. He charges Hamlet to *revenge his foul and most unnatural murder*. Whose? Who committed the murder?"

"Claudius!"

"His uncle!"

"Exactly. Thank you. This can be confusing, but the personal pronoun refers to the murder Claudius committed. Now I need four of you to act out this scene: two Hamlets and two Ghosts—"

Feona interrupted, her russet hair bouncing around her wide Elizabethan face. "What was with all the *Swear, swear!?*"

"Excellent question, Feona. We'll get to that. First, we need some of you to read this scene so we can take a close look at it." A few hands shot up—Feona's being one, of course. And Albert. I looked around the room for the ones who were paying the least attention.

"Okay, you three in the corner, Bermuda Triangle, Vincent, Gino, Jimmy, and…" I looked to the other side of the room, and called on Sage, the demurest young lady in the class. She sat as far away as possible from these three rascals, "You all get up here with your books."

"Bermuda Triangle, heh, heh," one of the girls muttered.

They stood and read 1:5, two of them as Ghosts and two Hamlets, each pair standing together as if they were one character, one speaking and one acting out the body language and gestures they imagined would go with the words. Sage and Vincent were Hamlet, giant Gino and little Jimmy were the Ghost.

"Now listen," I told the rest of the class, "while they are doing the reading, I want you to look at what the Ghost—Hamlet's dead dad, remember—says to his son; and also notice what he doesn't say. Highlight it in your books or write it down. Remember,

Hamlet was away at school when his dad died. Presumably Hamlet hadn't seen his father in a while, and his death came as a complete shock." They started:

> *HAMLET: Whither wilt thou lead me? Speak. I'll go no*
> *further.*
> *GHOST: Mark me.*
> *HAMLET: I will.*
> *GHOST: My hour is almost come*
> *When I to sulf'rous and tormenting flames*
> *Must render up myself.*

"Wait, sorry but Gino can you sound more ghost-y? Either scary or haunt-y or ominous? Ghosts don't talk like normal live people, do they? Give it a try." In a way I'm messing with them when I say stuff like that, but I'm also drawing off the theatrical conventions we all know and unconsciously expect.

> *HAMLET: Alas, poor ghost!*

Sage grabbed her head then clutched her heart.

> *GHOST: Pity me not, but lend thy serious hearing*
> *To what I shall unfold.*

Gino seemed paternal as he looked down at Sage. He was acting as well as reciting.

> *HAMLET: Speak. I am bound to hear.*

Here Sage gestured with upturned palms as if she were assuring a favorite friend she could be trusted.

GHOST: So art thou to revenge, when thou shalt hear.

"Better, better!" I acknowledged the booming ominous tone
Gino had adopted.

HAMLET: What?
GHOST: I am thy father's spirit,
Doomed for a certain term to walk the night
And for the day confined to fast in fires
Till the foul crimes done in my days of nature
Are burnt and purged away.

Jimmy, remaining mute, alternated between grabbing his heart
and supplicating the ceiling.

But that I am forbid
To tell the secrets of my prison house,
I could a tale unfold whose lightest word
Would harrow up thy soul, freeze thy young blood,
Make thy two eyes, like stars, start from their
Spheres,

"Come on guys," I encouraged, "don't wane off now! He's using
imagery to describe how freaked out Hamlet would be if he knew
how bad things really were in purgatory." The ghosts came back
to life a little bit.

Thy knotted and combinèd locks to part,
And each particular hair to stand an end,
Like quills upon the fearful porpentine.
But this eternal blazon must not be
To ears of flesh and blood. List, list, O list!

If thou didst ever thy dear father love—

Sage whispered in awe:

HAMLET: O God!
GHOST: Revenge his foul and most unnatural murder.
HAMLET: Murder?
GHOST: Murder most foul, as in the best it is,
But this most foul, strange, and unnatural.
HAMLET: Haste me to know 't, that I, with wings as swift
As meditation or the thoughts of love,
May sweep to my revenge.
GHOST: I find thee apt;
And duller shouldst thou be than the fat weed
That roots itself in ease on Lethe wharf,
Wouldst thou not stir in this.

"Wait," I said, "stop for a second. Do you see that Hamlet's dad just told Hamlet he'd be dull, and a wimp, if he didn't act on his father's command to revenge? That's harsh! Okay, keep going. Gino and Jimmy, do you want to switch roles? Jimmy, you talk now?" Jimmy took over, slowing occasionally over the unfamiliar syntax.

Now, Hamlet, hear.
'Tis given out that, sleeping in my orchard,
A serpent stung me. So the whole ear of Denmark
Is by a forgèd process of my death
Rankly abused. But know, thou noble youth,
The serpent that did sting thy father's life
Now wears his crown.
HAMLET: O, my prophetic soul! My uncle!

"Too flat, too flat," I interrupted. "He just told you your uncle killed your Dad. It doesn't have to be loud, but it must be full of emotion: disgust, shock, hatred, you choose. Try again." Sage whispered again, this time with the disgusted horror of someone who realizes things are way worse than they thought.

> *HAMLET: O, my prophetic soul! My uncle!*
> *GHOST: Ay, that incestuous, that adulterate beast,*
> *With witchcraft of his wits, with traitorous gifts—*
> *O wicked wit and gifts, that have the power*
> *So to seduce!—won to his shameful lust*
> *The will of my most seeming-virtuous queen.*
> *O Hamlet, what a falling off was there!*

"What does that mean? What is *a falling off*?"

"She really sank low," Jerome said from the sidelines.

"Yes! And here we see more examples of antithesis. The Ghost King says Gertrude has gone *from me...to a wretch*. He contrasts their *celestial bed* with a pile of *garbage*."

> *From me, whose love was of that dignity*
> *That it went hand in hand even with the vow*
> *I made to her in marriage, and to decline*
> *Upon a wretch whose natural gifts were poor*
> *To those of mine.*
> *But virtue, as it never will be moved,*
> *Though lewdness court it in a shape of heaven,*
> *So, lust, though to a radiant angel linked,*
> *Will sate itself in a celestial bed*
> *And prey on garbage.*
> *But soft, methinks I scent the morning air.*

"The cock crew!" shouted Albert. From his desk.

"Yes, see?" I said. "That confirms it. Reinforcement that ghosts can't stay out in the daylight."

> *Brief let me be. Sleeping within my orchard,*
> *My custom always of the afternoon,*
> *Upon my secure hour thy uncle stole,*
> *With juice of cursèd hebona in a vial*
> *And in the porches of my ears did pour*
> *The leprous distilment, whose effect*
> *Holds such an enmity with blood of man*
> *That swift as quicksilver it courses through*
> *The natural gates and alleys of the body,*
> *And with a sudden vigor it doth posset*
> *And curd, like eager droppings into milk,*
> *The thin and wholesome blood. So did it mine,*
> *And a most instant tetter barked about,*
> *Most lazar-like, with vile and loathsome crust*
> *All my smooth body.*

Gino rubbed his hands proudly up and down his generous torso, drawing laughs, while Jimmy took his time drawing out the last line.

> *Thus was I, sleeping, by a brother's hand*
> *Of life, of crown, of queen at once dispatched,*
> *Cut off, even in the blossoms of my sin,*

"Get louder here!" He did, booming,

> *Unhouseled, disappointed, unaneled,*
> *No reck'ning made, but sent to my account*
> *With all my imperfections on my head.*

O horrible, O horrible, most horrible!
If thou hast nature in thee, bear it not.
Let not the royal bed of Denmark be
A couch for luxury and damnèd incest.
But, howsomever thou pursues this act,
Taint not thy mind, nor let thy soul contrive
Against thy mother aught. Leave her to heaven
And to those thorns that in her bosom lodge
To prick and sting her. Fare thee well at once.
The glowworm shows the matin to be near
And 'gins to pale his uneffectual fire.
Adieu, adieu, adieu. Remember me.
                    (1.5.1-98)

"Okay, great guys, thank you," I said as they went back to their seats. 'Remember we need to look at what's said in the text; what's not said in the text; and what we can glean based on what we know about the characters and about human nature." I walked back to the podium.

"Let's look at what Hamlet's ghost father says to him. And what he doesn't say. You summarize the key points of what he says, and I'll write them down on the board. Try to list the things he says in the order he says them." I stood at the board with my chalk in one hand and my lesson plan with the chronological list of the main points in the other.

"That he's his father's ghost!"

"Yes."

"That he was murdered!"

"Yes—but he says something else before that. Anyone?"

There was a pause, then Feona said "that Hamlet is going to have to revenge once he's heard what the Ghost had to say."

"Yes! Yes!" I shouted and rang the green "Right" button

on the podium. "Look here, Hamlet says, *Speak, I am bound to hear*. Now look over to the left. Remember to look over to the left. There's valuable info there. Would someone read the note next to 'bound'?"

Vincent raised his hand and read "Bound: ready (the word also means 'in duty bound' and 'obligated,' which is the sense to which the Ghost responds in the following line.)"

"Yes," I said, "thank you. Here's poor Hamlet saying, 'I'm ready to hear you, Dad; and his dad's like 'Yeah, and you better be ready to revenge me once you hear my story.'"

I guess that's what happens when your dad's a king and is used to getting his own way. My dad was not bossy and he never guilted us into anything. At least not anything self-serving. My mother either, come to think of it. My dad was almost embarrassingly grateful for the visits from me and my sister, and he never seemed embittered or resentful that there weren't more. Sometimes he'd wistfully say, "I just wish we lived closer."

"Yeah, Dad, me too."

"Okay," I continued, "what else?"

"He tells him what Claudius did," Albert.

"Yes, and to review, what did Claudius do?"

"He poured poison in his ear," Jerome.

"While he was sleeping!" Bradley.

"Right! Did you notice anything else Hamlet's dear old dad said to his bereaved son the prince? What does he say about revenge?"

Boy, I am so mad at this Ghost right now. I never thought of the Ghost as more than a theatrical trope before, but now I'm thinking of him as a father back from the dead, and he's not a nice guy.

"Anyone?" I droned. "Anyone…?" I actually stole that from Mrs. Esther.

Nothing. Dead silence. "Okay, get ready to highlight important bits here," I said. "The Ghost finds Hamlet 'apt,' which is a compliment, but then tells him he'd be *duller…than the fat weed that roots itself in ease on Lethe wharf* if he didn't take action."

That's harsh, dead dad ghost.

Never, ever did my father degrade, demean, or insult me. Never. If he ever alluded to a fault or quirk I might have, it was with a gentle ribbing like that of an inside joke. He got away with saying things like, "Yes, but looks aren't everything," when I'd pester, "Dad, dad, aren't I funny?" and "I hear ya talking," when I'd prod, "Dad, Dad, are you listening to me?" But ridicule, intimidation, or cruelty? Never.

"Basically, he's saying Hamlet will be a wuss if he doesn't revenge his father. And look here," I said, getting excited and pointing to the page, "make a big circle around *Lethe wharf*. Here the Ghost suggests that Hamlet would be living on the banks of the river of forgetfulness if he is so lame as to not snap to revenge. It's funny, because one of the things that is often talked about in this play is Hamlet's delay."

"Where is that?" Meredith asked.

"It's right there on the other page, in the notes," pointed Catherine, sitting between her and Luis.

"You see, read the notes," I said. "It's overwhelming to see all the layers of meaning woven into even the most seemingly meaningless lines, but that's part of the greatness of Shakespeare. You feel like your head's gonna pop off. But in a good way."

I could see we only had about five minutes left. This is what I mean by Mr. Toad's Wild Ride. There's always too much to cover each day. That's a given. But this time around, with my dad fading towards death, I started to feel like I was being haunted. Things I never saw before kept jumping off the page. Words, lines, connections. For years I've told the kids that "every time you read a Shakespeare play you find something new," because that's what I'd always heard.

Now I realize I misunderstood the adage. It's not simply that the plays are so dense we can't catch every bit of wisdom and wit the first five or ten times we read them. It's that as our own life circumstances change, we pick up on nuances and themes that were always there but sailed right over our heads before. I think somewhere in the back of my mind I thought that once I knew the plays well, they wouldn't be able to surprise me anymore. Delight, sure. Impress, absolutely. But not surprise. Boy was I wrong.

Wrong, wrong, wrong.

"Folks, please notice that remembering is a prevalent motif in this play obsessed with death. At the end of their first visitation, the Ghost of Hamlet's father implores Hamlet *Remember me!* It seems an extraneous request. Hamlet is already preoccupied with his dead dad and his mother's *o'er hasty marriage* before the Ghost materializes. Now his father's ghost has regaled him with tales of such villainous horror that, of course, Hamlet will think of nothing else. Duh, Dad." A few chuckles.

I continued, "And just think how unfortunate it is that Hamlet is not permitted to go back to school or resume his normal life. He's trapped in the prison of his mind, haunted by bad dreams of his uncle Claudius' pernicious deeds. *Remember thee!* Hamlet cries out twice to the departed spirit, from this time forward he'll think of nothing else. Let's read it."

Remember thee!
Ay, thou poor ghost, while memory holds a seat
in this distracted globe. Remember thee?
Yea, from the table of my memory
I'll wipe away all trivial fond records,
All saws of books, all forms, all pressures past,
That youth and observation copied there;
And thy commandment all alone shall live
Within the book and volume of my brain,
Unmix'd with baser matter: yes, by heaven!
O most pernicious woman!
O villain, villain, smiling, damned villain!
My tables,

"*My tables* refers to what we'd think of as a tablet of paper and *meet* means apt or fitting," I explained, miming writing something down in a book. "*Meet it is I set it down,* means I should write this down. Keep it in mind. Okay, go back to *My tables.*"

—meet it is I set it down,
That one may smile, and smile, and be a villain;
At least I'm sure it may be so in Denmark:
[He writes]
So, uncle, there you are.

"Okay, hold on," I interrupted again. "So if your Hamlet has been writing this down, this is a nice place to have him put a firm period on the page and close his notebook."

Now to my word;
It is 'Adieu, adieu! remember me.'
I have sworn 't.
> (1.5.102-119)

"Great, thank you. To review, *Meet it is I set it down* means Hamlet thinks it's a good idea to write it down. This is the reaction of a scholar, not a drunkard (like Claudius) or a warrior (like King Hamlet), and it marks Hamlet as somewhat of an oddball within his community."

"Well, maybe that's why he wanted to go back to school!" said Albert.

"Yes! Wait a minute," I reached down for a star and walked over to his desk, "here you are, sir. Excellent point. Hamlet is often portrayed holding a book; he's the type of guy who writes things down. You can see him sort of obsessively jotting things down in his notebook."

I'm the type of person who writes things down, too. I'm afraid I won't remember them if I don't. Not sure why it never struck me before, but death is all about remembering. There we were in Costa Rica, two childless daughters pretty sure we were spending our final days with our beloved father. None of us wanted to talk about dying, or something as awkwardly obvious as how much he meant to us. Instead, like Larry and Dad did, the three of us sat around and talked about what we remembered. We wanted to hear Dad talk about his life, and he seemed, as he had for the past year or two, more than ready to stroll down memory lane.

"You remember the regular poker game I had in Huntingdon Valley, don't you?" he asked. "When I got all the corned beef and chips...."

"I do!" my sister said. "I remember because I was the puppy under the table." Her puppy phase.

I didn't remember that game until he mentioned it, but I sure remembered the Monday night game he had in the basement of our next house, in Northfield, New Jersey. As far as I knew, every household had a big tablecloth-size piece of thick Kelly green felt on hand for card games. What I most remember from that regular game was when he'd have a good night, Mom would get some money under her pillow. One night in the early 80's Mom got a $100 bill under her pillow, and Paige and I each found fifties under ours. It felt glamorous having a Dad who was a big spender. Later Larry told me that the extra money Dad made from hosting that game was important to our family. Not necessarily money from winnings, but from the weekly rake for the house. "Your Dad made about 10K a year from that game."

Northfield was the last house we all lived in together, and the backdrop for Paige's and my very different bumpy teenagehoods. I'm not sure how we got off onto other stories from that era, but probably just a natural result of going back to that time in our minds and looking around.

"Do you remember when I threw the phone at your head?" Paige said with a twinkle in her eye and more than a trace of glee. "You were such a jerk and deserved it to the degree I didn't even really get in trouble for it! You would *never* get off the phone. Never. No matter what. And I had a really important call to make for school."

There is something elemental and magical about sitting around remembering with the people with whom you've shared a lifetime.

"Remember when you had that boat you were working on in the back yard for two years?"

"Remember when you snuck out the second story window?"

"Remember when you taught me to drive the jeep on the beach?"

"Remember that beat-up green truck that I used to drive to my job at Steinbecks?"

"Oh my gosh, Steinbecks! I forgot you worked there."

Each of us was remembering the same years and moments a little differently but gazing backward enveloped us all in a dream-like haze. Together we were reliving times only we had known. Our family of four. Strained and broken at times, but our own little family.

Dad asked if we remembered going to the club every Friday night for the buffet, "Was that fun for you or was it something you had to do?" he asked.

"I loved it," I said, "but I don't remember it being a buffet as much as...well, yes, I do remember the Sunday brunch buffet. With unlimited bacon. I also remember going to eat there, getting the big menu, and ordering the same thing every time: shrimp cocktail, filet mignon, and a crème de menthe parfait. *Petit* filet mignon."

As the students left, I looked down at my notes and realized I never got to Feona's question about the Ghost insisting that Horatio and Marcellus swear, swear, swear not to tell what they had seen. I tried to think of a time that my father made me swear to do or not to do something. I could see him run his hands through his thick, wavy, graying hair, lean in with his forearms resting on his thighs, and plead, "Just don't lie to me. And don't be rude to you mother."

Swear.

I remember the first time I heard my father swear. I can picture him in his white V-neck undershirt and jeans, working in our house on Edgehill Road. I was around 10 or 11 years old; he must have been about 40. He wore tortoiseshell Wayfarers and a smile whenever he looked at us. He did so much work on that house. Turned the garage into a family room, built a separate garage on the other side of the driveway, a brick patio, put up wallpaper, made a breakfast room and soldered together a fruit-themed Tiffany-style lamp to go over the table. He planted roses, built me a balance beam and high bar, and even got us the very first Space Trolley in our neighborhood. To think now how much labor and love he put into that house. And we were only there for three years. One afternoon I heard a loud "Fuck!" from the floor of the breakfast room. I found out a moment later that he had hammered his thumb, and my first thought was, weird, why is he talking about *that* when he's so angry?

ACT TWO

The readiness is all

(5.2.237-238)

2: 1

By the mass, I was about to say something: where did I leave?

(2.1.57-58)

The next morning was gray. I was surprised to see Diane standing at her desk in the dark when I entered the classroom. She pulled her school sweatshirt over her head and my stomach lurched when I saw the lines of scars on the underside of her arms. In a flash I realized I'd never seen her in anything but long-sleeved uniform shirts.

"It's not what you think," she said matter-of-factly. "I was in a really bad car accident."

"I'm so sorry Diane." I found out later she was a passenger in a drunk driving accident and went through the windshield and back again. She had put her arms up to shield her face.

"It's okay. Do you mind if I study in here? It's quiet."

"Sure, feel free."

I took the Act 2:1 folder off the podium and sat down at my desk. The content was unemotional for me and perfectly geared to teenagers. I was looking forward to the respite. The scene opens with Polonius coaching his man Reynaldo how to act when he arrives in Paris to spy on Polonius' son Laertes. Teenagers can relate to parents being overly interested in their movements. The four-minute bell rang and kids started trickling into the room.

"Good morning; morning; morning," I said as they entered. "Did you pick up your returns? Reading responses and graded quizzes are on the desk."

After the quiz I launched in. "So, why is Polonius sending Reynaldo to Paris?"

"To spy on Laertes!" several students shouted out at once.

"Yes, exactly," I confirmed. "So, one at a time now. What's your opinion of what Polonius is doing? Meredith?"

"Well," Meredith said, looking down into her book then back up again, pushing her pale blonde hair behind her ear, "I think it's pretty dishonest of him. It's sneaky."

"Sneaky!" said Albert, pointing in the air towards Meredith. I semi-ignored him. As much I loved his energy, I needed to draw out some of the other students, and Duncan had been one of the kids who had shouted out that Polonius is spying. I wanted to capitalize on that and show him that I noticed he had said something.

"Duncan, you're in the dorm, right? What if your parents, all the way up in Canada, were wondering how you were doing at school? I mean the real story not just what you tell them in your Sunday calls?" Vincent kind of nudged him. "What if they asked one of their friends in town to check in on you at Stuart Hall? Maybe subtly ask one of the housemasters or RAs how the Canadians are doing? 'Are they as wild as they used to be in the olden days?'"

Duncan half laughed.

"Wouldn't you want to know how your kid, so far away, was doing?" I kept prodding.

"Well, yes," Duncan said, "but I wouldn't send someone to spy and tell rumors about them. That's just wrong."

"Yeah, man, that's wrong," said Vincent, his Harry Potter glasses slipping as he nodded vehemently.

"Yeah," boomed Gino from the corner, on Vincent's right. "Parents should trust their kids."

"Yeah!" said Jimmy Wong, looking up over his glasses with his pen in the air for emphasis. The Bermuda Triangle always perks up when we are talking about oppressive parents or kids getting in trouble.

"Okay, okay, so you guys say parents should trust their kids...."

"Well, maybe not all kids," Coleman chimed in.

"Ah, thank you. Good point. Maybe not all kids. What kids shouldn't be trusted?" I baited them. I realized it was a tricky question. I was leading them in one way or the other; I was trying to get them engaged in what was happening in the play and have some thoughts about it.

"He's been in trouble before!" called out Albert.

"Who?" I asked.

"Laertes!" he said, leaning over his tall desk into the center of the room.

"Yes!" I dinged the green yes button on the podium. "Exactly. Where did you get that?"

"He mentions that Laertes was already in a scandal," said Feona.

"Exactly. We get more information in this scene. Not only is it confirmed that Laertes is, in fact, in Paris, but see where it says *You must not put another scandal on him*? Don't miss these bits of backstory Shakespeare gives us. There are so many unanswered questions in this play, when we do get some hint of information, it's probably important."

Jimmy was raising his hand and bouncing a little in his seat.

"Yes, Jimmy?"

"I have the *No Fear Shakespeare*," he said pointing inside his book, "and it says here: 'Oh no, not if you say it right. I don't want you to say he's a sex fiend, that's not what I mean. Just mention his faults lightly, so they make him seem like a free spirit who's gone a little too far.'" Jimmy finished with a little giggle, and Meredith on his right leaned over to look at his book. She was shaking her head and had a funny smile on her face.

Oh my gosh, I really need to get myself a copy of *No Fear*

Shakespeare Hamlet. I don't forbid my students to use it, though I do require them to have the Folger Shakespeare Library version. If they care enough to know what is going on in the play, I'm not going to make a fuss about how they figure it out. The obvious pitfall is that they might not read Shakespeare's words at all, but at least they wanted to understand what was happening.

"Nice! Thank you, Jimmy. There's nothing wrong with the *No Fear Shakespeare*, but again, if that's the one you're reading at home, make sure you actually read Shakespeare's words on the left, not just the contemporary translation on the right." Now Gino was peering into Jimmy's book. One mention of sex fiends and that's what happens.

"Okay," I continued, "Polonius goes into a lot of detail about how he thinks young men act away from home. Let's read this passage together. Look at what he's suggesting. He's sending Reynaldo to spy on Laertes," I gestured up to the board to the word SPYING, "and notice that he is giving his man Reynaldo very specific acting advice," I tossed my hand back to the board where it says ACTING ADVICE. "And in both cases, with Laertes and with Reynaldo, there is a power structure here in which Polonius is the one is charge. His son and his manservant are meant to do what he says. Get it?" A few nods.

"Duncan and Luis, would you read from the beginning of Act 2: scene 1?"

POLONIUS: *Give him this money and these notes, Reynaldo.*
REYNALDO: *I will, my lord.*
POLONIUS: *You shall do marvellous wisely, good Reynaldo,*
Before you visit him, to make inquire
Of his behavior.
REYNALDO: *My lord, I did intend it.*
POLONIUS: *Marry, well said; very well said. Look you, sir,*

Inquire me first what Danskers are in Paris;
And how, and who, what means, and where they keep,
What company, at what expense; and finding
By this encompassment and drift of question
That they do know my son, come you more nearer
Than your particular demands will touch it:
Take you, as 'twere, some distant knowledge of him;
As thus, 'I know his father and his friends,
And in part him:' do you mark this, Reynaldo?
REYNALDO: Ay, very well, my lord.

(2.1.1-58)

"Okay, you can stop there. Thank you. So, what do you think about Polonius?"

"It's wrong," Diane said indignantly. "Spying is wrong. He should just be honest about checking up on him because he's worried."

"I don't know," said Sage, talking to Diane more than to me or the class, "if he's already been in trouble once...maybe Laertes isn't that honest either."

Mei-Mei, on the other side of Diane, leaned over and said, "Well, he is sending him money." Those three, Mei-Mei, Diane and Sage were becoming their own little peanut gallery. Unlike the Bermuda Triangle, though, they were talking about the text and making notes, instead of nudging each other and chuckling under their breath.

"When I was young I got in trouble a lot," said Jerome.

"Really?"

"I used to talk all the time in class, but my teacher said I was taking away other people's shine. So I stopped talking." Wow. "Then I lost my shine," he said quietly.

"Yeah, that happens," I nodded. "But you're shining now."

"I know," he smiled, "I'm making a comeback."

Some of the other students seemed to be getting bored with the side talk. Time to cut to the chase: "Is Polonius a good father?" I asked in a voice that invited them to shout out their thoughts.

"Yes, yes, I think he is!"

"Nope, nope, good parents don't need to spy on their kids."

I'm not so sure about that, but my father didn't spy on me. At least, not that I know of. And though he was given to long pauses in his stories, he rarely forgot what he was saying. I was more Polonius; I went off on tangents and completely forgot my point on a regular basis. I looked at the clock.

"Okay, let's move on. Reynaldo leaves and Ophelia enters. What is Ophelia upset about?"

"Hamlet's acting wack," said Coleman.

"Yeah," said Bradley next to him, "He's gone off the deep end." Luis is nodding in agreement.

"Good," I said, "and—"

"There's implied stage direction here," Feona called out.

"Yes, Feona, thank you. Where is that?"

"Hmmm...Act 2.1.84. *How now Ophelia, what's the matter?*"

"Okay, so explain how that is implied stage direction," I urged her on.

"Well, if the first thing he says is *what's the matter* then we know that she must look like there is something wrong."

Ding, ding, I rang the bell. "Exactly. Thank you." I pulled out the stars and, walking past Albert and the Peanut Gallery, peeled off one and transferred it onto Fifi's outstretched finger. "Now, one thing the girls already know because they've done a lot of Shakespeare with me is that Shakespeare gives us very few stage directions—"

"Directorial freedom," Diane piped in.

"Yes, exactly," I said, turning around and peeling off a star for her, too. "I think it's one of several reasons his plays have lasted so long—because there is so much what we call 'freedom for interpretation', or 'directorial freedom.' It lets actors and directors make Shakespeare their own." Diane, whose wide-opened almost-black eyes were looking up into mine, took the star onto her finger with a big beaming smile.

"Okay, what does Polonius think is the cause of Hamlet's madness?"

"Ophelia rejected him," said Catherine.

"That's so annoying," said Feona.

"Yes, it is so annoying," echoed Meredith, fake pounding on her desk. Yeah!

"Agreed!" I pointed in the air, looking around. "Hey—the rest of you—why are Fifi and Meredith saying it's so annoying that Polonius thinks the cause of Hamlet's madness is that Ophelia rejected him?" Yes, I know I repeated everything they just said. That's because they often don't listen when each other speaks. That's how they can get excited about saying something that was just said two comments ago.

"Let's look at this passage—make sure you highlight this bit, line 119. Would someone read for us?" Coleman's hand shot up. "Great, Coleman, start with Polonius."

> *POLONIUS: What, have you given him any hard words of late?*
> *OPHELIA: No, my good lord, but, as you did command,*
> *I did repel his fetters and denied*
> *His access to me.*
> *POLONIUS: That hath made him mad.*
> (2.1.119-123)

"Good, thank you," I said to Coleman, who was slouched down in his chair and gravelly voiced the whole time, but read with some feeling and changed his voice when he got to Ophelia, which got a great laugh. I told them, "This is the one time we see Polonius with some humility, admitting that he might have been wrong: or that his advice might have made the situation worse. Let's keep reading. Coleman, want to keep going?" He shuffled in his seat, looked at me then back at his book and said sure.

> *I am sorry that with better heed and judgment*
> *I had not coted him: I fear'd he did but trifle,*
> *And meant to wreck thee; but, beshrew my jealousy!*
> *By heaven, it is as proper to our age*
> *To cast beyond ourselves in our opinions*
> *As it is common for the younger sort*
> *To lack discretion.*
>
> (2.1.124-130)

"Okay, thanks, you can stop there. What's ironic about the passage we just read?"

"He's blaming Ophelia for following his directions!" said Mei-Mei quietly indignant.

"Yes," I said. "She can't win."

2: 2

Words, words, words

(2.2.210)

I may have overmedicated last night. My sister had mailed me some of her Xanax and I had some of my grandmother's Ambien. I slept right through chapel and part of first period. I didn't care. My body felt heavy and drugged, like there was a cushion between me and the rest of the world. I didn't have to teach until 9:15, so I took my time.

I couldn't Skype with my father yesterday afternoon. When I called, Maureen's voice warbled up and down as if she could no longer control volume and pitch. "It's been a bad day. Dad fell in the bathroom. He slipped off the toilet and hit his head on the sink. His head was bleeding and he looked awful, Erica, awful. I insisted on coming into the bathroom with him, but he refused."

"Oh no!"

"He's been so constipated because of the pain meds," she wailed. "He needed my help. He needed to go to the bathroom. He was so uncomfortable. Finally, he could go but he fell. It was a huge mess. Blood all over his face. He can't talk. I finally got him to bed. Oh Erica, he's a mess. My poor David!"

Act 2.2 gets two teaching days because it is long and so much happens. The first part of 2.2 is a language-heavy day, and I focus on unpacking for them what was going on between Hamlet and Polonius. I cued up three YouTube video versions of the fishmonger scene: the 1964 black-and-white Richard Burton and Hume Cronyn filmed stage play, Kenneth Branagh's 1996 film, and the BBC television version of the Royal Shakespeare Company's 2009 production with David Tennant.

The bell rang and half the class stood up. They looked about as energetic as I felt. Even though there was sun for a change, it was still cold outside.

"Okay now" I said, "let's officially greet each other and get started. Everybody up! Good morning everyone!"

"Good morning Miss Erica."

I gave them the quiz and began discussion by getting Feona and Albert to explain who Rosencrantz and Guildenstern are, and what was happening at the beginning of the scene. Then I launched into lecture mode.

"One thing scholars have noticed about this play is there are a lot of situations in which adults or authority figures are controlling or messing with the lives of their kids. In *Taming of the Shrew* the girls saw a lot about power structure and supremacy. The natural power structures in Shakespeare's time are parent/ child, master/servant (boss/employee now), husband/wife, and if we are in a royal world, which we often are in Shakespeare, monarch/subject."

"So, with everything else going on, this is also a play about authority and power structure. *The Taming of the Shrew* is a farce (an exaggerated comedy) so many of the laughs come from the inversion of the power structure. Servants getting one up on their masters, kids going behind their parents' backs and marrying who they want, wives being smarter than their husbands—and these inversions of the power structure get laughs. Interestingly, *Hamlet* is a tragedy, and the younger generation can't seem to get out from under the need to be dutiful and obedient to their elders."

"Act 1, which sets up the whole play, is full of references to knowing your duty and being obedient. At the end of Act 1:1, line 188, Horatio says it is *fitting our duty* to tell Hamlet they saw the ghost of the dead King Hamlet. That's subject to monarch. In 1.2, starting at line 54 Laertes tells Claudius *though willingly I came to Denmark to show my duty in your coronation…that duty done* he would really like his king's permission to go back to France."

Albert shouted out, "Hamlet says *I shall in all my best obey you, madam.* Meaning you but not him. Like he's not accepting orders from his stepfather," he finished with a satisfied smile.

"Yes, good," I said. "What else? Mei-Mei?"

"Ophelia has no choice but to obey. At the end of Act 1:3, line 145, she says almost the exact same thing to Polonius that Hamlet said to Gertrude: *I shall obey, my lord.*"

"Yes, that's when Polonius ordered her to stop talking to Hamlet. Now in this scene Polonius, like a good spy, is telling Claudius what he learned from Ophelia. Yes, Feona?"

"I found another obedience. On line 115 Polonius says *in her duty and obedience.*"

"Good, thank you. Highlight *in her duty and obedience* on line 115, and again on line 133 *obedience, hath my daughter shown me,*" I told them.

Fathers and daughters. Poor Ophelia. All this talk about dutiful daughters and obeying made me circle back to the question: What did I owe my father? When I used to dream about making a ton of money, I would imagine buying him a boat, or paying off the mortgage on his house. Or taking him on a cool trip. Or making all his financial worries disappear, like he had done so many times for me. Had I been a good daughter? I know he said I was, and everyone knows how much he loved my sister and me. But he also accepted whatever we gave him, and never said a word about wishing for more. Looking back, our whole relationship sort of rolled out organically, with no sense that he was the boss or that I owed him anything. He never conveyed any specific expectations as far as time, fealty, or deference. In fact, on the contrary, he expressed nothing but appreciation for whatever time we had together. And when I would ask what I could do for him, his answer would always be the same: "Just have a good life."

I looked down at my lesson plan. "How would you describe Polonius' behavior with the King and Queen here?"

"Obsequious!" A vocab word from the fall.

"Yes, Feona! Exactly." That girl remembers everything. "Yes Catherine?"

"May I go use the restroom?" She was gone a long time.

"Why obsequious, Feona?"

"Because he's always kissing up to the King and Queen and showing them how much he knows," she said, pointing in her open book and nodding her dark red curls. "He seems like he's always trying to impress Claudius."

"He thinks he's great," said Jimmy Wong on the other side of the room.

Thinks he's great. A know-it-all. Trying to be important. Those are things no one would ever say about my father. I don't think I ever saw him trying to impress anyone in my life. In fact, growing up in my house, "she thinks she's so great" was just about the harshest epithet you could give a person. I always knew my dad thought I was great; yet I also got the impression that acting like *you* thought you were great was a bad thing. "You're not showing off, are you?" he'd say, when regaled with a particularly self-aggrandizing story of something that happened at school or with friends.

"Yes, Jimmy, thank you! Polonius, as we determined in Act 1, likes to hear himself talk. We concurred that he did have some good fatherly advice. What's Polonius' job, by the way?" They have heard me say the name Polonius multiple times, but I bet half of them aren't 100% sure who he is.

"His job?" Mei-Mei echoed quietly.

"Yes." No raised hands and no shout-outs.

Mei-Mei looked around the room. "He's advisor to the King," she said flatly, as if everyone should know that.

"Yes, he's advisor to the King. Consigliere, as they say in *The Godfather*. So, he needs to be in the know." A few nods around the room, and a few mumbled "oh yeahs."

"In fact," I continued, "remember what he said to Laertes in Act 1:2 when Laertes was about to ask permission to go back to France?" Both Albert and Diane on my left started flipping back in their books—my dream come true.

"I got it!" said Albert.

"Great, would you read it?" I grabbed one of the plastic golden crowns off my desk and tossed it to him.

He adjusted the crown, stood with book in left hand, right hand waving in the air, and recited:

> *The head is not more native to the heart,*
> *The hand more instrumental to the mouth,*
> *Than is the throne of Denmark to thy father.*
>   (1.2.48-50)

Straight in front of me Luis and Bradley were smiling and nodding, Coleman was still slumped, but his eyes were wider than usual, and he had a smirk on his face. I checked the Bermuda Triangle and the guys on my right, and they were smiling too, but more like they were in on a private joke.

"Yes, thank you," I said. "One of the big unanswered questions in this play is just how much does Claudius owe Polonius for the throne? Did Polonius know about the plot to poison King Hamlet? Maybe Polonius is the one who acquired the poison. What was Polonius' role in the court during the reign of King Hamlet? We know he was around because Ophelia and Hamlet have a history, but was he the number one advisor to King Hamlet, too?"

"Wait, was he?" asked Sage.

"We have no idea. It doesn't say one way or another. This is a perfect example of how Shakespeare leaves out a lot of backstory, which lets each production make guesses and choices."

"That's annoying," muttered Coleman.

Sage had her hand on her chin, still thinking about it. "Because that would be really weird if he was," she said.

"I know. It certainly would open possibilities. One thing we know for sure is that Hamlet knows Polonius, and while Hamlet is a prince, and therefore of higher status than Polonius, Polonius is his elder, and counselor to the King."

"And Ophelia's dad," said Feona. "Don't forget that!"

"Yes, exactly. Yet something about the way Hamlet acts toward Polonius here makes Polonius ask him, *Do you know me, my lord?*"

"Implied stage direction," called out Meredith.

"Right. Clearly, he made some gesture or used some tone Polonius found unusual. As actors you have to figure out what behavior will make Polonius question whether Hamlet realizes who he's talking to."

"He calls him a fishmonger," Catherine said.

"Yes, exactly, what's that?"

"A seller of fish," Jimmy said.

"Yes, is that an insult?

"Yes," Gino said, awake in the corner. His Greek-Italian family runs a restaurant somewhere in Northeast Philly.

"Why?" I asked.

"Because he's supposed to be royal, not a fish salesman," Gino said, with industry expertise.

"Exactly." I explained the intricacies of the analogy, that fishmongers might smell fishy when they get home at night, and that the nature of their work requires them to sell the older fish first, but they must be honest enough to never sell spoiled fish, or they'd lose their customers.

> *POLONIUS: How does my good Lord Hamlet*
> *HAMLET: Well, God-a-mercy.*
> *POLONIUS: Do you know me, my lord?*
> *HAMLET: Excellent well; you are a fishmonger.*
> *POLONIUS: Not I, my lord.*
> *HAMLET: Then I would you were so honest a man.*
> *POLONIUS: Honest, my lord!*
> *HAMLET: Ay, sir; to be honest, as this world goes, is to be*
> *one man picked out of ten thousand.*
> *POLONIUS: That's very true, my lord.*
>   (2.2.187-196)

Talking about fishmongers made me think of my dad. He loved fishing. In a canoe on a pond in the Poconos, surf fishing in Ocean City, trolling for blues off the Atlantic City inlet. Going for pompano on Christmas Day one year, we broke down five or ten miles off Boca, with me, Paige, Uncle Larry, Chris and Terry in the boat. We had to send up flares. A Coast Guard helicopter eventually located us and called for a tow. When I was 25 and caught a sailfish, Dad was even more excited than I was: he kept mumbling something about being 25 and with his father when he caught his first sailfish.

I looked down to my lesson plan and back up at the class.

"So, Hamlet is messing with Polonius," I said. "You see how craftily Hamlet insults Polonius with *fishmonger*, and he does it again when he tells Polonius what he's reading. Hamlet is a wordsmith, and as opposed to Polonius, Hamlet does use art and wit (remember Gertrude told Polonius *more matter with less art*, and he said, *I swear madam I use no art at all?*) to craft his pregnant replies."

"Hamlet is crafty," said Jerome.

"Yep. He knows whatever he says and however he acts, Polonius will report it to the King," said Feona.

"Good point," said Albert.

"The question is, is Hamlet trying to seem nonsensical? Is he coming off as a smart alec, or someone so far gone he doesn't understand Polonius' questions? Yes Mei-Mei?"

"If you're crazy it's easy to control the moment. It draws people's attention."

"Yes, great point! It distracts people's attention, at the same time they don't take the crazy person seriously, right?" I saw a few nods. "And notice all the punning, echoing and double meanings here. Besides *Words, words, words*, what else does Hamlet repeat three times in this scene?"

"*Except my life!*" shouted out Albert.

"Yes, thank you!"

"*Except my life, except my life...except my life,*" he echoed. Thank the Lord for the Performing Arts students. This scene is always more fun than *To be or not to be,* or *Too, too, solid flesh.* That thought gave me an idea.

"Okay everybody, stand up. If you're doing this scene you have to decide how he's going to say these lines. Does he say the phrase differently each time, or monotonously like a zombie? Let go around and each of you say 'Except my life' once and try to say it differently than the person before you. Be as loud or quiet or weird or whimsical as you like. You got it?" Luis in the middle nodded and a wave of agreement rippled outward. "Great. Albert—you start, then Mei-Mei, then keep going around. And…action!"

That was fun, though some of the renditions were duds, and I had Coleman try again because his was so flatline.

"But I'm depressed," he said, with morning languor. Heh, good one.

I upped my tone and energy to signal we were going to do something different. "Okay, let's have two of you up here to read this exchange." A few of the usual hands went up.

"Nope, nope, I'll choose," I said, and called on Jerome and Luis, whose hands weren't raised and who hadn't acted yet. "Jerome, you be Hamlet, and here," I added, reaching for the smaller crown and handing it to him, "you wear this, because after all, you are a prince." He adjusted it on his head and straightened his shoulders. "Remember," I told him, "you've decided you're going to act crazy. You can't stand your uncle, and Polonius here is his nosey advisor, okay?" Jerome nodded, not looking up from his book.

Then I turned to Luis who was already out of his chair, book in hand.

"Okay, come on out here to the middle. Remember, you're Polonius, and you're on a mission to find out what's going on with Hamlet. Polonius considers himself a good judge of character and thinks he can figure out why Hamlet is acting crazy and then go tell the King. Okay?"

He nodded, "Where do I start?"

"Right here with *What do you read, my lord?*"

POLONIUS: *What do you read, my lord?*
HAMLET: *Words, words, words.*
POLONIUS: *What is the matter, my lord?*
HAMLET: *Between who?*
POLONIUS: *I mean, the matter that you read, my lord.*
HAMLET: *Slanders, sir: for the satirical rogue says here*
that old men have grey beards, that their faces are
wrinkled, their eyes purging thick amber and
plum-tree gum and that they have a plentiful lack of
wit, together with most weak hams: all which, sir,
though I most powerfully and potently believe, yet
I hold it not honesty to have it thus set down, for
yourself, sir, should be old as I am, if like a crab
you could go backward.
POLONIUS: *[Aside] Though this be madness, yet there is method*
in 't. Will you walk out of the air, my lord?
HAMLET: *Into my grave.*
POLONIUS: *Indeed, that is out o' the air.*
[Aside]
How pregnant sometimes his replies are! a happiness
that often madness hits on, which reason and sanity
could not so prosperously be delivered of. I will
leave him, and suddenly contrive the means of
meeting between him and my daughter.—My
lord, I will take my leave of you.
HAMLET: *You cannot, sir, take from me any thing that I will*
more willingly part withal—except my life, except
my life, except my life.
                    (2.2.209-235)

Words, words, words. We share with words, remember with words,
and connect with words; though we often don't remember precisely

what was said. That's why *meet it is to write it down*. That's why three weeks ago when I was lying in bed in the screened-in ground floor computer and laundry room at Casa Cantley, listening to the sounds of rural Central American insects and donkeys amplified to a jungle din in the dense, pitch black mountainside, I was making notes in my journal.

Dad and Larry were out front on the porch. It wasn't really a porch as much as a cement slab apron that went around the front of the house under the cover of an overhanging corrugated metal roof. For the second night in a row I laid in bed listening to them talk. Did I think they needed their alone time, or did I need a break myself? After a few minutes of diligently documenting the stories and sentiments of the day, I realized it was ludicrous to lie crying in the basement. I would probably never have the chance to sit alone with the two of them again.

I dried my eyes, went upstairs, and sat outside with them for about an hour until my dad had to go to bed. Good thing it was dark out on that porch; the reality of why we were there drowned my face in tears. Sitting with Larry and Dad, I wondered what it would be like to know that it was the second to last night you'd ever spend in the presence of your brother. Your best friend and your connection to your dead parents and childhood. Of course you would want to stay up all night and talk: to not let go.

That week in Costa Rica I counted each hour, morning, afternoon, dinner time and night as it went by. I recorded conversations and wrote down as many impressions as I could. I was so conscious of each moment with my father being right now and never again, time seemed to slow. I watched as the clock did the unforgivable. Minute by minute, it kept moving towards the end. The days were long, and sometimes they dragged, but each night when I went to bed, there was one fewer day left with my dad.

"So, Hamlet has said things that indicate he's not feeling too upbeat. Remember the first time we see him his mom is telling him to *cast thy nighted color off*—stop wearing black and being so dark and gloomy. And we saw Claudius tell Rosencrantz and Guildenstern that Hamlet's been acting out of sorts. Again, what is Hamlet upset about?" A couple of hands went up.

"Yes, J-rome?" He smiled.

"He's upset because his dead dad told him he was murdered."

"Yes! And what else?" I prompted.

"By his uncle, man. Who married his mom. Not cool."

"Exactly, thank you. And there's more. Not only does his dead dad give him that information, what else does he tell Hamlet?" Sage uncurled her long dancer's arm. "Sage?"

"He told him to get revenge. To punish Claudius," she said with quiet confidence.

"Yes, Jimmy?"

"I think Hamlet is smart to test Claudius to make sure first."

"Agreed! Because here's the problem: what's the evidence? Think about it. A ghost. Hamlet can't exactly go to the court and tell them the new king is a murderer; he knows because the ghost of the dead king, his father, told him. Plus—think about this—he doesn't know if Polonius or Gertrude are in on it! Hamlet's in a tough position. He doesn't know who to trust. Who remembers that line at the end of Act 1.5 where Hamlet says the equivalent of 'Why me?' It's a great line with a nice ring to it." I recited it to them.

> *HAMLET: O cursèd spite,*
> *That ever I was born to put it right.*
>   (1.5.210-211)

When I was down in Costa Rica I had the sense I had been born to help usher my father through and out of this world.

The last day of Larry's visit I was busy. I made breakfast and was getting adept at cooking bacon in the microwave. That day we hosted an early dinner for Dad and Maureen's expat friends, the kind of sixty-year-old Tommy Bahama-wearing rebels you'd expect to find living in the middle of nowhere and acting like it's paradise. Clearly they loved my father. They brought a party atmosphere with them, drinking Myers's rum batitos at 3PM and talking about how to get good cat food, pot and passable ground beef in this Third World country. In the last few years these friends had been a huge social highlight for Dad and Maureen. Although they maintained a general air of tropical ease that afternoon, from time to time I caught them gazing at Dad as if he were their favorite nephew who was heading off to war the next day.

I broiled local snapper with lemon and butter, which was quite good, and we played Five Crowns, a card game like Russian Rummy with thirteen rounds and a different wild card every time. My grandmother originally gave the game to Dad and Maureen, and it is now the hit of the San Isidro del Generale gringo community. I'm not sure if these friends ever saw my father alive again, but I know that was their last game of Five Crowns.

Throughout the week visitors stopped by. Locals who wanted to see and be with Dad because they knew he was on his way out. Friends who wanted to play cards with him, talk with him, smoke and drink with him, just be in his presence. No one talked about anything spiritual or life-and-death oriented. No overt comments about what he's meant to them or what a great guy he is. Just friends showing up and sitting there together. Maybe I imagined it, but I'm pretty sure I saw a glaze of appreciation and gratitude in their eyes. And his. A silently acknowledged awareness of the hugeness of it all. This was it. It was about to be over. No obvious saying goodbye, but getting a goodbye, nonetheless.

There's something about visiting a person who you know is dying; there's a level of respect and awe. This might be the last time you see them. The last. It's powerful to touch that person, alive right now. To ask them questions. Breathe their air. And know they'll soon be gone. Forever inaccessible. Gone.

"Don't say gone," my dad quoted, one night in the Costa Rican dark. He shook his head somberly, and then he and Larry burst out laughing. "Don't say gone" is a classic line in our family. In their 40s the brothers had rented a villa in Nassau with three other couples, living it up for a week with a chef and a housekeeper and lots of rum. One night they left the rental skiff tied up to the rocks instead of bringing it in.

"It was as calm as could be," Larry explained. "We figured we could get away with it." After dinner they all went to the casino, and while they were inside a huge storm whipped up. When they got back to the house around 2 AM, my dad went down to survey the stormy waters and seeing the shattered remains of the fishing boat, shook his head and pronounced it "Smithereens."

A local fisherman had rented them the boat. "That boat was probably all he had," my dad explained. "It was his livelihood. We had to go to him the morning after the storm and tell him his boat was gone," he paused, gazing back in time. Then he continued, savoring the punchline in advance, "The guy looked at us, that old fisherman with his big sad eyes. He shook his head slowly and said, 'Don't say gone.'"

"Any questions?" I asked. "Okay, have a good day everyone—and think about whether Denmark should trust Fortinbras or not."

Catherine took time packing up and stopped halfway between her desk and mine with her backpack slung over her shoulder.

"I'm sorry I was gone so long. I had to take a walk."

"Oh, okay, no worries Catherine." She was still standing there.

"Umm, can I talk to you?"

"Sure, what's up?"

"So, umm, I wanted to talk to you because I'm having problems with Bradley."

"Really? What's going on?"

"Well, we have a history. Remember the day we were doing that activity and he kept saying 'you know me, you know me, I'm always the depressed guy,' and kept looking at me to make sure I was listening?"

"Umm, sort of." Not really.

"Well, you might not have noticed because I didn't react, but I knew what he was trying to do. He knew what he was doing because he knew that I could tell what he was doing but was trying to ignore it because I didn't want to start a fight." I kept listening, waiting for the problem.

"So yesterday remember when they were playing with that Nerf football you had on the desk? He had the ball and wound up like he was going to throw it at me. Hit me with the ball as hard as he could. Luckily I saw him so I was able to move back a little bit, and it ended up bouncing against the desk. But if I hadn't moved I would have gotten hit in the face pretty bad. Or in my eye. I was so shocked. I was like, did that just happen? I was like darn, I wish Miss Erica had seen that. I would never come to you to share this except—"

"I'm glad you're telling me," I encouraged her, wondering where this was going. Letting a boy get under her skin seemed unlike her.

"I went home and told my parents, because I tell them everything, and they said the best thing to do was talk to you. I don't want this to be turned into a big thing, but basically I'm telling you because I don't want to be partnered up with him in a group again."

"Okay, I get it."

"Basically, to have another adult who, like—"

"Knows?"

"Yes, knows. The way it's escalating I worry something more will happen. That he'll do anything for the attention, to make sure I know he's mad."

"This is weird," I said, it didn't sound like the Bradley I knew.

"Well, it was never things he would say to me directly, it's not reportable stuff. I've known him for a long time, since freshman year. He's liked me since freshman year and he never asked me out. I asked him to Sadies, and I think he thought that was an in. I never led him on and finally he asked me out on a date a couple weeks ago, to the movies. At the end I told him I had a just gotten out of an intense relationship a couple of months ago and I don't want to date right now. I don't want to get hurt again. I could tell he was really angry. He's like 'See ya.' Then for the next two weeks whenever I'd see him there was no hi or anything. Lately he's being mean to my sister. They used to be friends; we used to all be in PreCal together. We were friends."

She seemed exasperated and confused. I tried not to dismiss this as something that would pass—I hated when grownups used to do that to me. I wanted to honor her upset without fueling it. Plus, this was the most she had ever talked to me at one time.

"Catherine, thank you for telling me. I'll do my best not to put you two together."

"Thank you, I'd really appreciate that."

"Now, that being said, you don't need to sit near him. Maybe you can sit somewhere you can't see each other at all."

"I thought of that," she nodded.

"It stinks when a guy starts treating us differently just because we're not interested in them—"

"I know, right?"

"But something to keep in mind: he's actually not required to be your friend. Or even to be nice to you. I mean, he's allowed to be mad at you. He shouldn't be nasty or throw stuff at you for heaven's sake. But realistically, you might be expecting too much if you're looking for him to be nice to you like he was before."

"Hmmm...I think I see what you mean."

"Believe me, I think it stinks," I told her.

"It does stink."

"It happens. Maybe just give him a wider berth for now, okay?"

"Okay, yeah, you have a point. I was trying to do that anyway."

"Okay darling, what else?"

"That's it Miss Erica. Thanks." I was sorry she was going through a tough time, but it was nice to think about someone else's problems for a few minutes.

2: 3

There is nothing either good or bad but thinking makes it so

(2.2.268-270)

Thursdays were my busiest teaching days and I had grad school Thursday night. I spoke to my father briefly when I got home on Wednesday; Maureen handed him the phone. It was so good to hear his voice.

"Hi sweetheart. I love you. I can't really talk," he said, and handed the phone back to her. The "Hi sweetheart" sounded just like him, but the rest sounded thin and strained, and I heard spurts of noise that sounded like gasping coughs as Maureen took the phone back from him.

I was replaying that call in my head when the bell rang.

"Okay, let's get started. Take out your books. So, who are Rosencrantz and Guildenstern and what was Hamlet's first reaction to seeing them? Yes, Duncan?" He's awake early today.

"They are his friends from school and he was happy to see them." His voice makes me feel like there's a man in the room, and his thick beard contributes to this illusion.

"Good. But let's be sure we know they are not college friends like Horatio. No, Rosencrantz and Guildenstern are childhood friends. Guys he grew up with. What are the words he uses that show he's happy to see him?" Duncan's hand went slowly halfway up. Really awake. "Yes, go ahead," I encouraged.

"He says *My excellent good friends!*"

"Exactly. Then they immediately start bantering and ribbing each other like old friends do. But notice how Hamlet's reaction to them changes. Let's get three of you up here to read this, it's much easier to understand. Duncan, why don't you come up and be Hamlet, and Vincent here is your buddy from home you haven't seen for a while." They laughed and started to unfold themselves out of their desks. "And Gino, you too. Come on up here. Now remember, you guys are childhood friends. You know Hamlet's parents, in fact they asked you to come and check on him."

"We're like spies, heh, heh," said Gino.

"Yes, you are! Exactly! And the question is, are you good actors? Will it be easy for Hamlet to tell something is up? Can you act like you aren't just here to get intel for his parents?" I added and turned to the rest of the class. "Now, while these guys are doing this, the rest of you watch, and think about whether you think they are being good friends to Hamlet or not, okay?"

On the side I reminded Gino and Vincent, "You're trying not to give away the fact you were sent for, and it gets awkward."

GUILDENSTERN: My honoured lord!

ROSENCRANTZ: My most dear lord!

HAMLET: My excellent good friends! How dost thou, Guildenstern? Ah, Rosencrantz! Good lads, how do ye both?

ROSENCRANTZ: As the indifferent children of the earth.

GUILDENSTERN: Happy, in that we are not over-happy; On fortune's cap we are not the very button.

HAMLET: Nor the soles of her shoe?

ROSENCRANTZ: Neither, my lord.

HAMLET: Then you live about her waist, or in the middle of her favours?

GUILDENSTERN: 'Faith, her privates we.

HAMLET: In the secret parts of fortune? O, most true; she is a strumpet. What's the news?

ROSENCRANTZ: None, my lord, but that the world's grown honest.

HAMLET: Then is doomsday near: but your news is not true.
Let me question more in particular: what have you, my good friends,
deserved at the hands of fortune, that she sends you to prison hither?
GUILDENSTERN: Prison, my lord?
HAMLET: Denmark's a prison.
ROSENCRANTZ: Then is the world one.
HAMLET: A goodly one; in which there are many confines,
wards and dungeons, Denmark being one o' the worst.
ROSENCRANTZ: We think not so, my lord.
HAMLET: Why, then, 'tis none to you; for there is nothing
either good or bad, but thinking makes it so: to me
it is a prison.
ROSENCRANTZ: Why then, your ambition makes it one; 'tis too
narrow for your mind.
HAMLET: O God, I could be bounded in a nutshell and count
myself a king of infinite space, were it not that I
have bad dreams.

(2.2.258-275)

This year I noticed all the references to ambition and dreams and marveled at how dreams and ambition and dead fathers seem to naturally go together. Back when I was in New York trying to "make it," one of the faults I found with my father was that he didn't seem to have dreams or ambition. No wonder it was so hard for me to live big, I'd think; both my parents were content with their lives. No drive, no dreams, no trying to make something happen. I now know the era of my own aching aspirations coincided with my father being deeply depressed. He was a man who was not built to be alone and the woman he had fallen in love with when he was out opening a casino in Deadwood, South Dakota, had dumped him. He bought them both Harleys and they planned to ride back to Florida together and get married.

Larry told me, "almost immediately after she got the Harley Davidson, she was out of there. He took it very, very hard. He couldn't understand it."

A few years later, he lost a big chunk of money on a little Italian restaurant he bought in Florida with his half of the money he and Mom got from selling their house. I couldn't believe it: what was he thinking? He had some experience in restaurants, but not in owning and running his own place. It hurts me to think of it now. When I went down to visit him and he proudly brought my sister and me to the restaurant, he was so excited. He'd learned that sautéing the pasta and sauce together in a pan before plating brings it to a much higher temperature than just taking the pasta out of the boiling water and putting the sauce on it like we did at home all those years. He always wanted his soup and his pasta to be hot. My throat tightened with dread and remorse. Did I have a lukewarm reaction to that cozy, rustic place? Had I only been there once? I think he only had it for six months.

I can't remember much about it. I hope I was enthusiastic. I've never been good at hiding my disdain or disinterest, and it makes me cry to think of how many times I eeked out a tepid response, or out-and-out dismissal, that might have hurt him. How did I not see he was really trying? How he was such a good sport about whatever life dealt him? Was he as wise as his patient, stoic demeanor indicated? How did I not know it was one of my father's dreams to own his own restaurant? I should have known. I guess I just never gave it much thought. He loved restaurants. As much as he loved movies. He'd get excited telling you about them. Larry said Dad had a vision of making it into a Joe Italiano's (a place he loved in South Jersey), somewhere everyone would come to. According to Paige he did a lot of the cooking himself; she said he made the best pizza in town, and the pasta dishes were great.

Tony's Pizzeria. Talk about *the heart-ache and the thousand natural shocks that flesh is heir to.* I acted like I knew everything, but I didn't know enough to see my dad as a man with a dream of having a pasta joint—the kind he always loved. I should have dropped everything and moved to Florida to help him make a go of it. I'd give anything to sit there and watch him make me a plate of linguini white clam.

Oh God. Can't we rewind?

He was a man, take him for all and all...

Can't we rewind and get back wasted time? The summer afternoons I spent hanging out in my friend's dark messy room when I could have been out on the boat with my Dad? Seeing him smile. Making him happy. *Had I but time!* (5.2.368). I never wanted to live in Florida, but if I could rewind I'd go back and help him. I could have given a year of my life to this man who gave me so much love and kindness and asked so little.

"Why do they find it hard to believe that Hamlet thinks Denmark—and the palace at Elsinore where he lives—is a prison?"

"Because he's a prince," said Gino.

"Yeah, he's rich," said Jerome.

"Exactly," I agreed. "Rosencrantz and Guildenstern are simple guys. They grew up with Hamlet. He's their rich and influential boyhood friend. They can't imagine a prince would feel trapped, and in their mind the only explanation can be, what?" Wait, give them a second. Another second. Nothing. "What do Rosencrantz and Guildenstern think is upsetting Hamlet?"

"His dead dad."

"His uncle married his mom like two months later!"

"Yes...okay, that's what Claudius and Gertrude think, but Rosencrantz and Guildenstern don't mention either of those.

Look at what we just read. Hamlet says Denmark's a prison, and what does Rosencrantz say? Sage, read that part again."

"*Why then, your ambition makes it one; 'tis too narrow for your mind,*" she said with poise. My ambition. It kept me away from my family—even though they were the ones who moved to Florida. If they had stayed in New Jersey or Pennsylvania…. Stop. Focus.

"So, what is this ambition R & G think Hamlet has?" I asked.

"To kill Claudius!" said Jimmy Wong. Ugh. Nice try.

"Well, actually, good point, that is something Hamlet wants to do, but R & G don't know that. What do we know from Act 1:2 that Hamlet wanted to do?"

"Go back to school," said Catherine.

"Right. Go back to school and hang out with his philosophical scholar friend Horatio. What would we think is the natural career path for a prince, especially an only child?"

"To become king?" guessed Meredith.

"Yes, exactly. See how he acknowledges he knows what they are suggesting, but not being king isn't what is bothering him. What's bothering him?"

"He has bad dreams!" said Diane.

"Exactly. And what do you think his bad dreams are about?"

"The ghost and his father being murdered," she said.

"And how he's going to get revenge," piped up Coleman.

"Yes, great. Now did you guys notice any familiar phrases in this scene?"

Meredith raised her hand, smiling. I nodded, and she recited *there's nothing either good or bad but thinking makes it so* with relish and air quotes. I've been saying that line to them since sophomore year.

My dad didn't quote Shakespeare like Mrs. Esther, but he did have his sayings and he did coin or perpetuate a lot of phrases that have echoed through my life. Some he'd say ironically with a smirk and an air of remembrance, like the punch line of a well-honed inside joke. Besides "Don't say gone;" there was "I hear ya talkin' kid;" "Life is better than the best movie;" "Is this the fun part?" "That's a good one," when someone said something funny, and "It sounds like another once in a lifetime chance!" referencing my refrain whenever I was trying to get money to go on some adventure. He'd say "I love it!" with a delighted chuckle when I told him about something cool I did; "You're a very thoughtful child," when I did something nice for someone; "Oh, reeely?" when I went on and on telling him something that might not have been very interesting, and "the Lord will help you, he always does," when I felt hopeless.

In 1995, when I was 29 and my father was getting prostate cancer treatments at Sloan-Kettering, he would pass the time visiting me where I worked, at Mezzaluna on Third Avenue and 74th. He stayed in a room at the West Side YMCA Monday through Thursday nights, in part because he thought it would be fun, and in part, he said, because he didn't want to do my sixth floor walk-up studio every day and sleep on a futon. His best friend Jerry told me my dad walked all over New York City during that time. "He knew the city better than anyone I knew," Jerry told me, years later. That struck me as so strange, since I was the New Yorker and he was the dad from Florida. I remember him sitting at the bar at Mezzaluna telling me about where he'd gone and what he'd seen. I hope I asked questions and acted interested.

In 1995 I was half his age, and I knew a lot less than he did, although I was convinced I knew a lot more. About New York and life. But even though I probably acted like a know-it-all sometimes, my father humored me, always taking my twenties angst and drama seriously. When there was no clear solution to my latest major dilemma, he would bring events back in perspective with a philosophy that would serve as a guiding premise all my life: "the only thing that really matters is what kind of a person you are." Like I said, he knew a lot more than I did.

"Ah yes, there's nothing good or bad but thinking makes it so, one of my favorite lines," I said. "What Hamlet says next, while not a soliloquy, is a wonderful monologue." I noticed Luis's brow clouding over. "Who remembers the difference between a soliloquy and a monologue? Feona?"

She dutifully recited, "All soliloquies are monologues, but not all monologues are soliloquies."

"Yes," I confirmed with a gratified smile. Luis wasn't looking any less muddled and now a few other boys were looking confused. "Think of it this way," I tried to explain. "SOLO is alone, so a soliloquy is someone alone talking. MONO means one, so it's one person talking, but they are not necessarily alone. That's why, yes, all soliloquies are monologues, but not all monologues are soliloquies. OK?" I asked, waiting for nods. "Anyway, there are some wonderful well-known lines in this next monologue. Albert, would you read it? And read it coming from a place of suspicion, disappointment and cynicism—because life stinks right now and you don't know who you can trust."

He was already up and easing his shoulders into place. "You want this?" I asked, holding out the crown. He waved off the idea or the need and began con brio. He stood like a young Dr. Emmett Brown with a full head of the same wild hair; only the lab coat and the DeLorean were missing to complete the scene. Albert read beautifully; fully articulating and savoring each word, even if he didn't seem to quite know what some of the phrases meant. He was even savvy enough to gesture to the ceiling at *this majestical roof*. It was terrific.

HAMLET: I will tell you why; so shall my anticipation
prevent your discovery, and your secrecy to the
King and Queen molt no feather. I have of late, but
wherefore I know not, lost all my mirth, forgone all
custom of exercises, and, indeed, it goes so heavily
with my disposition that this goodly frame, the-
Earth, seems to me a sterile promontory; this most
excellent canopy, the air, look you, this brave o'erhanging
firmament, this majestical roof, fretted
with golden fire—why, it appeareth nothing to me
but a foul and pestilent congregation of vapors.
What a piece of work is a man, how noble in
reason, how infinite in faculties, in form and moving
how express and admirable; in action how like
An angel, in apprehension how like a god: the
beauty of the world, the paragon of animals—and
yet, to me, what is this quintessence of dust? Man
delights not me, no, nor women neither, though by
your smiling you seem to say so.
                (2.2.316-334)

"Yaay! Thank you!" I didn't bother going into how Hamlet can
be seen to be describing the painted ceiling of the Globe theater
in London in this passage. Time was running out.

"Okay, next, let's look at the actors and the idea of hospitality. What did you say was Hamlet's reaction to the arrival
of the players?" Mei-Mei raised her hand. Still on a roll from
yesterday, yeah!

"He was happy," she said.

"How could you tell, Mei-Mei?"

"He welcomed them," she answered as if it were evident.

"Yes indeed. Anyone count how many times Hamlet said

the word "welcome" starting at 2.2.445? I saw some heads tilting into their books.

"Three!" said Catherine.

"Yes, would you read those first few lines for us, Catherine? And look at all those dashes, who remembers what they indicate? Yes Meredith?"

"A change of direction in who they're talking to," she said. Good memory.

"Yes, exactly, so imagine him going from one of the actors to the next, on down the line. Go ahead."

> *You are welcome, masters; welcome, all.—I am glad*
> *to see thee well.—Welcome, good friends.—O, my old*
> *friend! thy face is valenced since I saw thee last:*
> *comest thou to beard me in Denmark?—What, my young*
> *lady and mistress!*
>
> (2.2.445-8)

Welcome, welcome. That's a Dad word. "You are more than most welcome," was his standard response to "thank you, thank you, thank you!"

"Thank you," I said, when Catherine finished. "We see later that Hamlet tells Polonius to make sure the players are well lodged—look on line 553 where Polonius says he'll treat them as they deserve—in other words as the lower-class citizens traveling players were. But then see how Hamlet tells him, no, you must treat all your guests well."

God's bodykins, man, much better: use every man
after his desert, and who should 'scape whipping?
Use them after your own honour and dignity: the less
they deserve, the more merit is in your bounty.
    (2.2.555-9)

"That's Shakespeare on hospitality and being a good host. Remember, Shakespeare was first and foremost an actor: a member of a troupe. Yes, they had the theaters, but they traveled, too. It's worth noting that this play, arguably his most popular with actors and directors, is full of references to the art and business of acting. It's fun to think of Shakespeare putting in a plug for better treatment of traveling players."

Hospitality. I grew up thinking of my dad as a great host and the life of the party: a tortoise-framed suburban golfer out of 1970s central casting. He had Ted Kennedy hair, wore wild madras, Lilly Pulitzer, or tan-and-rust vertical striped pants, and danced a little dad's shuffle with his hands in loose fists and his arms bent at a 90 degree angle, chugging along back and forth with his feet. This image was probably cemented by a singular huge party they threw at our house when we lived outside of Boston and he ran the foodservice for MIT. He spent all weekend preparing. My Mom was cleaning and cooking, but what I distinctly remember was my father explaining to me — while standing in the kitchen in front of the stove – how he had borrowed racks and racks of heavy-duty institutional ceramic soup cups from work and was making a huge, hotel-sized aluminum stockpot of vichyssoise. He pulled up a chair so I could peer into the high pot. "Cold soup!" he said like it was the weirdest, coolest thing ever, "Can you believe it?"

     Dad would frequently comment on how many friends I had

and how social I was. "I don't know where you got it," he'd say. "You didn't get it from me and your mother."

"But Dad, you were so social. You used to have all those parties in Medfield."

"What parties?" he asked.

I told him about the borrowed dishes and the vichyssoise, and he laughed.

"Yeah, okay, that was one party, though. Only once."

I finally got to talk to Dad Thursday night as I was driving to my 7 PM class. I was calling every day since I got back from seeing him, which seemed embarrassingly obvious; we both knew why. He was drugged up, sleeping a lot in his chair, and Maureen said he was saying weird things. I wanted to hear him say something otherworldly. Some say "oh, that's the morphine talking," in these circumstances, but I suspect that sometimes morphine blurs the senses enough so a person can see and say things that are more real. I kept asking Maureen if Dad was saying anything specific, final truths or insights into the world beyond. After three days of not being able to talk, I was so glad to hear him, even though his voice sounded thin and far away.

"Hi sweetheart."

"Hi Dad. Hey, Dad, have you been seeing anything? I mean, have you had any hallucinations or anything?"

"You know, that's what's funny," he said, and sort of laughed. "I think it's all real."

Just like that, I knew it was all real. Whatever he was seeing, whatever was being unveiled, it was all real. I remember exactly where on the road the car was when he said it; the image of that telephone pole at that specific intersection is inextricably connected with the words, "I think it's all real." I wanted more, I wanted specifics. When I pulled into the University parking lot,

I sat there for a moment, my body tingling from what felt like a peek beyond this world. I dried my tears and went inside.

As soon as I sat down in my Teaching Literary Criticism class I opened up my notebook and wrote down what he said. I kept looking at the words, wishing there were more, even though part of me knew those few words were enough because they summed up everything.

I tried to write down a timeline. I think it was Tuesday he fell in the bathroom; thank God he didn't break anything. It was yesterday—yes, Wednesday—Maureen told me the doctor came on Wednesday and said *poco tiempo*. It was three weeks since we were there in Costa Rica, and a month since they told him there was nothing more they could do. After all those years of cancer and cancer treatments, my father had real pain. I could tell it was wearing him out. He still didn't talk about it, but I could tell it was getting harder and harder for him to be here.

Poco tiempo.

I slept through chapel again. I don't teach until 10AM on Fridays, so I took my time getting up and dressed and to school. I got to the third floor, opened the shades to let the gray in, and felt strangely outside of myself, dragging my body around the room, looking for that damn red pen I just had in my hand. After they took the quiz and we went over the answers, I went around the room and had them say One Thing You're Looking Forward To for the weekend, to use up time. I had written META THEATER on the board and wanted to explain the concept, but I couldn't find the energy. I felt dazed and my face was a little numb.

"Okay, take out your reading responses and your books," I said, starting around the room at Jerome. They had all done the homework. For the most part, I assign work, and they do it.

"Let's hear something from everyone." I reminded myself to say little in response. Hearing from everyone took twenty minutes. Then I hoisted my body up and did my part. I explained meta by using the TV show *The Office* as an example, which made many of them sit up in their chairs and smile.

"Like *The Taming of the Shrew*, there is a lot of talk about acting in *Hamlet*. *Taming* talks more about the roles we all play," some of the girls nodded, remembering back to November, "whereas *Hamlet* talks about the profession of being an actor. And Hamlet says he's going to use a play to find out the truth about Claudius."

"*The play's the thing!*" Albert called out.

"*Wherein I'll catch the conscience of the King*—yes, exactly! And those are the last words of Act 2."

"Rhyming couplet!" shouted Feona. Random shout-outs are better than talking amongst themselves and not paying attention, that is for sure.

"Meta is huge right now. Have you ever heard someone say "'that's so meta'?" I asked. I heard a few affirmative-sounding murmurs behind and turned to explain. "In this case 'meta' means self-referential. So, *Hamlet* is meta-theater because it's a play that spends a lot of time talking about acting. How should humans act? Are we good at taking on roles and direction or not? Hamlet warns Horatio that he's going to start acting crazy. Then actual traveling actors show up, and we see that part of being a well-educated noble is knowing theater and having acted, at least at university. Hamlet himself is a theater buff. He knows these actors as if he's hung out backstage or in the pub with them. He's even read and practically memorized their old reviews! We see him come alive, he's in his element, using the lingo. He has theater expertise. Okay, the bell's about to ring. We'll talk more about actors and acting next week—over the weekend you'll finally get to the *To be or not to be* speech—pay close attention to what it's about. Also look for Hamlet as an acting coach, the advice he gives. Have a good weekend—and I hope to see you at the Oratorical on Sunday!"

The Oratorical is an annual night of student speeches produced by the English Department. I had been coaching my three speakers for months. Mom had arrived the night before to visit my grandmother and I wasn't going to do anything other than the Oratorical and be with Mom this weekend.

When I called Maureen around dinner time, she said it was really bad. Dad had been asking the Lord to take him, but he wanted to wait until my uncle Walter got there.

"Erica, I have to get off the phone—call back in a few hours, okay?" When I called back, she sounded calmer.

"He felt nauseated but didn't want me to give him the suppository. Once I gave it to him, he was much better." More information than I needed, but she had no filters left. "He's sleeping."

My other uncle, Walter, was set to leave for Costa Rica early the next morning and arrive at their house around 4pm. I hoped to God he would get to my dad in time.

O, O, O, O, Dad....

> *O day and night, but this is wondrous strange*
> (1.5.185)

That was Friday night.

At 7:30 on the cold, rainy Saturday morning of March 29, 2014, the phone rang and woke me. The screen said "HLC." Of course I knew. As we had prearranged, Maureen called Larry, and Larry called me.

"Hello?" I said with quiet dread.

"Erica, this is the call. This is it. He's gone."

Don't say gone.

"When?"

"I'm not sure. This morning. Sometime after midnight. Around one I think. I wanted to wait until morning to call you. You'll call Paige?"

"Yes, yes, I will. Thank you." I hung up.

I couldn't move.

I felt suspended; not connected to any one surface, but not floating, either. I knew I was still in bed under two big duvets, but I couldn't feel my body, I couldn't move my arm, and I couldn't feel the bed.

I sat like that for at least five minutes.

Slowly thoughts started forming. Dad probably died a little after I fell asleep on Friday night. That felt important. I had been semi-conscious most of the night thinking about him. Now I told myself what had really happened was he had been flitting around the edges of my dreams, passing through my room on his way out of this world.

I heard myself emit some strange whithered yalp.

My next thought was a visceral craving: I need my Mommy. Thank God she was in town. Thank the dear Lord God. I dressed and started walking towards my grandmother's retirement village across town wearing my slippers. I called Paige and told her. We talked all the way to my grandmother's, which takes about twelve minutes. I could tell there was cold all around me, but I couldn't feel it.

When I arrived, I was still talking to my sister. I knocked on the guest suite door, walked in, and found my Mom in her nightgown, cozied up in bed reading. I mouthed "It's Paige," and made a thumbs down sign, shook my head and felt my face crumble again. I passed my Mom the phone and sat on the edge of her bed. How lucky I could climb onto my mother's bed on this worst of all days.

Dad died. He died. Dad. Our Dad. She understood. She was upset too. After a few minutes I went upstairs to my grandmother's apartment to tell her. My grandmother was 91 at the time.

At this stage in her life Mimi resided mostly in the electric recliner in her living room. I sat on the floor at her feet, took her hand, looked up into her face and told her: "My dad is dead."

"Oh no, I'm so sorry, sweetie," she said. Something like that. We hugged, and sat in silence, my head resting on her knees, feeling completely known, held and understood. For minutes. Finally, I lifted my head and she spoke with the wisdom of the ages.

"Well," she said, looking down into my middle-aged girl eyes, "it's gonna be strange."

> *HORATIO: O day and night, but this is wondrous strange.*
> *HAMLET: And therefore as a stranger give it welcome.*
> *There are more things in heaven and earth, Horatio,*
> *Than are dreamt of in your philosophy.*
> (1.5.185-188)

March 29th was a blur of texts and calls and the frightening sense I was on the edge of an abyss. I finally talked to Maureen that night. She told me that in his last twenty-four hours he kept saying "Bye! Bye!" to her, and sort of waving her off. And she kept saying, "I'm not going anywhere. I'm right here." He also told her several times "Don't touch me." I think that hurt her. But I have heard that sometimes it's harder for a person's spirit to leave their body when someone they love is holding onto them.

"Wow. What else did he say? Did he say anything else?"

She was sobbing so hard, but it was obvious she wanted to talk.

"Oh Erica, it was so awful. I just turned away for a minute. For a minute. He kept saying 'Bye! Bye!' so finally I said, okay, 'I'm going into the kitchen, but I'm not leaving.' Erica, ohhh, all of a sudden I heard some noise from over in his chair and I then realized it didn't sound like he was breathing any more. I ran over there, and, oh Erica, he was gone!"

Oh God. Don't say gone.

The authorities wanted to bury him that same day; that's what they do down there. But Maureen explained to them that they had to wait until hermano, hermano, hermano got there. They understood and would bury him on Sunday.

"Did he say anything else? I mean before that, when he was saying bye?"

"Yes, oh my gosh, yes, it was amazing. He said, 'Don't forget to call Jerry on his birthday, April 7th.'" I smiled through the tears. His best friend from the first day of first grade.

"Yeah, and then he said, 'Tell Larry, you got four queens, you gotta go all in!'"

"No way!" I cried.

"And then you know what? The very last thing he said to me?"

"What?"

"Erica, he seemed so light and calm and he said with a smile, 'Bye! I'll catch up with you at the end of the week.' That's what he said! So cheerful and upbeat. Oh, Erica—" she wailed. "David...my David...."

O, O, O, O!

ACT THREE

My father died within 's two hours

(3.2.134-135)

"Oh Erica, it was sooo weeeeiird. So awwwwful. He kept telling me 'Bye!' Like he was shooing me away. 'Bye, bye,'" she quoted him, mimicking a cheerful, light-hearted Dad voice. "I told him I'm not going anywhere. I'm right here.' And then, oh then, Erica it was so terrible, it hurt my heart so much…ohhhhh…. He told me not to touch him!"

That first conversation with Maureen crackled with an electricity that felt paranormal. Ghostly. I never experienced anything quite like it. The air was thick and slow and my skin tingled. Especially my forehead. Even though all I had were her words in my ear, *in my mind's eye* I could see a movie of what had happened. We were thousands of miles apart but as she told me the details of his final hours, I felt like I was in their house on that Costa Rican hillside. I could see her pacing the white tile floor of the kitchen-dining-room-living room while she talked. I could tell she was looking at his empty chair when she described his last breaths and the moment at which she realized he wasn't breathing anymore. The sound of her bawling and wailing filled my head; but I could also hear the awe and wonder in her voice. She had been there. In the room, in the midnight hours, when he left. She heard his last words. And as she repeated them to me, I could see his shrunken, almost corpse of a body, wearing loose-fitting shorts—long stained from working around the house and yard—and one of his many old Guy Harvey or Harley Davidson tee-shirts, stretched out across his recliner between the front door and the TV, his mouth agape, gasping for air.

"He was in so much pain, Erica," she groaned like she was about to double over from physical anguish by proxy. It was as if she was trying to explain to me the only reason she let him go. She was bereft, and sounded borderline hysterical, but she also sounded grounded in a way that had been missing in the weeks leading up to his death. Something seemed to have subtly shifted. It was as if seeing how much my dad was suffering at the end helped Maureen let go just enough for my father to leave.

As much as I hated the idea of him suffering, I accepted that some pain was going to be part of his departure process. My dad was so gracious in his final weeks. He kept saying "You know, I've been very lucky. After 20 years of cancer, I never really had any bad pain until recently."

Lucky. Yep. Now we could say it. We had been lucky. Uncle Larry had said multiple times, "I just don't want him to suffer," and of course neither did I. For years I feared my father would have a long, drawn out, scary, painful decline, so when it all happened so relatively quickly, there was an element of relief. I had spent so many years getting used to the inevitability of losing my dad: *Thou know'st 'tis common; all that lives must die, passing through nature to eternity*; there was no point in peevishly opposing it now.

> *'Tis a fault to heaven,*
> *A fault against the dead, a fault to nature,*
> *To reason most absurd, whose common theme*
> *Is death of fathers, and who still hath cried,*
> *From the first corpse till he that died today,*
> *"This must be so."*
>   (1.2.105-110)

In those first few days after he passed, more than one person asked me if I was upset I hadn't been there when he died. People seemed to think it was weird, but I felt mostly okay about it. I mean, that had been the plan. Not to go back. And since they bury the body the same day down there, I would have had to be in Costa Rica just waiting for him to die for days if I wanted to be at the interment. Instead, I focused on celebrating his life at the funeral I knew we would have for him in Jenkintown, PA.

Hmmm. Funny. Hamlet wasn't there when his dad died either. He was busy at school, just like me. No doubt he "got the call" too, though I'm sure it was delivered on horseback by some royal messenger. But King Hamlet's death was unexpected. Prince Hamlet had no warning; no chance to say goodbye. No "one last good week," as Maureen kept calling our visit. Poor Hamlet. And though that goodbye at the bus station was the saddest, most unnatural moment of our lives together, my father somehow made it seem like it was natural his children were leaving him. He seemed almost peacefully preoccupied. It was as if saying goodbye to his children wasn't the most important thing. Maybe saying goodbye to life was.

3: 1

Where's your father?

(3.1.141)

The Monday after Dad died I was *creeping like snail unwillingly to school*, watching one salt-stained boot hoist itself in front of the other. Dad was dead. My first fatherless Monday.

He died on Saturday. Or Friday maybe. I didn't know because I didn't know the hour. But I guess it was after midnight, so I guess it was Saturday.

That was the longest Saturday of my life. So many friends and neighbors materialized. So many eras and epochs were traversed and transcended. So much soul and spirit energy coursed through my mind and body and house. Every surface of my skin was tingling. Sort of vibrating. Not numb. More like buzzed. The tactile feeling of being drunk. My mind didn't feel intoxicated though. More like stunned. My head felt detached from my body as if I had lifted it off and it was having a strangely separate experience somewhere else. I welcomed friends and family, I thanked them for coming over and for whatever they brought. I recounted his final words. I heard myself say things, and I heard visitors talking to each other, but the voices all sounded one or two rooms away.

Tom offered to drive me to school but I wanted to walk. I wanted to feel the cold. I wanted to walk up the hill and sift through how I was going to approach the day. I walked through gelatinous air. The world seemed slower. After passing a house or two I found myself looking around to see if anything had changed since Friday. Strange. The world, now irrevocably altered, had the audacity to look exactly the same.

As I got to the path along the Pike, I thought about what was I going to do in class today. What was the least amount of teaching I could get away with? After doing *To be or not to be* I could talk about actors, acting, and holding up a mirror to nature. Yes, yes, that would be perfect. Give them some stock background on Shakespeare as an actor; I could do that off the top of my head and with no emotion. I'd tell them he was a member of the Lord Chamberlain's Men acting troupe, and how Shakespeare didn't make his money off publishing his plays, but rather off his share of the box office.

It was a relief to enter the school's empty halls. I got to the third floor and opened my office and classroom without seeing anyone. Then I heard my friend Kira—the science teacher and the only one who is here by 7 AM every single day—coming down the hall towards my office. She tilted her head, stared into my gaze with empathic sorrow, and held out her hands. I shook my head, felt my face crumble to a deep frown, and let myself be enveloped in her mama bear hug.

After she left, I shook off my grief spasm and was glad to see the graded quizzes and reading responses from Friday already collated and laying on the desk. The Act 3:1-2 file was on the podium. I erased the homework assignment on the board for Seniors and drew a circle with a line through it. No homework for the next three nights. I wobbled back to the podium and opened the file folder.

Where's your father? was written across the top of the first page.

Oh shoot. I forgot about that. *Where's your father?* Hamlet asks Ophelia in 3:1.

"Dead!" I cried out, like in "Shakespeare in Love" when Gwyneth Paltrow as Juliet awakes and swoons "Where is my Romeo?" and her nurse in the audience shouts out "Dead!"

Hot tears swelled up from the top of my spine and pushed through the back of my eyes. I let them come.

Where's your father?
  In the ground in Costa Rica.

I thought of Ophelia's words from Act 4 after Polonius dies: *I cannot choose but weep to think they would lay him i' th' cold ground* (4.5.74-75).

They buried him in the colorful cemetery at the end of their red dirt road on March 30th, the day after he died. It's amazing how many legal procedures surround death. I started seeing how the business of death was an essential part of life. How come I never realized that until now? Until now I skimmed over the technicalities of death like unfamiliar words in a mystery I was hurriedly reading to find out whodunnit. I've been so busy living the stuff in the middle that I had little awareness or respect for the beginning and the end of life. Well, no more, I can tell you that. Now the end is all I can think of.

According to Maureen the police had to be notified. They came and made a report; there's always an official investigation of a death. A doctor must be consulted, and a death certificate filled out. Once your loved one dies, logistics and legalities take over. I recognized the imperious role the government plays at the end of a human life. Eventually you need a death certificate to get anything done: to dispose of the body, deal with Social Security, collect insurance.

Their hilltop neighbors knew, I guess everyone knew, the gringo americano had died

"Everyone loved David," Maureen kept saying. "The kids, old men, all of them poor as dirt, but so sweet, so kind. Simple, good folks. Generous. They have nothing, but they are so generous. They share whatever they have. They help you. Your Dad loved them and they loved him. He would always give the kids candy."

My dad never learned Spanish, but his favorite phrase was "Vaminos, donde va?" When someone spoke Spanish to him, he would lift his shoulders with a kind smile, hold out his hands palms up and say "Lo siento, non habla espagnole." I'm not surprised that his warm personality transcended language barriers, the way he shared the oranges and grapefruit with the neighbors, the nine hummingbird feeders he had decorating the back porch, and the way he said "confeeti, confeeti" like a proud dad on Halloween when he would return home from the States with candy for the kids who lived on their road.

According to both Maureen's and Walter's account, there were at least seventy-five people—ticos, in addition to their expat friends—who came to the cemetery to pay their respects. They lined up, a long impressive parade leading to the temporary sunshade covering the gaping grave. Each person carried a flower, and each stopped to greet Walter and Maureen as they approached the graveside. Then one by one they dropped their flowers into his grave, crossed themselves, and turned to join the gathering group of mourners outside of the tent. Everyone told Maureen what a nice man Dad was, and what a big heart he had. They just kept saying things about his corazón. Corazón.

Once the classroom was ready I went into my office and turned on my laptop to check emails. Compliments on the Oratorical. Condolences about my dad. I checked Maureen's Facebook. There was a picture of Dad posted to her timeline by someone I didn't know. He looked so old: gray and fading; smiling in sort of a patient dreamy way; sitting on his recliner holding a baby, and the caption read "Don David te llevare siempre en mi corazón."

It's so strange. I used to think "You never know what's around the corner" was a wishful cliché, and that most lives weren't that surprising. But it's true, we don't know what lies ahead. There is no way Dad could have imagined he would be buried on a hillside in the middle of Nowhereville, Costa Rica, and that he could have scores of locals commemorating his passing with flowers, tears, and the gift of their presence. I could picture the cemetery perfectly because I went to see it a few weeks earlier. I gazed through the chipped, blue-painted wrought iron gates and visualized it as his final resting place.

I don't know if I'll ever feel a need to go visit my father's grave. Maureen keeps saying she wants us to come down. My sister says she thinks she'd like to go at some point. If she does, I'll go with her. I don't want to think about it right now. It's too soon to tell if a trip down there—to where he was but isn't anymore—would just be awful or would be sort of nice. I feel like it's going to take a long time before it would be nice, but you never know.

I could hear the hall slowly come to life with the sounds of teenage girls and their Monday morning excitements and woes. I kept working in the dark with my door open. Rarely will a kid come into a classroom if the light is off, and I didn't want to call attention to myself. I went down to chapel late, hoping to have as few interactions as possible, and I sat in the back. By the time second period came around I had finished my coffee and felt ready to go. Nothing like show time to snap me out of my misery.

"Okay, everybody up! Up, up, up! It's Monday—look alive! Are you ready?" I asked. "Let's do this. Official Greeting time. Good morning everyone!"

"Good morning Miss Erica."

"Thank you. Please be seated. So, who went to the Oratorical last night?" Hands went up. Bradley was one of the MCs and there were comments and compliments bouncing around the room for him and the different speakers. I just let them talk amongst themselves.

We used up the next ten minutes taking the quiz and checking reading responses. They had read *To be or not to be* over the weekend and I had told them to watch as many different YouTube versions of the speech as possible.

"Okay, I said," pointing to the board, "here's what's happening today. We're going over the *To be or not to be* soliloquy—"

"Hey Miss Erica," said Imani, "did you see the Adrian Lester one? I liked that one," she drawled.

"Ha, yes," I said. "Not only did I see the YouTube version, but Peter Brook's Adrian Lester *Hamlet* was the first live version of the play I ever saw."

"Cool."

"Anyway," I continued, "today we are going to look at more spying, more implied stage direction and more acting advice. What's Claudius and Polonius's plan?"

"They are going to spy on Hamlet," said Meredith.

"Yeah, they are setting him up," Catherine said, turning to Meredith to commiserate.

"Exactly," I confirmed. "Do you agree with Claudius? Is it well within the rights of parents to spy on their kids?"

"No!"

"Not okay."

"Depends…."

"Depends on what?" I asked.

"Well, like, if they already have a history of getting in trouble," said Meredith.

"Okay, gathering intel on your kids—like Polonius sends Reynaldo to do—is one thing. What about setting them up?" I asked. I was not really looking for an answer, just planting a seed. "That's what happens here. They totally set Hamlet up."

"Yeah man, not cool," said Gino.

Vincent next to him was nodding. "Definitely not."

"What did you say the *To be or not to be* soliloquy is about?" I asked.

"Suicide!" Meredith called out.

"He's depressed," said Catherine.

"Life sucks!" said Luis. I winced. Sweet Luis?

"Life sucks and then you die," muttered Coleman with a smirk, a nod to Luis, and a glance up to see if I was paying attention.

"Okay. How about let's not use 'sucks' though? I'm going to read this—girls, those of you who did this for your soliloquy feel free to pitch in."

I still don't have it all memorized, but I wandered around the room and looked at each of them during the parts I did know by heart. The speech is taped onto the podium, so I just glanced down when I needed to.

"Do you have that whole thing memorized?" asked Coleman when I finished.

"No," I said, "but Diane does!" She smiled, looking like a black-eyed Pippy Longstocking.

"Well, I'm not sure if I still do," she said with a half-smile.

"You have to!" I exhorted her. "You have to remember it for the rest of your life! After all that work you put into it," I added, referring to the fact that winter term the girls were required to memorize a speech of at least 18 lines from either *The Taming of the Shrew* or *Hamlet*, and Diane memorized all 35 lines of *To be or not to be*.

"Remember I told you I'll give you extra credit if you memorize five lines or more."

"How much?" asked Coleman, sitting up.

"Yes," said Mei-Mei quietly, "how much?" She was jotting it down.

"Hmmmm, good question. One extra credit point for the first five lines, and one point for every line after five."

"To our final grade?" Bradley asked, in disbelief.

"Uh, no," I said, "that would be insane. I'll add those points onto any points you lost on the quizzes or the test, okay?" Lots of rumbling and turning side to side to check in with each other, and a few questions about whether someone who already memorized it for the exam last term could still get extra credit for it this term.

"Of course!" I said, smiling at Diane. She seemed surprised. "If they still remember it, they can get the points. Why not?"

"I'm doing it. I'm definitely doing it," said Bradley, making a note in his planner.

"Okay, back to the most famous soliloquy in the most famous play in the English language. I would submit to you that this speech is not about Hamlet contemplating whether to kill himself or not. He's exploring the reasons why we don't kill ourselves. If we unpack the language we see that he touches on everything hard about life." I took them through line by line and went over every unclear word or phrase.

To be or not to be—that is the question:

"Right off the bat, he's talking about existence. BE-ing human, BE-ing alive."

> *Whether 'tis nobler in the mind to suffer*
> *The slings and arrows of outrageous fortune,*
> *Or to take arms against a sea of troubles*
> *And, by opposing, end them.*

"*Nobler in the mind*. Is it a better idea, is it more honorable, to just take all the crap life gives you, or should you fight back? Here's where it gets interesting because the word 'opposing' sounds like you're standing up to your troubles. Choosing to fight against the indignities of life instead of sitting on the couch night after night feeling sorry for yourself. The language that follows next does not suggest a fight. It suggests that opposing your troubles equals ending them, which equals:"

To die, to sleep—

"To me this is very interesting because Hamlet is suggesting the *slings and arrows of outrageous fortune* are so endemic to human existence, that to end your troubles, you must actually end your life. You see what I mean?" Albert, Feona, and the entire Peanut Gallery, were paying seemingly rapt attention, giving quick nods of comprehension. I looked to the other side, and from Luis and Imani, through the Bermuda Triangle, there were foggy expressions. "You see what I mean?"

"Yes." "Nope." "Not really." "Um, can you say it again?"

"Absolutely. Jot these notes down in the margin."

To die, to sleep—
No more—

"This suggests that once you die all you do is sleep. There is nothing else. Oblivion. You're done."

and by a sleep to say we end
The heartache and the thousand natural shocks
That flesh is heir to—'tis a consummation
Devoutly to be wished.

"There it is again. Basically, he's iterating that to be human—to have flesh—is to inherit heartache and pain."

To die, to sleep—
To sleep, perchance to dream. Ay, there's the rub,

"Meaning, there's the snag or the problem or the glitch."

For in that sleep of death what dreams may come,
When we have shuffled off this mortal coil,
Must give us pause.

"We don't know what kind of dreams we are going to have on the other side! What if we have bad dreams? *Must give us pause* means we better think about whether we really wish we were dead."

There's the respect
That makes calamity of so long life.

"If you look at the word respect, you see it's just another way to say re-look at."

"Like spectacle!" Albert called out.

"Yes, exactly. Or spectacles, an old-fashioned word for glasses. Things you see with. Next Hamlet details life's universal hardships."

For who would bear the whips and scorns of time,
Th' oppressor's wrong,

"That's pretty straightforward."

the proud man's contumely,

"That means rude language. The things an arrogant person might say to humiliate you."

The pangs of despised love,

"Meaning when you love someone who doesn't love you back, and in fact, they wish you'd leave them alone." Giggles. I resisted looking up at Bradley or Catherine.

the law's delay,

"The lack of justice in this world."

The insolence of office,

"How people in official positions are petulant and difficult because they know they can get away with it."

and the spurns
That patient merit of th' unworthy takes,

"*Patient merit of the unworthy*. Think of the people in this world who control some aspect of your life or tell you what to do. Chances are many of them you think don't deserve to be the boss of you, and yet—they are."

When he himself might his quietus make
With a bare bodkin?

"*Quietus* is peace, or reckoning, and *bare bodkin* is a dagger. He's saying, who would put up with all this when he could escape it by killing himself? Of course, this is a rhetorical question. I think it's interesting to see Hamlet's musings shape up to be more 'Even though life's really hard; here's why we don't just end it,' than, 'Should I kill myself or not?' You see the distinction?" Nods.

Who would fardels bear,
To grunt and sweat under a weary life,
But that the dread of something after death,
The undiscovered country from whose bourn
No traveler returns, puzzles the will
And makes us rather bear those ills we have
Than fly to others that we know not of?

"He's saying we don't kill ourselves because we aren't sure what is on the other side. If we can consciously reason—meaning we haven't had a psychotic break or aren't crippled by the hopelessness and despair of depression." I added that part last year because these days almost everyone knows someone who has committed suicide. "Most of us choose to stick with what we know rather than fly off to the unknown. *The undiscovered country.*"

Thus conscience

"He means the process of thinking, of being conscious, not so much "conscience" like guilt. But of course, back then suicide was illegal, so he could mean guilty conscience as well."

does make cowards of us all,
And thus the native hue of resolution
Is sicklied o'er with the pale cast of thought,

"We would take matters into our own hands, but once we've thought about it long enough, we are like, naah."

And enterprises of great pitch and moment
With this regard their currents turn awry
And lose the name of action.
(3.1.64-96)

I assigned them each two to four lines of the speech.

"Okay, now that you have your lines, I want you to stand up and pace around as if you're contemplating the meaning of life and repeat your lines out loud at least five times. At least five times. Get comfortable with shaping the words in your mouth. Think about which words you're going to emphasize when it's your turn to speak. Get into the rhythm of it. Remember how we did the work with heroic couplets and iambic pentameter? Ba BUM, ba BUM, ba BUM, ba BUM, ba BUM."

"Can we do it like rap?" asked Luis.

"Absolutely!"

"Really?" asked Coleman.

"Yes, that's a great idea. It's all about the rhythm. Okay, ready? Go!"

In a few seconds a din rose from the students saying their disparate, overlapping lines, some louder than others. "Hey," I shouted, "pace around. Be upset. Do something with your hands."

Some of them, like Albert and Feona, and Meredith, and even Mei-Mei, got right into character using gestures. The rest shuffled around at first and kept looking to see if the others were doing it. I scanned the room and made eye contact with those whose eyes weren't in their books. Eventually everyone was doing it. Gino and Jimmy, the biggest and the smallest in the class, kept intentionally bumping into each other.

"Now everyone circle up! Let's recite this soliloquy with as much abandon and emotion as you can. When it's your lines, step into the circle to say them, and add some movement or gestures. Diane, you got this—Go!"

She took center stage and pen in hand, alternated between making notes and resting the pen tip pensively on her lip. After a few moments she launched in as if she was sharing the contents of her journal. At *that is the question* she tipped the pen to the audience.

"Great, great!" I called. "Keep going!"

Meredith paced back and forth and exuded a tense explosiveness she never shows in real life. At the end of the soliloquy they clapped for themselves.

That was fun. About halfway around the circle I sidled over to the podium, which I had moved to the corner, and checked what was coming next on the lesson plan.

Where's your father?

Ugh. My father. Dammit. Another rush came from the base of my neck and pressed a wave of tears against the back of my eyes. Hold off. Hold off. I stared down at the page, then out the window. I missed a few of the lines, and they were nearing the end of the speech. I returned to the living.

"Great everyone, have a seat. After *To be or not to be* we have Hamlet and Ophelia. What does Hamlet keep telling Ophelia?" I nodded and smiled at Luis. He never shouts out

"*Get thee to a nunnery!*" Jerome and Luis said in unison.

"Why do you think Hamlet is so angry at Ophelia?" I asked.

"She set him up, man," said Jerome, shaking his head.

"That's right" chimed in Albert from the opposite side of the room. Those two spent most of the class looking at each other across the room; I wondered if they were friends, or just happened to sit in each other's direct sight line.

"Do you think Hamlet knows they are being watched?" I asked. "A lot depends on how good an actor Ophelia is." Nothing. Silence. "What do I mean by that?" Still nothing.

"I was saying that in this nunnery scene, you can play it like Hamlet knows they are being watched, or as if he doesn't. One thing that might give it away would be if Ophelia wasn't a good actor. What do I mean by that?"

"Well in the movie she looked sketchy," Albert said, bouncing, as usual. He never just sits.

"Yeah, yeah, she did!" said Sage, pointing at Albert in agreement. Luis and Bradley nodded. "Good job remembering! What made Ophelia look sketchy? Catherine?"

"She kept looking around behind her and seemed nervous."

"That's true," Jerome conceded.

"You saw it too?"

"We watched it in our room." When he said "our room" Jerome pointed across to Albert who was smiling and nodding proudly.

"Wait," I said, "you guys are roommates?" I resisted the urge to say, "That's so cute," and tried not to look so surprised.

"Oh yeah," said Albert proudly. "Second year." I heard a few chuckles but nothing overtly derisive.

"Okay, excellent. If you're directing this scene, you must decide how Ophelia feels about the role she's being forced to play. Is she good at hiding her feelings from Hamlet? Is she a good accomplice to the spying fathers? Those *lawful espials*? Your Ophelia could be trying to let Hamlet know they were being watched.

I realized I hadn't thought about my dad for the last five minutes, and I was going deeper into this scene than usual.

"Remember Hamlet's just said the worst thing you can possibly say to an ex." Silence. They weren't expecting me to stop there. "Think about it. What is the absolute worst thing you can say to a former boyfriend or girlfriend?"

"You never loved them," said Catherine.

"Exactly!" I said, looking in turn at every one of them as if she had just said the truest thing ever. "Boys, you read Hamlet's lines; girls, Ophelia's."

"Are we all reading at the same time?" asked Mei-Mei, her hand in the air and face down in the book.

"Yes, yes, all together. We'll just do it nice and loud and clear to hear it, then you'll vote on Ophelia's attitude and reactions in the scene, okay? Go!"

> *HAMLET: I did love you once.*
> *OPHELIA: Indeed, my lord, you made me believe so.*
> *HAMLET: You should not have believed me, for virtue*
> *cannot so inoculate our old stock but we shall*
> *relish of it. I loved you not.*
> *OPHELIA: I was the more deceived.*
> *HAMLET: Get thee to a nunnery. Why wouldst thou be*
> *a breeder of sinners? I am myself indifferent honest,*
> *but yet I could accuse me of such things that it*
> *were better my mother had not borne me: I am*
> *very proud, revengeful, ambitious, with more offenses*
> *at my beck than I have thoughts to put them*
> *in, imagination to give them shape, or time to act*
> *them in. What should such fellows as I do crawling*
> *between earth and heaven? We are arrant knaves*
> *all; believe none of us. Go thy ways to a nunnery.*
> *Where's your father?*
> *OPHELIA: At home, my lord.*
> (3.1.125-141)

Yesterday when I tried to pick up the text I couldn't focus on the words; my eyes just scanned the pages; my highlights, and different color underscores from past years barely registered. I bought the audiobook on my phone and played it while I walked around the neighborhood.

Yesterday my dad was buried. In a grave in Costa Rica. What a difference a day makes. Dad used to love singing "What a difference a day makes, twenty-four little hours…." *Heaven and earth, must I remember?*

Less than 24 hours ago they put my father in the ground. The image was creepy and the reality difficult. Only a day ago? Friday, two days ago, he was still alive.

"Look at what happens at 3:1.163, once Hamlet has left. Ophelia cries *Oh what a noble mind is here o'erthrown!* She's just had a traumatic experience with her ex-BF. What's her dear old dad's reaction?"

"They don't care," Feona called out, waving her book in the air, russet curls bouncing.

"Why? What makes you say that?"

"Because they totally blow her off."

"That's true!" I said, ding dinging the green buzzer. "Will you read that—the part between the dashes?"

"—*How now, Ophelia? You need not tell us what Lord Hamlet said; We heard it all.*—"

"You guys remember what the dashes mean?" I asked.

"Change of direction," Sage said.

"Exactly. They watch while Hamlet freaks out on Ophelia. She has to keep the act up. Then Hamlet leaves and they talk about his behavior. What's missing here?"

Diane's hand slowly went up and I nodded her on.

"They don't even thank her for helping them," she said, tossing her hands palms up in dismay.

Ding, ding, I hit the buzzer. "Thank you! Exactly! They use Ophelia as a pawn to set up Hamlet, then they just brush her off. Her father wasn't worried about her at all." I peeled her off a star and asked "What's Polonius worried about?" as I walked over and gave it to her. "Polonius, the King's consiglieri?"

Still nothing.

"We said he doesn't seem to care about his daughter. What does Polonius care about?" I asked.

"Being the man to the King." Jerome said that. "He's the ultimate wingman," he added, glancing around for confirmation.

Ding, ding. Ding, ding, I banged on the green buzzer twice, and reached into the podium.

"Thank you!" I said, presenting him one of the big stars. There were knowing chuckles when he used the word "wingman." He liked that.

"Whoa, dude," said Albert. "Good point, good point," he told his roommate.

When I got back to the podium Jerome was still smiling and deciding where to put his star. I checked the clock and changed the subject.

"Let's jump to the next scene: 3.2.21. According to Hamlet, what is *the purpose of playing*? In other words, why do we put on plays?" It was written on the board. I hoped someone would get it. "Yes, Albert?"

"*To hold a mirror up to nature!*" he said.

"Yes, yes," I nodded, " *to hold, as 'twere, the mirror up to nature, to show virtue her own feature, scorn her own image, and the very age and body of the time his form and pressure.* What does that mean, Albert?"

"Hmmm...good question," he said, intentionally stroking his clean-shaven chin. "I got this," he said, interjecting a pregnant pause. "It means to show the audience what they are—like satire," he finished with a confident nod.

"Exactly. Shakespeare's not talking about holding a mirror up to nature, like the trees in the woods. He means to show humans what their nature looks like. And yes, Albert, like with satire, to make social commentary. I love thinking about Shakespeare taking this opportunity to speak to both the Globe audience and his fellow actors about how it should be done. This is literally a manifesto on the art of acting. Look at the beginning of 3.2 where he tells them to play it like he wrote it:

> *Speak the speech, I pray you, as I pronounced*
> *It to you, trippingly on the tongue*

"not to overact to get a bigger response from the groundlings, on line 9:"

> *it offends me to the soul to hear a robustious,*
> *periwig-pated fellow tear a passion to tatters, to very*
> *rags, to split the ears of the groundlings, who for the*
> *most part are capable of nothing but inexplicable*
> *dumb shows and noise. I would have such a fellow*
> *whipped for o'erdoing Termagant. It out-Herods*
> *Herod. Pray you, avoid it.*
> (3.2.9-15)

"*Out-Herods Herod*—that's a good one! My dad used to play Herod in the Christmas tableaux every year," said Meredith. "I think because he had dark hair and a beard."

"I know! *Out-Herods Herod* has such a good ring to it. Like *Hecuba to him or he to Hecuba that he should weep for her.* And look at line 40 where Hamlet tells the actors not to add lines or go for their own laughs."

> *And let those that play*
> *your clowns speak no more than is set down for*
> *them*

I looked at the clock: less than five minutes left. I'm surprised no one asked me about the homework yet. Coleman and Bradley must have seen me glance at the clock, because they were shifting in their seats and reaching down to pack up. This action spread like a ripple to the girls in the Peanut Gallery on my left.

"Okay," I raised my voice to reign them in. "We've got four minutes left. One more question for you and then some information. Question: What does Gertrude think of the Queen in the play?"

Niente.

"Stick with me, guys! Remember I asked you to look for familiar lines? What did Gertrude say when Hamlet asked her what she thought of the Queen in the play?"

"Oo, oo, oo!" called out Albert. "*The lady doth protest too much methinks!*"

"Yes, excellent," I pointed to him. "And what is the Player Queen *protesting*—or insisting upon? Yes Catherine?"

"That she won't remarry after her husband dies."

"Yes," I rang the green bell. "Exactly. Hamlet's play really hit close to home, huh?"

"Yeah, man, really," nodded Jerome. "Yo Hamlet, that was pretty salty." I looked at the clock. One minute.

"Salty?" I asked.

"Yes, salty!" said Gino. Luis was nodding.

"You guys know this word?" Pretty much everyone nodded or said yes.

"Was it 'salty'?" I asked.

"Oh yeah," sang a chorus of voices.

"We'll come back to this scene—and 'salty' later. The bell's about to ring so, let's talk about the homework…."

Surprised groans all around.

"There is none. My dad died this weekend…."

Gasps, widened eyes, sympathy sounds. I took a deep breath and continued. "...and I'll be taking the rest of the week off. No reading. You'll have a sub and he's going to show you the Branagh version of the movie from beginning to end. Then next week we'll pick up where we left off. Okay?"

The bell rang. I made it. Mr. Toad's Wild Ride. I felt more alive in the past hour than I had in days, and I could feel the invigoration draining from me as the students shuffled out of the classroom, several of them slowing past the podium to say they were sorry about my dad, including Diane, who seemed particularly empathic, and a little shaken.

"Miss Erica, I'm really sorry," she said. Her eyes clung to mine with a deep sadness. "It's really hard."

"Yeah, it is. Thanks sweetie."

Once I doled out the DVDs to the various subs, I exited the building into five days of timelessness. Paige arrived Monday night. We went to the church of Our Savior in Jenkintown, a few towns over. We saw my grandfather's stained-glass window and met with the pastor there. I told him our father was the son of the man whose memorial window is there at the end of the front pew and that I'd like to have my father's service here at his childhood church. He was an altar boy. Maybe in June. Maybe Father's Day weekend.

We went to visit Mom's childhood friend who knew my parents from the beginning, and who I hoped would give my father's service. We hung out at my grandmother's and then ate at Outback Steakhouse, where we used to take Dad as a treat when he was on his trips to Florida getting his "bone juice." We moved in slow motion through the ritual of ordering and eating. Halfway through, my sister and I leaned up against each other in the booth.

"Petit filet mignon," I said, and sighed. "That's something I always remember from Dad at the club. He'd say, 'You can order whatever you want, and you don't have to finish it.' And Mom, you'd be like, 'David!'" Paige smiled and nodded.

"Hey, Mom," I asked. "Did you ever wish you had a son? Did Dad want a son?" I don't know why I had never thought to ask before.

"Well," she said "you know, it's funny. We talked about it after Paige was born. I asked your Dad, do you want to try for a boy?"

"And what did he say?"

"He said, no, he figured it was probably easier to be a good dad to daughters than to a son, so we stopped there."

The company of my Mom and sister cushioned the *thousand natural shocks* of realizing Dad was gone. Paige stayed until the weekend, and we wandered from room to room playing cards with my grandmother, or looking at old pictures, insulating ourselves against death with sweatshirts, blankets, and ice cream. Mom left the day after Paige, and I passed the second Sunday in a row alone in bed, staring into the dark reality of the rest of my life without my dad.

I remembered my spiritual ace in the hole, Kirstin. Kirstin was a gifted Reiki healer, Jin Shin, and IEP practitioner, and she was known for getting messages from the other side. A few days after Dad died I reached out to her. She said,

I am so sorry for your loss. I understand the pain of the loss of a parent. I lost my mom a few years ago. If you ever want to talk, I am here.

As I mentioned on the message, I saw the announcement in the Post *and wondered if that was your dad. Over the next 24 hours, I would occasionally connect with your dad. I saw him smiling and he was relieved and at peace (I am thinking this means he had a long illness perhaps).*

I saw a vision of him on a porch during the lazy days of long ago

summers. He was shelling peas. (May seem random but I feel like this was symbolic.) Then I saw a young Erica next to him helping. The interesting thing was that the clothes everyone was wearing would have been from the 30s or 40s.

Then I heard him say "sweet pea."

Sweet pea! A warm wave washed over me. They used to call us sweet pea. Now it's sweetie or sweetheart. I sat there mesmerized at the message. My parents always had gardens, always cared about fresh seasonal food. Lazy summer days. I felt little and pure and enveloped with familial love. Kirstin's email continued:

The language of flowers associates the following meanings with sweet peas: blissful pleasure, delicate pleasure, good-bye, departure, adieu and thank you for a lovely time. Sweet peas derive their name from the Greek word lathyros for pea or pulse, and the Latin word odoratus meaning fragrant. Sweet peas are the flowers most closely connected to the month of April.

Another time I saw him as a young man walking up to some people then shaking your grandfather's hand (it felt like your mom's dad). More on this when we talk, too hard to explain via email. There was a young boy next to him then an older girl. They were all very happy to be with each other.

Even though her visions and messages amazed me, I never for a moment doubted they were real. *There are more things in heaven and earth, Horatio, than are dreamt of in your philosophy.*

"They were all very happy to be with each other."

A month ago we were with each other. Dad took long naps every day we were in Costa Rica, and did his best to eat a little bit, play cards, and visit. In the early evening one night after Larry left, the three of us sat in the sunroom to play more Five Crowns. Maureen was downstairs on her videogames as she had been for hours, mostly all afternoon. Who could blame her?

I had an idea.

"Why don't you guys teach me how to play poker?" I suggested. My sister inherited the family gambling gene and I think she's a good player. At least she knows the game and likes it. She got my dad's razor-sharp math brain, and the two would play pub poker together. Over the years I'd heard them share poker stories peppered with arcane references that went over my head.

He looked across at my sister, tilted his gaze and said, "I don't think we have enough time," and shook his head. "No offense."

They burst out laughing.

"Hardy, har, har," I said, and then laughed for real.

I don't think we have enough time. Meaning, you guys are leaving in a few days and that's not enough time to teach Erica poker. She won't catch on. Typical family ribbing yet my throat tightened and my face winced to hold in the tears.

I don't think we have enough time.

He was right. We definitely didn't.

3: 2

To hold, as 'twere, the mirror up to nature
(3.2.23-24)

It was Monday again. Part of me felt light and grateful I hadn't come to work for almost a week. What a luxury. I was lucky. Yet it still felt too soon to be back to normal life. My quotidian commute and workday tasks seemed ridiculous, even cruel, when I was grappling with the meaning of life and death.

My classroom felt dark and ghostly; cushions were still strewn around the floor from the movie watching. My notes were still on the board from last Monday. For the central quote at the top of the other board I wrote in big yellow caps: *My father died within these two months.* Then I took the pink chalk and drew a line through "months" and wrote "days?" and then crossed that out and scrawled "hours?"

"Good morning everyone!"

"Good morning Miss Erica!"

"How was the movie?" I heard a few mumbled comments, then Feona, Bradley and Catherine piped up that they really liked it.

"Yeah, it was good," said Meredith.

"Everybody died, though," said Jimmy Wong.

"Yeah," said Gino. I hadn't heard from these guys in forever. Time to put them on the spot a little bit. Roust the rest of the Bermuda Triangle.

"Vincent, what about you? What did you think of the movie? The ending?" He looked up and his face unfolded into an impish grin.

"The sword fighting was awesome," he said. "It went on for a long time."

"Yes, yes," I affirmed. "That is something you decide when you put on your own *Hamlet*. How long is the duel? How many parries between lines?"

"That fall was awesome," bellowed Duncan.

"Dude!" Albert called from the other side of the room. "Yeah it was!"

"Wait," Coleman said, curling up out of his slouch a little. "What fall?"

"Laertes!" voices chimed. Thank you, Kenneth Branagh. And thanks Shakespeare for putting in sword fighting. And pirates.

"Okay, that was the ending," I said, "which we will get to before we know it, but for now, let's go back to where we left off last week: Act 3." I turned and gestured to the homework board. "Please notice what you need to read tonight: finish Act 3: scene 2 and read 3:3 as well. Keep your eye out for:

Why is Hamlet so irritated with Rosencrantz and Guildenstern?

What does he accuse them of ? (Look for the musical instrument metaphor)

Where is Claudius planning to send Hamlet and why? Who's going to help Claudius carry out his plan?

"Any questions? Nope? Good. Let's review what we covered in the first part of Act 3:2. Remember we got to see Hamlet as an acting coach in the hold a *mirror up to nature* speech. Critic and scholar Harold Bloom says this is as close as we may get to Shakespeare's own voice talking." I reached into the podium and pulled out a small, thin paperback.

"In this book *Hamlet: Poem Unlimited*, Bloom talks about how Will—Kempe the star clown in Shakespeare's acting troupe the Chamberlain's Men—was 'notorious for his jigs, stage business, and improvisations' (73). Remember 3.2.40 where Hamlet says *And let those that play your clowns speak no more than is set down for them.* We can see here Shakespeare wants the actors—including the clowns—to play as he wrote it—don't add stuff!"

"Also," I continued "there are other references to acting. Notice Shakespeare has Hamlet use a play, *a fiction*, to divine the truth? Look back on 2.2.634 where Hamlet says *The play's the thing wherein I'll catch the conscience of the King.* Here we have Shakespeare—the actor, playwright and shareholder in the Globe—suggesting that plays bring out the truth."

"Basically, according to Shakespeare, there are a lot of good reasons to watch plays. When we consider how 'meta' or self-referential *Hamlet* is to the business of acting, we must always remember Shakespeare was first and foremost a member of an acting troupe, and an entertainer. He saw everything through the lens of a professional actor. *Hamlet* is one of his most popular plays in performance. Perhaps all the references to the life and work of actors is part of what make this particular play perennially popular with actors and directors." It seemed like most of them were listening. Ish. I kept going.

"We noticed 'everyone is a critic' (which is a famous saying, in case you haven't heard it before), which implies everyone knows or thinks they know how to do something better than it was done. Maybe Shakespeare was skewering his own critics. Polonius critiqued the Player's speech when he interjected *This is too long* and *Mobled Queen is good*" (2.2.523, 528).

"Notice how it is assumed that part of good breeding and education is knowledge of the theater and classic plays? Before Hamlet's play *The Mousetrap* starts, at 3.2.109 Polonius mentions he played Julius Caesar at university *I was killed—Brutus killed me.* Shakespeare's *Julius Caesar* came out in 1599 and Hamlet in 1600, so when Shakespeare references Julius Caesar in Hamlet, he is actually promoting his other play. Shakespeare the Marketer. Yes, Double I?"

"Hamlet is really bossy," she said.

"Really?"

"Yeah. He's really superior. He's telling everyone what to do."

"That's true." This was interesting; I decided to go with it. "Well...he is the prince, so he is technically superior, that's one thing. Hamlet's got a plan though. He's trying to make something happen." I threw it out to them. "What's he trying to make happen?"

"Kill Claudius?" said Jerome.

"Well, no, not right now. First, what does he want to do? What's the project he's working on? What's Hamlet organizing? We just talked about it."

"The play," said Duncan, like it was so obvious why was I even asking.

"Right. The play. And why's he putting on the play?"

"*The play's the thing*!" shouted Albert, pointing in the air.

"Exactly. *The play's the thing wherein I'll catch the conscience of the king.* Meaning what?" They looked comatose. I'm not sure if it was because it was an easy question, because they weren't listening, or because it was Monday morning. "Hey, wake up. Review time: why is Hamlet putting on the play? Mei-Mei? Please, help me out here."

"Well, he's putting on the play to see if Claudius is really guilty or not. It seems like kind of an unreliable plan, but..." she trailed off.

"Yes, thank you. And you've got a point, but I don't want to go there right now. Anyway, back to Double I," she perked up, "you're right, Hamlet is bossy and controlling. He's acting like a director of a play. Literally."

"Ha, ha, Mr. Waelchli!"

"Kenneth Branagh kind of reminds me of Mr. Waelchli," I confessed. I usually avoid commenting on my colleagues, but the Performing Arts teacher and musical director is a true character at the school, and I consider the comparison flattering.

"Let's do this scene. There's a lot going on. Notice on 3.2.269, Ophelia knows the elements of Greek tragedy. She teases Hamlet that his narration of the play they are watching makes him *as good as a chorus, my lord.*"

I had been talking for a long time; time to get them up. I had truncated scripts for *The Mousetrap* scene from a Folger workshop I attended a few years ago in Philly. The setup is a little complicated: understanding the dumb show and play-within-a-play takes explaining, but ultimately it comes together when they actually do it, and it's one of the few scenes with enough parts to include everyone.

"We need a Hamlet and an Ophelia." An idea was coming to me based on something I recently read. "Did you guys pick up on how raunchy Hamlet was with Ophelia?

"Yeah."

"Yeah."

"Hamlet you dawg."

"Right? His mother says, hey come next to me, sonny, and Hamlet says, oh no, here's *metal more attractive.* Side note: guys, that's one thing you never, never want to do." A couple laughs. Mostly female voices. "Seriously, you never want to tell your mom another woman is more beautiful than she. Especially someone younger." There were a couple of serious nods among the guys.

"The last time Hamlet and Ophelia were together they had that big fight, remember? *Get thee to a nunnery?* I want to try two girls playing Hamlet and Ophelia. Over 200 women have played the role of Hamlet, including way back to the 1700s. Feona, you be Hamlet" she made a fist like she was psyched, "and Catherine, you're going to be Ophelia." Giggles.

"Now, you still love this guy. He was awful to you last time, and now he's flirting with you in front of your Dad, and the king and queen. It's important you play the proper Elizabethan girl, yet you love and are attracted to Hamlet. Hamlet," I turned back to Feona, "Whatever you think about Ophelia and the fight you had before, you have this show you're putting on, and you acting crazy—*putting on an antic disposition*—is part of the show."

"Am I wearing a crown?" asked Feona.

"Ha! Good question. Up to you. Depends on what kind of a statement your Hamlet is trying to make. Okay, let's do this," I directed. "Just Hamlet and Horatio," played by Mei-Mei, "on stage right now. The rest of you, in the wings," I showed the characters where they should sit, grabbed an empty desk in the back and cried: "And…action!"

> *HAMLET: There is a play tonight before the King.*
> *One scene of it comes near the circumstance*
> *Which I have told thee of my father's death.*
> *I prithee, when thou seest that act afoot,*
> *Even with the very comment of thy soul*
> *Observe my uncle. If his occulted guilt*
> *Do not itself unkennel in one speech,*
> *It is a damnèd ghost that we have seen,*
> *And my imaginations are as foul*
> *As Vulcan's stithy. Give him heedful note,*
> *For I mine eyes will rivet to his face,*
> *And, after, we will both our judgments join*
> *In censure of his seeming.*
>   *HORATIO: Well, my lord.*

If he steal aught the whilst this play is playing
And 'scape detecting, I will pay the theft.
[Sound a flourish.]
HAMLET: They are coming to the play. I must be idle.
Get you a place.

(3.2.80-97)

"Okay, Horatio, you go off to the side. Find a spot where you have a clear view of Claudius' face while he's watching the play. Vincent? You're sound effects?"

"Yep!"

"Get ready. Bradley, go ahead with the stage directions."

[Enter Trumpets and Kettle Drums. Enter King, Queen,
Polonius, Ophelia, Rosencrantz, Guildenstern, and other
Lords attendant with the King's guard carrying torches.]

Duncan was an imposing king with purple crown, a scepter from someone's old medieval project, and arms linked with Sage, who was playing Gertrude. Feona played Hamlet with all the dramatic flourish of a flamboyant community theater director.

KING: How fares our cousin Hamlet?
HAMLET: Excellent, i' faith, of the chameleon's dish. I
eat the air, promise-crammed. You cannot feed
capons so.
KING: I have nothing with this answer, Hamlet. These
words are not mine.
HAMLET: No, nor mine now. [To Polonius.] My lord, you
played once i' th' university, you say?
POLONIUS: That did I, my lord, and was accounted a
good actor.

Luis puffed up his chest. Perfect.

> *HAMLET: What did you enact?*
> *POLONIUS: I did enact Julius Caesar. I was killed i' th'*
> *Capitol. Brutus killed me.*
> *HAMLET: It was a brute part of him to kill so capital a*
> *calf there.—Be the players ready?*
> *ROSENCRANTZ: Ay, my lord. They stay upon your*
> *patience.*
> *QUEEN: Come hither, my dear Hamlet, sit by me.*

"Pat the chair, Gertrude, pat the chair," I prompted. Sage patted the chair.

> *HAMLET: No, good mother. Here's metal more*
> *Attractive.*

"Ooooooo," I taunted.

"Burn," said Coleman under his breath.

> *Hamlet takes a place near Ophelia.*
> *POLONIUS: [to the King] Oh, ho! Do you mark that?*
> *HAMLET: Lady, shall I lie in your lap?*
> *OPHELIA: No, my lord.*
> *HAMLET: I mean, my head upon your lap?*
>   (3.2.98-121)

"Go lay down on her!" Giggles. Catherine's Ophelia was the perfect degree of awkward, confused and disgusted. She kept rolling her eyes, looking around to see if anyone else realized what Hamlet was doing.

OPHELIA: Ay, my lord.
HAMLET: Do you think I meant country matters?
OPHELIA: I think nothing, my lord.
HAMLET: That's a fair thought to lie between maids'
legs.
OPHELIA: What is, my lord?
HAMLET: Nothing.
OPHELIA: You are merry, my lord.
HAMLET: Who, I?
OPHELIA: Ay, my lord.
HAMLET: O God, your only jig-maker. What should a
man do but be merry? For look you how cheerfully
my mother looks, and my father died within 's two
hours.
OPHELIA: Nay, 'tis twice two months, my lord.
HAMLET: So long? Nay, then, let the devil wear black,
for I'll have a suit of sables. O heavens, die two
months ago, and not forgotten yet? Then there's
hope a great man's memory may outlive his life half
a year.
[The trumpets sounds. Dumb show follows.]
            (3.2.122-141)

"Trumpet! Trumpet!" I shouted, and Vincent made a loud,
belated trumpet noise.

[Enter a King and a Queen, very lovingly, the Queen
embracing him and he her].
            (3.2.145-146)

The Player King and Queen were played by Jerome and Gino
respectively. It was visually hilarious watching them mime the

actions as Bradley narrated them, but he was going too fast. "Slow down, slow down! Start again. It says *very lovingly*. Let's see that, guys!" More giggles.

> *She kneels and makes show of*
> *protestation unto him. He takes her up and declines his*
> *head upon her neck.*

"Hey, decline your head! Come on!" They laughed, but Jerome as the Player King leaned his head on Gino as his Queen's neck. "That's it! Keep going."

> *He lies him down upon a bank of*
> *flowers. She, seeing him asleep, leaves him. Anon*
> *comes in another man, takes off his crown, kisses it, pours*
> *poison in the sleeper's ears, and leaves him. The Queen*
> *returns, finds the King dead, makes passionate action. The*
> *poisoner with some three or four come in again, seem to*
> *condole with her. The dead body is carried away. The*
> *poisoner woos the Queen with gifts. She seems harsh*
> *awhile but in the end accepts his love.*
> *[Players exit.]*
> OPHELIA: *What means this, my lord?*
> HAMLET: *Marry, this is miching mallecho. It means*
> *mischief.*
> OPHELIA: *Belike this show imports the argument of the*
> *play.*
> *[Enter Prologue.]*
> (3.2.146-161)

Nothing happened. "Who's Prologue?" asked Bradley.

"Oh," I said, "sorry, that's you. You're like the narrator now, announcing what is to come so the audience understands it." Bradley obligingly stepped up to the edge of our stage. "Go ahead, Hamlet."

> HAMLET: We shall know by this fellow. The players
> cannot keep counsel; they'll tell all.
> OPHELIA: Will he tell us what this show meant?
> HAMLET: Ay, or any show that you will show him. Be
> not you ashamed to show, he'll not shame to tell you
> what it means.
> OPHELIA: You are naught, you are naught. I'll mark the
> play.
> PROLOGUE:
> For us and for our tragedy,
> Here stooping to your clemency,
> We beg your hearing patiently. [He exits.]
> HAMLET: Is this a prologue or the posy of a ring?
> OPHELIA: 'Tis brief, my lord.
> HAMLET: As woman's love.
>   (3.2.162-175)

"Oooooooo…." I said, making a sizzle sound like we did back in the day. Do kids still do that?

> [Enter the Player King and Queen.]

> PLAYER KING: Full thirty times hath Phoebus' cart gone round
> Neptune's salt wash and Tellus' orbèd ground,
> And thirty dozen moons with borrowed sheen
> About the world have times twelve thirties been

Since love our hearts and Hymen did our hands
Unite commutual in most sacred bands.
> (3.2.176-181)

This part is long. Even longer in the uncut play, but Gino's falsetto and the humor of seeing two guys play it helped keep it somewhat interesting.

PLAYER QUEEN: So many journeys may the sun and moon
Make us again count o'er ere love be done!
But woe is me! You are so sick of late,
So far from cheer and from your former state...
Where love is great, the littlest doubts are fear;
Where little fears grow great, great love grows there.
PLAYER KING: Faith, I must leave thee, love, and shortly too.
My operant powers their functions leave to do.
And thou shall live in this fair world behind,
Honored, beloved; and haply one as kind
For husband shalt thou—
PLAYER QUEEN: O, confound the rest!
Such love must needs be treason in my breast.
In second husband let me be accurst.
None wed the second but who killed the first.
> (3.2.193-204)

"Ooooooo...." I crooned again.

HAMLET: That's wormwood!

"Okay, Hamlet, jump down to line 253 where Hamlet says *Madam, how like you this play?*

HAMLET: Madam, how like you this play?

Come on Gertrude, wake up. "Gertrude?"
    "Oh yeah," said Sage, "sorry, hee, hee."

QUEEN: The lady doth protest too much, methinks.
HAMLET: O, but she'll keep her word.
KING: Have you heard the argument? Is there no
offense in 't?
HAMLET: No, no, they do but jest, poison in jest. No
offense i' th' world.
KING: What do you call the play?
HAMLET: "The Mousetrap." Marry, how? Tropically.
This play is the image of a murder done in Vienna.
Gonzago is the duke's name, his wife Baptista. You
shall see anon. 'Tis a knavish piece of work, but
what of that? Your Majesty and we that have free
souls, it touches us not. Let the galled jade wince;
our withers are unwrung.
    (3.2.253-267)

"Great job everyone! We still have ten more minutes so don't start packing up. Go back to the beginning of the scene. I hope you noticed at some point between Act 1.5 and Act 3.2 Hamlet has apparently told Horatio what the Ghost said about being murdered. See where he says:"

One scene of it comes near the circumstance
Which I have told thee of my father's death.
    (3.2.81-82)

"Did you notice the reference to time when Ophelia and Hamlet were talking at the play? Yes, Mei-Mei?"

"He said his father's been dead for two hours," she said. "That was one of my reading questions. Why would he say that? It's not true." I looked around with a raised eyebrow.

"Personally I think Hamlet is losing it," said Gino.

"Possibly," I said. "Luis?"

"He means it feels like it was so recently. Like exaggerating. Like we'd say 'two seconds ago' when it was weeks ago." Ding, ding, I rang the bell. And peeled off a star sticker for him.

"Yes, thank you! Exactly. And Ophelia corrects him, *Nay, 'tis twice two months, my lord.* Most productions have Hamlet take a thoughtful pause there, as if he's being dragged into the reality of clock time again. Then he snaps out of it and sarcastically cries in response:"

> *Oh heavens, die two months ago and not forgotten yet?*
> *Then there's hope a great man's memory should outlive his life half*
> *a year.*
>   (3.2.138-141)

I stood still at the podium and gazed out the window. Long pause. Energy shift. Then, using a genuinely curious tone:

"How long are you going to mourn your dead parent?" Pause, pause, pause. Nothing. There never is. "When does their death stop feeling fresh?" I pause again and make eye contact with each of them. "After a week?" Groans, shakes of heads. "A month? Two months? How long do you think it is going to take for you to get used to the idea that your mom or dad is dead?"

A quiet hand unfurled at the end of an elegant arm.

"Yes Sage?"

"I heard this thing somewhere...I can't remember exactly

how it went, but something like if that person has been in your life for 18 years, it's going to take at least 18 years to get used to living without them."

"Yes," I said, dinging the bell. "I've heard that one and I like it!" She deserved a star. Lots of stars today.

"I can tell you that my dad's been dead for over a week now, and I feel like I'm in a time warp. I've lived a lifetime since it happened. At the same time, I can't believe it's already been more than a week. It's also strange that time keeps moving on at all. You'd think when something so huge happens, the world would just stop. At least for a day or two. But it never does. It never does."

"That's true," Diane said somberly.

"Time marches on," said the fake Michael J. Fox.

"Yes, Coleman, precisely!"

"Star?" he asked with hopeful eyebrows.

"Oh yeah!" I peeled one off and placed it on his outstretched finger. "Any other quotes or clichés about time?"

"Time waits for no man," said Duncan. Star.

"Time after time!" said Catherine. Meh. Okay, star for Cyndi Lauper and the 80s.

"Time heals all wounds," said Gino. Well, we'll see about that. "Star?" Gino asked. Yes, stars all around. Soon everyone was getting in the game. They wanted their stars!

"Time out!"

"Time to go!"

"Time flies!"

"Tempus fugit" (that was Albert).

"Time after time."

"Someone already said that."

Over in her corner I saw Feona start singing, slowly and not too loudly, "Time, time, time, is on my side...yes it is."

Ha! Well said young mole! I couldn't help it, I started to sing a verse from a Little Feat song "Well they say, time loves a hero... but only time will tell if he's real, he's legend from heaven...."

I lost all track of time in the days following my father's death. And strange things started happening. I thought I heard his voice. Not clearly: more like a vibration than words. I experienced the sensation I was standing on one side of a curtain and Dad on the other. When I talked to Uncle Larry on the phone I said, "Wow, I can't believe it's been a week."

"Really? It seems like a month to me," he said, sounding exhausted.

I wasn't sure whether it felt like more or less than a week. Calendar-based reality no longer seemed to apply. I was swallowed by a senseless space, *an undiscovered country* between my heart and what Hamlet refers to as *my mind's eye*, that clock time couldn't touch. When I got home that night I opened my Life Organizer and numbered every Saturday for the next few months so each week I could see how many weeks he'd been dead. I didn't want to lose track.

3: 3

But 'tis not so above; There is no shuffling;
there the action lies in his true nature

(3.3.64-66)

It was Tuesday and time for the second half of Act 3:2 and Act 3:3. I wrote on the board the highlights for the day and checked my email. There was a message from Diane with the subject line "yesterday in class." My stomach lurched. When I see a subject line like that from a student I immediately think something's wrong. It's like being called to the principal's office. What did I do? Am I in trouble? Did I sink too far down into gloom and doom yesterday? I clicked on the message and prepared for the worst.

> *Good evening,*
>
> *I just wanted to thank you for the discussion about death in class today. It was something I needed to hear especially now. It's been almost 6 years since I lost my sister coming up in May, and I have been thinking of her a lot lately. I have been going through the grieving process at a slow and steady pace over the years, and I found this discussion helped settle some uneasiness. I just wanted to thank you for bringing it up. I enjoy coming to your class every day.*
>
> *Thanks again,*

Six years. She must have been 11 or 12. And I, a 47-year-old woman, am struggling with the death of my father. When nature's *common theme is death of fathers.* Did Diane's sister die in the same car accident that tore up her arms? It's humbling to realize how much we don't know about our students' lives. Six years. Hamlet talks a lot about time and how long his father has been dead. In his first soliloquy he laments his mother has already remarried when his father is *but two months dead.* Then he contradicts himself saying, no it hasn't been quite two months, and a few lines later it's *within a month,* and *a little month!* and again *within a month… she married.* The text is ambiguous whether Hamlet is repeating himself out of disbelief or disorientation, but I discovered those two numbing sensations are constant companions of deep sorrow.

I was always aware of the time references in the play but, now that I was trussed up in the foggy world of grief, I was struck by the way Hamlet's calendar confusion mirrored my own. I related to his musings and laments. Hamlet's wisdom reminded me how much our philosophers, storytellers and songwriters throughout the ages have already figured out about what it means to live a life. I thought about all the immortal characters and philosophers who left us their stories and theories. Nick Carraway and Gatsby; Elizabeth Bennet and Mr. Darcy; Jake Barnes and Lady Brett Ashley. Holden Caufield. Janie in *Their Eyes Were Watching God.* Aeschylus. Shakespeare.

As I tried to adjust to the idea that my father was gone, disbelief and disorientation dazzled my ability to determine what was real and what was *the very coinage of my brain.* Maybe death and its attendants were enhancing my perception of reality. I saw clearly that love, heart energy, and moments are what matter; what last; what are remembered. Not days, weeks or months. Memories crunch time into images and clips in the highlight reels of our lives.

"Okay, let's hear something from everyone," I said, once the quiz was taken and the reading responses checked. I gave Diane a wink and mouthed "thanks for the message." "Yes, Duncan?" He had the physique of a high school lacrosse defenseman and his legs were stretched out under and way beyond his desk. His beard and deep voice held such authority I had to keep reminding myself he was a kid.

"Hamlet's messing with Polonius again—heh, heh—this time about the clouds."

"Good job! I love this bit. It seems so nonsensical reading it, yet if you imagine it, or see it acted out, it's hilarious. What else?" I asked.

"There was more spying!" said Gino.

"I know, right?" said Bradley, nodding to him.

"What is the deal with all this spying?" piped in Luis.

"All they do here is spy," said Feona, knowingly engaging in hyperbole.

"These guys are terrible parents," said Jimmy.

"Wait, why terrible parents, Jimmy? You don't think your parents have some spies here from Korea checking up on how you're doing?" A few chuckles. He smiled from behind his thick glasses and weaved his head back and forth.

"Yeah, heh, maybe," he conceded.

I called on Mei-Mei who had raised her hand.

"Well yes, but still, this is worse. They are setting Hamlet up again. This is not the same as parents checking up on kids who are...who are away at school." Ding, ding.

"Yes, Mei-Mei, you are 100 percent right. Good distinction." Star bestowal. "I wonder if Shakespeare is making a statement about how controlling parents are, or how the more powerful the parents are, the more they think everything is their business?" I saw a few nods and left the idea sit for a moment.

"What was Claudius trying, unsuccessfully, to do in Act 3:3?"

"Pray!"

"Ask for forgiveness."

"He said *my offense is rank, it smells to heaven,*" called out Albert.

"That means he believes in Heaven!"

"Good point," I said. "So why is he having trouble praying?"

"He's guilty," growled Duncan.

"True, but the guilty can still pray. There's something else here. Look at 3.3.55-60. Imani, would you read those lines for us?"

> *But, O, what form of prayer*
> *Can serve my turn? "Forgive me my foul murder"?*
> *That cannot be, since I am still possessed*
> *Of those effects for which I did the murder:*
> *My crown, mine own ambition, and my queen.*
> *May one be pardoned and retain th' offense?*
>   (3.3.55-60)

"You can stop there. So, why can't he pray?"

"Duncan?"

"Claudius is a lot more remorseful than I thought he would be, but not enough for me to regret him getting killed."

"Interesting," I said. "Clearly Claudius's conscience is getting to him, but what we want to know is why. Is he afraid to get caught? Does he sense things are closing in on him? Vincent?"

"Hamlet should have gone for it. Claudius wasn't even praying anyway."

"I know, right?" I said. "Frustrating! Let's think about this. What would happen if Hamlet did kill Claudius in that moment? Imani?"

"He'd probably be unsatisfied, and he'd probably be unsatisfied to the point where he kills himself," she said. Okay, not what I was thinking or where I wanted to go with it, but nice try.

"Hmmm, that's possible. That's a psychological reaction. Let's think about the technical aspects of Hamlet committing murder. Jimmy?"

"He will be in line for the throne?"

"Okay, listen, sometimes I ask these questions like what would happen if bla bla bla and it's hard to answer, but let's be Sherlock Holmesian in our reading of *HAMLET* because that is really what Shakespeare's work asks us to do: think two, three, four steps ahead. If Hamlet killed Claudius in that moment, then what? Logistically. What would happen next?"

"He would stop having bad dreams," Sage said.

"Nice thinking, Sage. But even before that. Listen up. I'm Hamlet, I kill Claudius, swoosh," I stab the air with my Sword of Truth. "Now what? Right now, what's next?"

"Where do you put the body?" Gino called out.

"Exactly. Don't you guys watch crime shows? If you succeed in hiding the body, then you have to explain the disappearance of the king. Why didn't he show up for supper?" Ha ha, that's funny. *At supper...where he is eaten.* "If you just say I'm not going to hide it, here it is, how are you going to justify what you've done? What's your explanation if you're Hamlet?"

"He killed my dad?" said Meredith, catching herself as she said it and slowly starting to smile.

"Ha! How do you know that, Hamlet?" I asked. There were a few muffled laughs of realization.

"Oh, a ghost told me," Meredith sang, waving her hand in the air.

"Exactly!

"I heard him praying!" tried Jerome.

"Oh, that's good," I said. "'I heard him confessing his crime,' that would be cool; that's a good interpretation," I said, getting excited about the possibility, but not wanting to go down the mental rabbit hole of what that would look like and if it could really work. "It is traditionally played as if Claudius and Hamlet can't hear each other. In the text Hamlet says Claudius is praying; he doesn't say I just heard Claudius confess. Back to what Albert said: Claudius references Heaven several times in this scene. Look on 3.3.61-64 where he talks about the difference between morality on earth versus in Heaven."

> *In the corrupted currents of this world,*
> *Offense's gilded hand may shove by justice,*
> *And oft 'tis seen the wicked prize itself*
> *Buys out the law.*
>   (3.3.61-64)

"What's Claudius saying about evil deeds?" I asked. Nothing. I waited. Still nothing. Eventually some looked around. I repeated the question, and saw Jimmy Wong dig into his *No Fear Shakespeare*.

"What is the *wicked prize*?" I asked.

"The crown!" Albert called out.

"The queen!" countered Feona.

"Both!" said Catherine, firmly.

"Yes. The power of the throne gives him immunity from the law. In other words, his sin won't get punished because he's the King. Is that true in real life?" I asked. "Do the rich and powerful get away with stuff the rest of us don't?" A few nods.

"Oh yeah," added Jerome.

"It's also important to know it was treason to accuse the king of a crime. Which of course is part of what puts Hamlet in such a bad position. So, who can Hamlet tell that the king is a murderer?"

"No one," said Imani. She was trying.

"Horatio," said Bradley. "He told Horatio."

"Yes, he did. And so far, Horatio is the only one Hamlet trusts."

"Claudius just wants the Queen and the crown," Jimmy said.

"Interesting. Do you guys agree? Do we sometimes decide the reward for a crime (the *wicked prize*) is worth whatever civil or moral law we break?" I let the question hang for minute. "Not so in Heaven, though," I continued.

> *But 'tis not so above:*
> *There is no shuffling; there the action lies*
> *In his true nature...*
>   (3.3.64-66)

Shakespeare's plays provide insight on Elizabethan superstitions and religious beliefs about the afterlife. In my undergraduate Shakespeare class at Columbia, James Shapiro said that *Hamlet* grapples with Christian conscience problems. Claudius is ambitious enough to kill his brother for the crown, yet he knows what he's done is wrong. He knows the scripture repudiates his crime, and knows he's made a trade that will only last while he's alive. *Above* there will be *no shuffling*, he says; he knows he will be judged for his actions when he gets to the other side.

Religious upbringing was a defining factor in my life. It wasn't until I came to the Academy of the New Church my junior year of high school that I discovered there were God cynics. Friends who had every right to be skeptical, considering some of the horribly flawed humans who were doling out God, and the many harmful things done in His name through the ages. As the years went by, I came to respect how an individual's attitude towards religion, and God, is often a reaction to how they were raised, or a personal experience.

When someone finds out where I work, they often ask, "Are you really religious?" Maybe it's my imagination but I often think I hear a twinge of disbelief in their tone. For many people, being "religious" does not have a good connotation. Understandable. One of my greatest gifts was being raised by people who believed in God, but who never used God against me. Not for discipline, nor to make me feel guilty, nor to make me do or not do something.

The other day Maureen told me that about a year before my father died he picked up his Bible—"the leather bound one from when he was an altar boy"—and read it from cover to cover in six months. My dad was a huge reader so in that regard it was not particularly notable.

She said, "When I asked him close to the time if he wanted an Episcopalian priest to come see him, he said no."

My dad didn't need a priest; he had God.

"Let's do the first few lines of Hamlet's soliloquy. Albert, why don't you do it. Stand behind Duncan. Duncan, put this crown on. You were such a good King during the play." They got ready; Albert having weighed two other swords before the one he stuck with.

"Please note," I added, "the staging of this shows Hamlet entering and drawing his sword, as if Claudius can't hear him. If you're making a movie you can do that in a voiceover. For a live stage play you need to accept the theatrical conceit they can't hear each other. Okay, go!"

HAMLET: Now might I do it pat, now he is a-praying,
And now I'll do 't.
[He draws his sword.]
And so he goes to heaven,
And so am I revenged. That would be scanned:
A villain kills my father, and for that,
I, his sole son, do this same villain send

To heaven.
Why, this is hire and salary, not revenge.
> (3.3.77-84)

"So, what's Hamlet's concern here? Jerome?"

"He doesn't want to send Claudius to heaven! That's harsh, Hamlet."

"Ha. Why does he think he'd be sending Claudius to heaven?" I prodded.

"Because he's praying," Albert shouted from across the room. "Like deathbed repentance."

"Exactly. Duncan, can you read Claudius's last two lines?"

KING: My words fly up, my thoughts remain below;
Words without thoughts never to heaven go.
> (3.3.102-103)

"So he wasn't really praying!" Bradley realized.

"Nope."

"Ugh," said Coleman. "Hamlet could have done it."

The bell rang. The week was more than half over. Two more days and my dad will have been dead for two weeks. *Nay, 'tis twice two months, my lord.*

3: 4

I took thee for thy better

(3.4.39)

I wasn't just seeing ghosts; I was seeking them. Maybe that's why when I got home on Wednesday I decided to listen to the Kenny Rogers song "The Gambler." My dad took us to see Kenny Rogers in Atlantic City in the early 80s. It was my first concert and I couldn't believe we were seeing the real Kenny Rogers sing the songs we listened to on the radio. Now I kept playing the song. At the beginning of the song I'd smile with fond recollection; by the end my chest heaved and I was gasping for air. The guy dies right there on the train. "And somewhere in the darkness, the Gambler he broke even, and in his final words I found an ace that I could keep."

Like Hamlet, as the finality of my father's death was sinking in, what I wanted more than anything was to rewind and see him one more time, and not just in *my mind's eye, Horatio*. Maybe this is why, like Hamlet, we are more willing to believe in ghosts once someone we love deeply has gone to the other side. The more I longed to summon my father's ghost, the more I'd listen to songs that reminded me of him. Since I moved to Pennsylvania (or is it since I've been married?), I'd gone for months at a time when I'd forget about music. Forget to avail myself of the emotional depths it can access, its cathartic powers, its ability to modulate mood. These days I needed music.

By Thursday we were at Act 3:4 and I could see the end. I started driving myself to school more often. It was still hard to get out of bed; I needed every extra minute. It was still cold and gray. I felt the cold deep in my bones, still wore my parka though everyone else shed theirs, and the walk from the parking lot to the ground floor entrance of the school was a cringe against icy vapors. I could hardly believe there had been those days, right when he died, that I didn't feel the cold. As I reached the school, I would keep my head down and minimize human interaction; I saved everything for the classroom.

I was looking forward to today because it was the killing of Polonius: I love teaching that scene.

As Bradley unpacked his backpack, he said, "Miss Erica, this is like a Denmarkian *House of Cards*!"

"Yes," I said, "absolutely. Though I think *House of Cards* is more like *Richard III* or *Macbeth*. *My vaulting ambition that or'leaps itself*." I scanned the room. "Okay, okay—everybody up! Good morning everyone!" I said with both arms wide in the air.

"Good morning Miss Erica!"

"So," I began, "Rosencrantz & Guildenstern bring up the question of loyalty. The other day we did a side-by-side comparison of Rosencrantz and Guildenstern versus Horatio. Who remembers the differences between these friends? Bradley?"

"Horatio: Hamlet was friends with him in university, like they found each other, but Rosencran and Guildenburg were childhood friends who were forced to play together."

I didn't correct him. It's my private chuckle. So classic.

"Yeah! I love 'they found each other.' You know...we're lucky, we're from a small town and a small school, and it often works out. You may end up lifelong friends with some of the kids you grew up with. But sometimes you don't find best friends until college or even later. What else, Sage?"

"Also, Rosencrantz and Guildenstern obeyed the parents because they have an obligation to, but Horatio doesn't know the parents; he doesn't have as much obligation to spy."

"Exactly. This gives me an idea. We don't know whether the

King and Queen even knew Horatio before, whereas they were the ones who summoned Rosencrantz and Guildenstern to the castle. Why did Horatio come to Elsinore?"

"Hamlet's father's funeral," said Jerome.

"Yes, Horatio came on his own," I explained, "unbidden. Who remembers what Horatio says when Hamlet asks him *what make you here at Elsinore?*"

"He jokes he likes to skip school," said Mei-Mei, in her small, sweet voice with subtly stilted English.

"Yes, good!" I flipped back in the book. "See here on 1.2.176, Horatio says *A truant disposition, my lord,* instead of coming right out and saying *I came to see your father's funeral.* Imagine you run into a friend whose parent has died recently. Remember we talked about how we might make a joke or change the subject because, this person just had a big loss, they might not be thinking about it right now and we don't want to bring up a sore subject? And in contrast, why did Rosencrantz and Guildenstern come to Elsinore?"

"Because the King and Queen wanted them to spy on Hamlet," Albert shouted out.

"Yes. That's interesting. Why didn't they come to the funeral? Hamlet's father was the King, they're old school friends…." I hadn't thought of this before. Ever. "Old friends usually come back to town when their friends' parents die. That's the kind of friend Horatio is. He shows up." I was tempted to mention *Who's There?* from the beginning of the play, but I didn't have time.

"Moving on, why does Gertrude want to talk to Hamlet?"

"He's in trouuuble," Gino said, like he was telling a much smaller, wimpier kid his mother was calling him.

"Yes, yes, why?" I prodded. No immediate answer. "Why are Gertrude and Claudius upset with Hamlet?" No comment. "Why is Prince Hamlet in trouble?" Still niente. "Guys, what just happened in the previous scene? Remember? Here on this very stage," I gestured to the center of the room. "Yes, Jimmy?"

"The play, he is in trouble because of the play."

Feona started waving her hand. "Yes Feona?"

"It's interesting, even before the play they were planning to send Hamlet to Gertrude's room, and Claudius was planning to ship him to England."

"That's right," I smiled, and gave her a star. "Okay, let's hear from everyone. What do you think about Gertrude now?"

"She's sketchy," said Coleman from his slouch.

"I don't think she knew," said Luis.

"I think she's starting to regret being with Claudius, which is the right thing, so I like her more," said Bradley.

"I like that she appears to be listening to Hamlet's story," said Duncan.

"I think she's torn and feels like she has to choose between Claudius and Hamlet. She also thinks Hamlet has completely lost it," said Meredith.

"Why does she think he's lost it?" I asked.

"Because he's hallucinating! Seeing ghosts!"

"Okay. Why does the Ghost appear to Hamlet?"

"Yes, well, to remind Hamlet about his purpose of revenge," said Vincent. "And he wants Hamlet to stop scaring his mother."

"Yeah, that's what I said," said Jerome, looking down at his reading response. "He tells him to stop threatening his mother."

"What does the Ghost think about Gertrude's reaction?"

"He's satisfied with it. He feels bad and tells Hamlet to comfort her," said Mei-Mei.

"Yeah, going off what Mei-Mei said, she looks surprised, so he thinks she's probably innocent," said Sage.

Catherine seemed relieved to find evidence Gertrude might not be as bad as feared. "It says on 3.4.28 *amazement sits upon her face.*"

"Did you guys get the extra credit question? What does Hamlet tell Gertrude not to do? Diane?"

"Don't sleep with Claudius and don't let him seduce you," she said.

"And don't tell the King that Hamlet's only acting crazy," said Gino.

Next, they were going to make up their own versions of killing Polonius, another exercise I learned at a Folger workshop.

"We will have two different acting troupes: the 1's & the 2's," I explained. "The 1's will do the first half of the scene, 2's the second half." I had them count off and get into groups. "1's over here, 2's over here. Let's go over the directions on the handout. There's a list of elements to incorporate into the scene, as well as the lines to include. You have 10 minutes to make your plan—be creative and entertaining!"

The scene they get is heavily cut, and the directions state that their renditions must: capture the general idea of what happens, bear the mark of their group's creative vision for interpretation, be entertaining, and include the provided lines from the text. In addition they have to include: a tableau at the beginning of the presentation, a tableau at the end of the presentation, at least one moment of direct address to the audience, at least one unexpected entrance or exit, 10 seconds of silence, a moment of laughter, a contemporary prop, at least one moment of unison movement, a moment of crying, and a whisper.

The scholars and teachers at the Folger have devised a way for the students to get inside this turning point of the play and make the scene their own. The exercise gets them up speaking the language and working together.

"Okay, 1's, Albert, Sage, Feona, Bradley, Catherine, Jimmy, Vincent, and Jerome, go into the next classroom and prepare there. Here," I said, handing them the large piece of black

Naugahyde I use to cover my A/V cart, "You can use this for an arras." Someday I should get a real tapestry. "Oh, and don't forget a sword."

"Yeah, yeah, sword!" said Jimmy, lunging towards the pile on the desk.

"Okay, 2's, Mei-Mei, Diane, Coleman, Luis, Gino, and Duncan, you guys stay here. Your part of the scene starts after Polonius is killed, so someone is must play the dead body." I forgot to tell them: "Remember, everyone in your group has to do something, so figure ways to get everyone involved. The extra bits you have to add can help with that." It never ceases to amaze me the way a natural leader always comes to the fore to pull the group together, and how much the kids get into it within the first three minutes. It's Folger's ideas for the additions that make the kids think outside the box and give their renditions a manic, silly feel.

After eight minutes on their own I checked in. "How's it going? Two more minutes okay?"

"No! Agggh, no!" they said, like they always do. I just say two minutes to get them going—they always say they need more and I give it to them. After four more minutes I called everyone back and we saw the scenes. Feona was a terrific Gertrude to Albert's Hamlet. Albert was completely insane, frenetic, and all over the stage with his long limbs flailing between Gertrude, the arras and the fourth wall.

> HAMLET: *Now mother, what's the matter?*
> QUEEN GERTRUDE: *Hamlet, thou hast thy father much offended.*
> HAMLET: *Mother, you have my father much offended.*
> QUEEN GERTRUDE: *Why, how now, Hamlet!*
> HAMLET: *What's the matter now?*
> QUEEN GERTRUDE: *Have you forgot me?*

HAMLET: No,
You are the queen, your husband's brother's wife;
And—would it were not so!—you are my mother.
HAMLET: Come, come, and sit you down; you shall not budge;
You go not till I set you up a glass
Where you may see the inmost part of you.
QUEEN GERTRUDE: What wilt thou do? thou wilt not murder
me?
HAMLET: [Drawing] How now! a rat?
POLONIUS: O, I am slain!

Jerome had fun being Polonius and getting slain. Catherine and Bradley held the arras. Oh shoot, they were in the same group. But it happened at random via counting off; I can hardly be expected to control that. The best part was when, Vincent, who was behind the arras next to Jerome's Polonius, fell at the same time as the murdered Polonius, dragging the arras down on top of them. Then laying on the ground, Vincent took the piece of fabric, white side out, put it over his head like a ghost, stood up and floated out the door. Oh. My. Gosh. Polonius' ghost! Brilliant.

"No way!" I cried out. "Awesome," I said, shaking my head and smiling from the back. This is the fun part. I believe this collaboration will help the play stick with them. Or at least plant the seed that hey, we can make Shakespeare our own and even surprise our teacher.

Sage and Jimmy were the unexpected entrance: police investigators who had been called to the scene because they heard "what sounded like a murder going on in here." Ha!

QUEEN GERTRUDE: O me, what hast thou done?
HAMLET: Nay, I know not. Is it the king?
QUEEN GERTRUDE: O, what a rash and bloody deed is this!

HAMLET: A bloody deed! almost as bad, good mother,
As kill a king, and marry with his brother.
QUEEN GERTRUDE: As kill a king!?
HAMLET: Ay, lady, it was my word.
[He pulls Polonius' body from behind the arras.]
Thou wretched, rash, intruding fool, farewell.
I took thee for thy better. Take thy fortune.
Thou find'st to be too busy is some danger.
Leave wringing of your hands: peace! sit you down,
And let me wring your heart;
                  (3.4.11...43)

Whoops, I forgot to point out to them the implied stage direction, so as happens about half the time in this scene, Hamlet tells Gertrude to stop wringing her hands, and she's doing nothing of the kind.

"Great, great!" I cheered. "I loved the ghost of Polonius! Now troupe two, come on up and take your places. And...action!" I cried. This time Coleman was Hamlet and Diane Gertrude. I was glad to see the imposing height and russet beard of Duncan in the role of the Ghost, Luis was the dead body, and tiny Mei-Mei and zorbic Gino looked hilarious side by side as Rosencrantz and Guildenstern who in this rendition had been hiding in Gertrude's room, working overtime on the spying.

HAMLET: Have you eyes?
Ha! Have you eyes?
You cannot call it love; for at your age
The hey-day in the blood is tame...
Eyes without feeling, feeling without sight,
Ears without hands or eyes,
QUEEN GERTRUDE: O Hamlet, speak no more:

Thou turn'st mine eyes into my very soul;
These words, like daggers, enter in mine ears;
HAMLET: A murderer and a villain;
A slave that is not twentieth part the tithe
Of your precedent lord;
GHOST: Do not forget: this visitation
Is but to whet thy almost blunted purpose.
But, look, amazement on thy mother sits:
O, step between her and her fighting soul:
QUEEN GERTRUDE: Whereon do you look?
HAMLET: On him, on him!
QUEEN GERTRUDE: To whom do you speak this?
HAMLET: Do you see nothing there?
QUEEN GERTRUDE: This is the very coinage of your brain:
HAMLET: it is not madness That I have utter'd:
Confess yourself to heaven;
Repent what's past; avoid what is to come;
And do not spread the compost on the weeds,
To make them ranker.
QUEEN GERTRUDE: O Hamlet, thou hast cleft my heart in
twain.
HAMLET: O, throw away the worser part of it…
go not to mine uncle's bed;
Assume a virtue, if you have it not.
Refrain to-night,
And that shall lend a kind of easiness
To the next abstinence:
I must be cruel, only to be kind:
QUEEN GERTRUDE: I have no life to breathe
What thou hast said to me.
HAMLET: I must to England; you know that?
                    (3.4.75...222)

"The ghost came back. What do people think of people who see ghosts?" I asked.

"They crazy," Imani sang under her breath.

I prodded. "Are ghosts the same as spirits?"

"My aunt sees spirits," Jerome said. "She is kind of psychic and people come to her to talk to people who died." A few snickers.

"Really?" I said. "That's cool."

"She doesn't talk about it though."

Mei-Mei piped up, "My grandmother has dreams about my grandfather all the time. I think that's why she stays in bed so much. My parents think she's depressed. I think she just wants to see her husband."

Imani, eyebrows raised, muttered, "I don't want to see no ghosts."

I didn't bother correcting her grammar.

In these past few days my mind meshed with the play, shuffling through the characters, checking each for their counterparts in my own life. Ray (my stepfather) was no Claudius. He's faithful and loving and a true father figure, not an interloper or a fake. Maureen was neither a Claudius, nor a Gertrude. Although it could be said of her that *she hung on* my dad *as if increase of appetite did grow by what it fed on.* If anything, Maureen was most like the Player Queen, who was scared to death to lose the earthly presence of the love of her life. My God, I've never known that feeling. I wasn't even scared to lose Dad. I should have been.

Obviously not everything in *Hamlet* synced up with my life. My father hadn't been murdered and I hadn't been charged with revenge. The only impossible task I had was getting up every morning to teach. And no ghost, only my thoughts, were telling me to do that.

Earlier that morning when writing on the board, I found myself wondering if my obsessive need to make everything in

Hamlet connect to my dad's death was a manifestation of what the Buddhists refer to as man's search for meaning in an effort to alleviate pain. *Hamlet* was becoming my new religion, a pain killer of sorts. Living in the play transported me from my specific loss and let me live surrounded by impersonal timeless truth about life and death.

"I love this part. Hamlet says *Take thy fortune* (meaning, his fate—accidently stabbed because he was spying) *thou findest to be too busy is some danger.*"

"Busy as in busybody. Victor, what's a busybody?"

"I've heard of it, but I don't really know."

"Anybody know what a busybody is?"

"I guess, like um sexually, like you know…" Meredith grasped for words.

"Uh, good guess, but no." I couldn't believe no one knew what a busybody was.

"Someone who is nosey? Like a person in everyone's business?" asked Feona.

"Yes! A gossipy busybody, those old ladies who say, 'Hmm, saw you walking and holding so-and-so's hand—are you engaged?' That's what a busybody is! This is straight up calling Polonius out for being in everyone's business and it got him *hoist with his own petard*! Write this down in the margin please. Busybody. Now you know what a busybody is. You don't want to walk out into the world and not know what a busybody is. What else" I scanned the text. "Victor?"

"On 3.4.6 when he says *I'll silence me even here*, and then later he's eternally silenced by Hamlet."

"Yes, good eye. Another connection I never made."

"It's foreshadowing," Catherine said.

"Yes, and later it becomes a pun, in a way. Okay I think we got it all." I glanced at the lesson plan, saw HOIST WITH HIS OWN PETARD, and looked at the clock. I'd have time.

"Now turn towards Hamlet's visit with Gertrude, starting at 3.4.222. This is a line you'll want to use forever."

I must to England, you know that.
QUEEN: Alack,
I had forgot! 'Tis so concluded on.
HAMLET: There's letters sealed; and my two schoolfellows,
Whom I will trust as I will adders fanged,

"*Adders fanged*, I like that line," said Albert.

"I know, right? Meaning he'll trust Rosencrantz & Guildenstern how?"

"Not at all," he said, poking the air with each word.

They bear the mandate; they must sweep my way
And marshal me to knavery. Let it work,
For 'tis the sport to have the enginer
Hoist with his own petard; and 't shall go hard
But I will delve one yard below their mines
And blow them at the moon. O, 'tis most sweet
When in one line two crafts directly meet.

"Has anyone heard *hoist with his own petard* before?" A few nods. "Yes, Albert?"

"It's like getting paid back," he said.

"Yeah, payback, baby," said Jerome. They laughed.

"Yes. That and more. Look at the notes." I saw pages turning. "A petard is an explosive and when something is hoisted, it's lifted up. If you picture it, this is powerful imagery. The engineer—bomb designer—blows himself into the air with his own clever device. Basically, *hoist with your own petard* is when your own tools and methods are used against you."

"Like getting a taste of your own medicine!" said Albert.

Ding, ding, I rang the green bell, "Exactly! It's payback plus. Hamlet is foreshadowing what he's going to do to Rosencrantz & Guildenstern on the way back to England, and the truth is that Polonius was hoist with his own petard, too. His spying got him killed."

The bell rang. I made it through the first week.

ACT FOUR

My father—methinks I see my father

(1.2.191)

Monday morning. I woke up to a late-night email from Maureen pleading for Paige and me to send money for a headstone for Dad.

"He has to have a stone. I can't stand the idea of him lying in an unmarked grave." As I lay in bed reading her emails, a fresh combination of pathos and guilt swirled in my gut. Of course Dad will have a headstone. But what's the rush? Why right now? My stomach ached.

It was already May. There was a visible disk of sun cresting above the fieldstone facade of the school in the mornings when I walked to school.

I entered the classroom that was mine, all mine, and looked around. Lucky me: some teachers have to share a classroom. This was my own Denmark and I had left a big quote at the top of the board:

Take you me for a sponge, my lord?

I sat, opened to Act 4:1-4 and checked the lesson plan. This was going to be good.

4: 1-4

#wormfood

Act 4:1-4 is a series of short scenes after the murder of Polonius; the pacing escalates as it would in a harried search for a dead body. A few minutes before class, Luis rushed in wide-eyed and panting.

"I just got into school," he exhaled, bending in half.

"Is everything okay?"

"Last night on the way home from the game I saw this— there's this old lady in my neighborhood, she walks on the road every day and every night. I saw her, this guy, he didn't see her. Boom he hit her." He looked ashen.

"You saw it? You saw her get hit?"

"Yes."

"Is she okay?"

"I'm not sure, I'm still not sure. But she's alive. The ambulance came. I waited until the ambulance came. Once I got home I was too shook up to do my homework. I'm sorry."

"Don't worry," I said. "Go get some water."

A minute later the bell rang and students arrived. On her way in Feona said, "Hey Miss Erica, I saw a great play this weekend—and I'm not saying that just because you're my teacher."

"Oh really? What did you see?" I asked.

"*On the Town!*"

"Wait, on Broadway?"

"Yep!" she smiled wide. "The Performing Arts Portfolio class went. It was amazing!"

"Was that your first Broadway show?"

"Yep, it was so cool!"

I sang "New York, New York it's a wonderful town," imagined the movie scene in the shipyard, which cheered me up, and started class by hearing One Good Thing about everyone's weekend.

"It was a gorgeous day yesterday, wasn't it?" I said. "Did you guys get outside? Did you get outside, Jerome?"

"Oh yeah I did," Jerome's smile widened across his face as if he were remembering, "I was playing some two-on-two with my cousins."

"I had to drive into Philly," said Gino, "and it was the perfect time in the afternoon when you just roll down the windows and crank up the tunes."

"Excellent," I relished the image, smiling. "Isn't that great? Rolling down the windows, feeling the breeze and not being cold? I did that, too."

"I went to a Gettysburg lacrosse game," said Catherine. "It was such a great day for it. And my brother got his first goal!"

"Did you get outside Miss Erica?" asked Jimmy.

"You better believe it!"

"I think I might have saw you."

I've been accused by some of the American students of being too critical of ELL's grammar. Correcting grammar is my job, but I decided not to break the flow of the conversation.

"You saw me?" I echoed.

"Yes, down by the elementary school. You rollerblade?" Jimmy asked.

"Yes, I rollerblade, though not much around here." Then to change the subject I recited:

Take you me for a sponge, my lord?

Talk about a line that speaks *trippingly on the tongue. Take you me for a sponge, my lord?* I love that line. I grabbed the wizened yellow sponge from the chalk tray and pretended to squeeze it in the air.

> *HAMLET: Ay, sir, that soaks up the King's countenance,*
> *his rewards, his authorities....*
> *When he needs what you have*
> *gleaned, it is but squeezing you, and, sponge, you*
> *shall be dry again.*
> (4.2.14...21)

"That's another thing you could do for extra credit. Bring me one of those old-fashioned sponges from the ocean to use as prop for next year," I said.

"Miss Erica, what was the answer to question three on yesterday's quiz?"

"Oh yes, thank you—a lot of people missed that one. The question was 'Why did the ghost come to Hamlet in Gertrude's closet? Turn to 3:4.127 where the Ghost tells Hamlet *This is to whet your almost blunted purpose,* which is the perfect kind of quote to be on the test, by the way. It's also nice to know that "whet your appetite" is not spelled W-E-T. Have you heard the expression before, 'this just whets my appetite'? You haven't? Well that's why I'm here. A whetting stone is what you use to sharpen a knife. So if something "whets your appetite" you get a taste and want more." Luis was nodding, Bradley and Diane confirmed with their notes from last week, and the eyelids of the Bermuda Triangle drooped.

"So, the answer is...?"

Silence. Ugh.

"Why did the ghost come back, Vincent?" Jimmy and Gino were visibly jolted hearing someone in their inner sanctum put on the spot.

"To remind him of his goal to revenge his father," said Vincent, looking almost surprised he knew the answer.

"Exactly," I confirmed. "Then the next line, *But look, amazement on thy mother sits!* Make sure you have this highlighted. What's the ghost saying?"

"She looks surprised," Diane called out.

"Yes, and that would indicate what? Yes, Mei-Mei?"

"That she's not in on it," said Mei-Mei quietly but confidently, as usual. I don't think she ever says anything she is not 100% sure is correct.

"Yes," I said, "exactly. The ghost is relieved to see Gertrude looks surprised to hear he was murdered by Claudius."

"There's a tenderness here," said Diane.

"Yes," I said, "agreed. Earlier in the play Hamlet talks about how in love his parents were. Here's something to think about. It's wonderful to have parents who love each other and are happily married. If you add to it that these are very powerful people, very busy people (they are the King and Queen), their son might not get much attention."

"I never thought of that," said Feona.

"Bradley, what was it you said about the ghost?"

"I think she could still fake looking surprised."

Luis looked over at him and nodded.

"True, true, good point, bro," said Coleman, clearly awake, though still slumped in his chair.

"Absolutely," I said. "With interpreting each one of these characters, the big question is, how good of an actor are they? Do they look like they believe what they are saying? Okay, let's move on. Remember when we finished up last week I had a bunch of notes on the board about Rosencrantz and Guildenstern? We want to keep thinking about what kind of friends Hamlet has," I pointed to "Hamlet's Friends" on the board behind me. "I want you to be making connections all the way back to the first line of the play, which is what?" I called out.

"Who's there?" at least five voices spoke in unison, thank goodness.

"Who's there!" I repeated. "It's not possible that Shakespeare, with all the layers of meaning that he puts into everything, much less the layers of interpretations scholars have made over the years, is merely having Barnardo ask *Who's there?* because he heard someone and can't see who it is. It can be seen as a larger question for the play, and life: Who's there, who's paying attention? Who cares about me and my life? Is anybody out there? Who can I trust? And for Hamlet, who shows up for him at this terrible time?"

"You've got two sets of friends," I counted on my fingers, "Rosencrantz and Guildenstern who are his childhood friends, and Horatio, who Hamlet says his soul chose for himself."

"Where's that?" asked Diane?

"Towards the beginning of 3.2, line 67."

Friends. Dad used to comment on how many friends I had. He said it like he was impressed, which was funny because I never saw him as someone with a small number of friends.

"Let's hear your reading responses," I prompted.

"I noticed at the beginning of Act 4 Claudius asks Gertrude 'where's your son,'" said Catherine. "He keeps changing it, right?" said Albert, more to Catherine than me. "Sometimes it's our son sometimes it's your son."

"Yes," I said. "You could say that reveals he's distancing himself from Hamlet, but it could also be respect to Gertrude when they're alone."

"It was interesting when he called the King a thing. Isn't that really rude?" asked Coleman.

"Yah, yah," said Jimmy, "dissin' him big time." Foreign students love our slang.

"Is that what's happening here?" I asked. "Is Hamlet being rude to Claudius?"

"He's saying he's a joke," said Luis. Reductive. But not bad for not having read.

"Maybe," I said, "but I think there's more to it. Hamlet is getting philosophical. He's saying the king," I grabbed one of the plastic golden crowns from the desk, "is a thing of nothing," and I tossed the crown to the floor. "Feona?"

"It's kind like he's separating the King from the man," she said.

"Exactly. The kingship is an entity. A job, a position. Of nothing. What is royalty? This is a huge issue in this play." Greatness vs. Goodness was written on the board. "This play talks about greatness a lot. It's not surprising when the titular character is a prince, royalty. Greatness is an issue. Even in our culture we can relate. These days, what is greatness associated with? Celebrity, fame?"

"Fame," said Jerome. "Definitely fame." Luis and Jimmy were nodding.

"Think about Greatness vs. Goodness. What does it mean if you're Alexander the Great? If you're Caesar? If you're *Hyperion to a Satyr?* Guess what? In the end, we're all wormfood." I turned and banged on WORMFOOD on the board.

I flashed to an image Maureen had put in my head of my dad's corpse being dressed in the fancy, white, tropical-style short-sleeve shirt his friend Jerry had given him. My shoulders shivered a bit and I shook off the vision.

"Yes, Diane?"

"He doesn't tell Rosencrantz and Guildenstern anything because they really haven't experienced anything…"

I wondered where she was going with this. "…anything, concerning…" it was obvious she was grasping for words, "anything concerning grief. They wouldn't understand what Hamlet's going through. They are with the King, not helping Hamlet. Hamlet's like, why talk to someone who doesn't know what I'm going through, who hasn't experienced it?" That was firsthand experience talking.

"Yeah," I said slowly, "They're kind of…shallow."

"Yeah," she nodded.

"Jimmy?"

"Back to why he doesn't tell them where the body is. When you bury someone you have closure so maybe Hamlet didn't want Claudius to have closure."

"Oh, I like that. Good one. Bradley?"

"In scene 3, line 37, Claudius asks where Polonius is and Hamlet says in Heaven, which is surprising because I thought he'd say in Hell, since he doesn't like him."

"Ha, ha, good point. And what comes next is the best! Can you read that whole chunk for us Bradley? From your seat? Wait, I'll prompt you and read Claudius' lines. *Now Hamlet, where is Polonius?*" I said.

> *HAMLET: At supper.*
> *KING: At supper where?*
>   (4.3.19-21)

Supper…. Supper. *Not where he eats….* As soon as I heard Bradley say those words my mind went to the last meal I made for my father. Spaghetti. The last spaghetti he would ever eat. I made it the way Mom used to, with sautéed onions and green and red peppers and Kraft cheese in the green shaky container, a staple in our household growing up. It was on the table in Costa Rica for our last supper. Dad loved his pasta. I wish I had made linguine and white clam too.

I zoned back into the classroom and realized Bradley was finishing the passage and I had another line.

> *HAMLET: Not where he eats, but where he is eaten. A*
> *certain convocation of politic worms are e'en at*
> *him. Your worm is your only emperor for diet. We*
> *fat all creatures else to fat us, and we fat ourselves*
> *for maggots. Your fat king and your lean beggar is*
> *but variable service—two dishes but to one table.*
> *That's the end.*
> *KING: Alas, alas!*

Close call, I almost missed my line.

> *HAMLET: A man may fish with the worm that hath eat*
> *of a king and eat of the fish that hath fed of that*
> *worm.*
> *KING: What dost thou mean by this?*
> *HAMLET: Nothing but to show you how a king may go a*
> *progress through the guts of a beggar.*
> *KING: Where is Polonius?*
> *HAMLET: In heaven. Send thither to see. If your messenger*
> *find him not there, seek him i' th' other*
> *place yourself. But if, indeed, you find him not*
> *within this month, you shall nose him as you go up*
> *the stairs into the lobby.*
> *KING: [to Attendants.] Go, seek him there.*
> *HAMLET: He will stay till you come.*
>   (4.3.22-43)

"Yes, Albert?"

"They think Hamlet's crazy so he gets away with telling Claudius go to Hell!" he giggled.

"Exactly!" I said, smiling and nodding. "Just think how many kids have wanted to say 'Go to Hell!' to their stepparent." I saw a few knowing nods, and a few smirks. "Or their king, or boss."

"So Polonius doesn't get a good burial?" asked Coleman. "What does that mean?"

"Good question. Hopefully everyone got the answer to the question, what is 'Claudius' first reaction to hearing about the killing of Polonius.' He says, *O heavy deed!* Then he says: *It had been so with us, had we been there.* Meaning what?" I asked. "Double I?"

"He was with us just a few minutes ago?"

"Uh, no—"

"That could have been me!" Albert shouted.

"Exactly. It's confusing but the 'It' Claudius refers to is Polonius' murder, and when he says 'us' and 'we' he is using the royal we. Claudius says if he had been hiding instead of Polonius, he would have been stabbed instead. Claudius is saying, 'whoosh, close call.' Diane?"

"His first thought is of himself and his own safety," she said, sounding surprised.

"Right. Claudius's first thought is of self-preservation, and then of what his subjects are going to say when they hear. Imani?"

"I was shocked Gertrude told Claudius immediately." She seemed to think she was onto something and continued, "and then she said *a rat a rat* when she was the rat. I don't know if that means anything."

"Oh, yeah, well, Gertrude was quoting Hamlet because he had said, "*a rat, a rat.*"

"I know, umm, well...I just thought, she was kinda ratting him out."

I banged the bell. "Yes, absolutely! I see what you're saying. Good! We need to look at this. Who thought, when they read this, wow Gertrude, you just ratted out your son?"

A few tentative hands went up.

"I think she's two faced," said Vincent.

"You think she's two-faced, why?"

"She's playing both sides," Vincent said.

"She might be trying to see how Claudius is going to react," Gino said to him.

"I think she's trying to protect herself," said Jimmy. Go Bermuda Triangle!

"Gino, what did you say?" I asked.

"I said I sort of expected it."

"We need to go back to Act 3:4 where Hamlet tells Gertrude what to do and what not to do. Can someone read this? Sage?"

Not this by no means that I bid you do:
Let the bloat king tempt you again to bed,
Pinch wanton on your cheek, call you his mouse,
And let him, for a pair of reechy kisses
Or paddling in your neck with his damned fingers,
Make you to ravel all this matter out
That I essentially am not in madness,
But mad in craft.

(3.4.203-210)

Bradley's hand went up.

"Gertrude was in shock and trying to process it," he said.

"But she doesn't say anything about Claudius killing King Hamlet," Catherine countered.

Jerome chimed in, "Yeah, that's what makes me think she already knew."

"Yes, okay, but let's get to the point because class is almost half over. We need to answer the question: Did Gertrude rat on her own son? Look at what Hamlet asks her to do and not to do. Who remembers?" I counted Hamlet's directives off on my fingers:

#1 - don't go back to bed with him, line 204

#2 - don't let him seduce you, line 207

#3 - don't tell him I'm just acting crazy, line 209

He doesn't say don't tell him I killed Polonius. Why?"

"Well, it's not like she can hide it. I mean, Polonius is dead, he was hiding in her room, who else would have killed him?" Thank you, Albert!

"Exactly! Some things you can hide and some things you can't. You can't hide the fact there's a dead body, and it didn't happen by accident, and Gertrude didn't do it. When we are looking for motivation for Gertrude, it can look like she ratted out her son for killing Polonius. But really, there was no point trying to hide it. She did not tell Claudius, 'Hamlet knows you killed his father.' She didn't tell him everything."

"Why can't Gertrude see the ghost?" asked Jimmy Wong. It was a good question. I pretended like I had never considered it.

"Hmmmm...can ghosts choose who sees them and who doesn't?" Some of the kids looked at each other as if they were supposed to know the answer. "Remember what I told you in the beginning? How to deal with questions the play raises? Look at what happens and what doesn't. If Gertrude is genuine and she doesn't see the King's ghost, I guess the answer is, yes, ghosts can choose." I took a breath and looked around. Everyone seemed fine with this premise. I had a fresh thought.

"Ghosts in Shakespeare are a great opportunity to take advantage of the directorial freedom his works allow. What are the two main contributors to directorial freedom for interpretation?" Nothing. "Remember?"

"Minimal stage direction and limited backstory," Mei-Mei recited, after flipping through her notes.

"Exactly. If you were mounting *Hamlet*, what would it be like without an actor playing the ghost? If the audience, as well as Gertrude, doesn't see what Hamlet sees? What then?"

"He seems way more crazy!" Albert bounced up and down on his stool. "He's hallucinating!"

"Exactly. You see how unanswered questions point us in certain directions? Remember in Act 1 we wondered why the ghost appeared to the watchmen first? Why did he appear outside instead of inside the castle?"

"If the guards see the ghost first then Hamlet has evidence he's not just hallucinating," said Coleman.

"To see if Hamlet wanted to talk to him. The guards tell Hamlet. That way if Hamlet didn't want to talk to his dad, he wouldn't have to," Luis said.

"Good point. When the question is why did somebody do *this*, we need to ask, why didn't they do *that* instead? Or what would have happened if they had done something else? That's where Jimmy was taking us. What if the ghost had gone straight to Hamlet? Imagine, your father died recently, you didn't get to say goodbye. Now you see his ghost. And he tells you your uncle, who you hate, who has married your mother, and who insists on calling you son, murdered your dad. If that were to happen, you might think you're losing it. So appearing to the guards first is confirmation that the ghost is not *the very coinage* of Hamlet's brain. This gives a lot of what is called 'agency' to the ghost. This implies ghosts can choose things."

"Why wouldn't the ghost want Gertrude to see him?" asked Jimmy, not ready to let go.

"Good question. Any ideas?"

"He doesn't trust her." "He's mad at her." "He still loves her and doesn't want her to get more upset."

"Okay, we are running out of time. We still need to hear from Catherine and Meredith."

"I thought it was funny how Hamlet called Claudius *my mother*, kind of making fun of him," said Catherine.

Meredith said, "The citizens of Denmark were loosely aware of what was going on, like they thought Hamlet and Claudius were unstable, and they wanted Laertes to be king, who's not even part of the family."

"Right, some of them, anyway. Apparently Laertes could raise an army—or a posse, if you will—by telling his story. Laertes has found a bunch of *lawless resolutes* who say *Laertes shall be king! Laertes king!* because what's happening here is wrong. Good noticing."

"What else—Bradley?"

"I have two things. Little side note, going off what Catherine said, I thought it was interesting how Hamlet, when he left, said *Farewell, dear mother*, so I feel like there's kind of a theme going there with calling Claudius a girl. It might be a dis, I don't know."

"Totally," I said, nodding. 'Could you read that? Start with *I see a cherub*."

> HAMLET: *I see a cherub that sees them. But come, for*
> *England.*
> *Farewell, dear mother.*
> KING: *Thy loving father, Hamlet.*
> HAMLET: *My mother. Father and mother is man and wife,*

> *Man and wife is one flesh, and so, my mother.—*
> *Come, for England. [He exits.]*
>   (4.3.56-62)

"Thank you."

"Also," Bradley continued, "this soliloquy at the end, Hamlet's soliloquy, I'm trying to wrap my head around it. I feel like he's trying to figure out what is greatness. He's thinking about it, like how all those soldiers will fight for this little worthless piece of land and they're all going into the ground. What they're fighting for...what seems like their honor, whether it's actually there or not. At the end he decides that for him to be great, he has to think only bloody thoughts or something like that? Which makes me think he's decided he's going to kill Claudius or at least try."

"Yes! He's going back to the old pagan, Beowulfian idea of greatness. Follow the bro code. It's ironic he takes us through this whole soliloquy and all its issues as Bradley pointed out, and it's all about acting and not acting, and then at the end he says *my thoughts bloody or be nothing worth,*" I said, stressing the word *thought.* "Yes Catherine?"

"Is that like a Freudian slip that he says 'thoughts' instead of actions?"

"Could be, could be!" I smiled and nodded. "What else? Did you get the answer to why did Shakespeare have Hamlet cross paths with Fortinbras and his army?"

"I just said so Hamlet can remember he needs to take action," said Bradley.

"Yes, and it's a reminder this whole force is coming towards Denmark. This soliloquy, by the way, gets cut by many productions. Look what he says starting at line 49. ... *Examples as gross as earth surround me* (everywhere I look I see examples), *witness this army,* (which means, look at this army), *led by this delicate and tender prince* (so he respects Fortinbras), *whose spirit with divine ambition puffed.* What's he saying about Fortinbras' motivation here?"

"It's from God?" said Jimmy.

"Yes. Hamlet sees it as God-directed," I said. "*Exposing what is mortal and unsure,* that means life, *to all the fortune death and danger dare, even for an eggshell.* Why an eggshell? Here's an egg," I said, drawing a large oval on the board. "How do I turn it into an eggshell?"

"Crack it!" I heard a couple of voices say.

"Crack it? Like that?" I asked, drawing a zigzag across the middle of the egg.

"Yeah!"

"Now watch," I said and I drew a line under the zigzag, erased the top of the egg, drew a smiley face on the bottom, and put dots on top of the points of what was now, clearly, a crown. I love doing this. I heard oohs and ahhs of realization.

"Can you believe it?" I exclaimed. "An eggshell—the crown! It's just a thing," I reached down for the plastic crown I had thrown to the floor earlier, waved it in the air, and tossed it back on the ground. "Like he said earlier, *the king is a thing, ...of nothing.* I didn't make that up, by the way. My college Shakespeare professor, James Shapiro, showed me that. Totally blew my mind. Okay, what else?"

"What if Claudius had become king but didn't marry Gertrude, would Hamlet still be so upset?" asked Coleman.

"Hmmmm. Did you guys hear Coleman's question?"

"I was wondering if Claudius became king but didn't marry Gertrude would Hamlet still be so upset? Did Hamlet want to be king?"

"This is one of the many questions this play brings up that really aren't answered, but we can guess. What do you guys think?"

"Well," Sage said, as if we had forgotten a crucial point, which perhaps we had. "Once the Ghost told Hamlet about the murder, I think he would still be pretty upset."

"Legit, legit," said Coleman, looking over from his slouch to her straight-backed poise in the Peanut Gallery to his right.

"Yes," I said. I had never thought of this before. "That's absolutely true. Sage?"

"Then Claudius wouldn't care if Hamlet stayed at court or went back to Wittenberg."

"Wait a minute," said Bradley. "Maybe that's why he married Gertrude, to keep Hamlet sort of, you know, in the family."

"Yes!" I said. "Or to minimize the possible rivalry for the throne. I mean this way he already has Hamlet's mother on his side. And he uses that. Good!"

"Hey, did he really want to go back to school or did he want to do what Laertes did, get an army together and come back and take over?" Jimmy asked.

"Excellent question," I said. "This is the kind of question you ask when you're trying to get into the mindset possibilities of your characters. Yes, Sage?"

"I'm sorry, Miss Erica, can you explain what you mean by getting into the...what did you say...the mindsets of the characters? What does that mean, exactly?"

"Good question. I mean that even if the audience or the other characters don't know how, say, Hamlet or Gertrude feel about something, the actors who play Hamlet or Gertrude need to know." The faces did not look enlightened. Did I not make sense? A teacher trick when this happens: "Could someone give an example of what I'm talking about? Albert?"

"Well, if you're going to play Gertrude, you need to decide whether you knew that Claudius killed your husband or not." Albert had been in the school plays and, not surprisingly, was an animated and engaging actor.

"Exactly. Can you explain why?"

"Well...you have to act and if you don't know what's in your character's head, how are you going to know how they will react to something?"

"Does that make sense? Good. What else?"

"I'm curious how Ophelia is going to react when she finds out Hamlet killed her father," said Jerome.

"I think Hamlet not telling where the body is, is trying to make Claudius angry. Like he's trying to seem crazy," said Mei-Mei.

"I know," said Diane, "it's annoying. Claudius has to ask 'where is the body?' like ten times. It reminded me of when parents keep asking the same question over and over. He must be getting angrier and louder each time." Yes!

"Luis, how about you?" I didn't have any checkmarks next to his name. He smiled.

"I noticed that Rosencrantz and Guildenstern are always seen together."

"Ha, yes, you are right about that. They are Tweedle Dum and Tweedle Dee," I said. "Let's take a close look at their interaction with Hamlet while looking for the body of Polonius. Anyone want to be Hamlet?" They looked around at each other. No volunteers. I needed a strong reader, but someone who could be funny and irreverent. "Okay, Jerome, you be Hamlet, Mei-Mei, you be Rosencrantz, and Sage, you be Guildenstern." Jerome looked surprised then popped out of his seat and picked up his book.

HAMLET: Safely stowed.
GENTLEMEN: within Hamlet! Lord Hamlet!
HAMLET: But soft, what noise? Who calls on Hamlet?
O, here they come.

[Enter Rosencrantz, Guildenstern, and others.]

Mei-Mei and Sage picked up where Vincent and Luis left off, but they were shy about it.

> *ROSENCRANTZ: What have you done, my lord, with the dead body?*
> *HAMLET: Compounded it with dust, whereto 'tis kin.*
> *ROSENCRANTZ: Tell us where 'tis, that we may take it thence*
> *And bear it to the chapel.*
> *HAMLET: Do not believe it.*
> *ROSENCRANTZ: Believe what?*
> *HAMLET: That I can keep your counsel and not mine*
> *own. Besides, to be demanded of a sponge, what*
> *replication should be made by the son of a king?*
> *ROSENCRANTZ: Take you me for a sponge, my lord?*
> *HAMLET: Ay, sir, that soaks up the King's countenance,*
> *his rewards, his authorities. But such officers do the*
> *King best service in the end. He keeps them like an*
> *ape an apple in the corner of his jaw, first mouthed,*
> *to be last swallowed. When he needs what you have*
> *gleaned, it is but squeezing you, and, sponge, you*
> *shall be dry again.*
> *ROSENCRANTZ: I understand you not, my lord.*
> *HAMLET: I am glad of it. A knavish speech sleeps in a*
> *foolish ear.*
> *ROSENCRANTZ: My lord, you must tell us where the*
> *body is and go with us to the King.*
> *HAMLET: The body is with the King, but the King is not*
> *with the body. The King is a thing—*
> *GUILDENSTERN: A "thing," my lord?*
> *HAMLET: Of nothing. Bring me to him. Hide fox, and*
> *all after!*
> *[They exit.]*
>   (4.2.1-31)

"Okay, Act 4, scene 3, part of which Bradley and I read earlier. Meredith, you be Claudius." I knew she could capture the angry parent energy needed here. "Come on up. The first part, you can just talk to these guys on the right as if they are your attendants, okay? Let Catherine be Rosencrantz, Duncan you be Guildenstern, and Coleman you're Hamlet." He smirked and unfolded himself. Come on fake Michael J. Fox.

> KING: *How now, what hath befallen?*
> ROSENCRANTZ: *Where the dead body is bestowed, my lord,*
> *We cannot get from him.*
> KING: *But where is he?*
> ROSENCRANTZ:
> *Without, my lord; guarded, to know your pleasure.*
> KING: *Bring him before us.*
> ROSENCRANTZ: *Ho! Bring in the lord.*
> *[They enter with Hamlet.]*
> KING: *Now, Hamlet, where's Polonius?*
> HAMLET: *At supper.*
>   (4.3.12-20)

"Come on, Coleman. 'At supper,'" I imitated his flat drone. "You sound dead. Act crazy or something. Bring some life to it!"

"I was trying to act like he didn't care. Like he was blowing it off," Coleman said.

"Well...that's a cool idea. I take it back. But figure out how to do 'I don't care' in a way so the audience does care. Maybe put some movement or gestures into it? Take it again, Meredith, at *Now Hamlet.*"

> KING: *Now, Hamlet, where's Polonius?*
> HAMLET: *At supper.*
> KING: *At supper where?*

*HAMLET: Not where he eats, but where he is eaten. A
certain convocation of politic worms are e'en at
him.*

Speaking the word *worm* the fake Michael J. Fox became funny
and philosophical.

"Much better—good! Keep going."

*Your worm is your only emperor for diet. We
fat all creatures else to fat us, and we fat ourselves
for maggots.*

He emphasized *worm* and *maggot*.

*Your fat king and your lean beggar is
but variable service—two dishes but to one table.
That's the end.
KING: Alas, alas!
HAMLET: A man may fish with the worm that hath eat
of a king and eat of the fish that hath fed of that
worm.
KING: What dost thou mean by this?
HAMLET: Nothing but to show you how a king may go a
progress through the guts of a beggar.*

Meredith grabbed Hamlet by the shoulders and almost shouted

KING: Where is Polonius?

I think I heard a gasp or two. Yes!

HAMLET: In heaven. Send thither to see. If your messenger
find him not there, seek him i' th' other
place yourself. But if, indeed, you find him not
within this month, you shall nose him as you go up
the stairs into the lobby.
KING: [to Attendants.]
Go, seek him there.
HAMLET: He will stay till you come.
[Attendants exit.]
KING: Hamlet, this deed, for thine especial safety
                (4.3.19-44)

Now she came up to him and put her hand on his shoulder.
Nice touch. Very avuncular. Coleman wriggled out from under
Meredith's grip. Perfect. They were getting it.

"Good, good, you can stop there. Meredith you captured how angry
and desperate Claudius is at this point. Now, 4:4 is when Hamlet
sees Fortinbras in the distance. When Hamlet finds out what the
Norwegian Prince is doing, it sets him off on yet another soliloquy."

How all occasions do inform against me
And spur my dull revenge.

"Hamlet's basically saying everywhere I look there's an example of
someone who's doing more than I am for my dead dad. In this case,
it's Fortinbras, who's off seeking to get his dead dad's lands back."
        I've been saying the phrase "dead dad" a lot.

What is a man
If his chief good and market of his time
Be but to sleep and feed? A beast, no more.

"Hamlet wants to do the right thing, but he's not sure what the right thing is. He is caught between the ancient father-son revenge code and his own conscience. He's questioning the meaning of life."

Wake up. Get Dressed. Eat Breakfast. Brush Your Teeth. Go to Work. Is this quotidian monotony what it means to be human? Now that I was swallowed by the dense, chill cloud of death, all these day-shaping essential tasks seemed empty. Meaningless. Rote. Yet, post-my father's death, I don't know how I'd ever get out of bed or bathe if I didn't "have to."

"Miss Erica?" Mei-Mei's voice sounded far away. "This sounds like the *to be or not to be* speech."

"Yes! Good eye. And not surprising since throughout the play Hamlet is obsessed with the questions 'Why are we here?' and 'What is right action?'"

The bell ringing caught me off guard, and within thirty seconds I was standing alone in the room.

Mei-Mei came into the classroom after school, looking almost afraid. She said she wasn't sure if what she said today (about security guards being low on the social ladder) had offended anyone.

"Not that I noticed."

She got weepy and warbled: "I'm not sure what's happening or why I came to talk about this...but I'm sick, too." Oh great. Germs.

"I don't think so—do you remember what you said?"

"No, not really. I, I, I just have a hard time knowing how I come off." She said she was stressed, and she hadn't gotten into any schools and it was getting late.

"Aww, don't cry," I said, resisting the urge to move closer to this wet-faced walking virus. "Or do cry. Let it out. It's good to let it out." She did that for a while and I started to feel guilty about sitting behind my desk.

"I'd give you a hug, but no offense, I do not want to get sick." She nodded understanding. "You've been away from home for a while, right? You didn't go home for Christmas?"

"Yeah, yeah but I knew that. I knew I wouldn't go back until the end of the year." More held back sobs.

"Are your parents coming for graduation?"

"Noooo!" she wailed, waving her arms up and down and folding and unfolding herself dramatically.

"I'm sorry, that's so hard." I got up and hugged her, germs be damned. She held on tight for five full seconds then pulled away.

"Um, Miss Erica? I really like *Hamlet.*"

"Good I'm glad."

It seemed like more students talked to me about their family this year, which on one hand made sense, but ironically, if there was ever I time I felt I had nothing left to give to anyone else's problems, it was this spring. If you could call it spring. When I asked Mei-Mei what she liked about *Hamlet* she surprised me.

"My father really likes it. He's glad I'm studying it."

"Have you talked to him about it yet?"

"Only a little. But I know he likes it."

"Hey," I thought, "you should do your *To be or not to be* speech for him."

"No, it's not good enough," she said.

"Ohh, come on. Did you ever get the whole thing?"

"No, but I think I'm going to for extra credit."

"Do it!" I said, and she smiled, turned, and quickly shuffled out of the room with her head bent towards her book.

4: 5-7

O, this is the poison of deep grief; it
springs all from her father's death.

(4.5.80-81)

Tuesdays are my least favorite day and to spread *compost on the weeds* I woke up late. Probably because it was charcoal gray and damp outside. A great day for drowning or being rescued by pirates, I thought, anticipating the lesson ahead.

Drowning. Rescued at sea. Dad almost drowned once. Well, probably more than once considering all his maritime mishaps, but I'm thinking of one time with me. I had almost forgotten. It was in Nevis, in the West Indies, where I was living and working. My parents were still together enough to come visit me, and Dad and I took out one of the catamarans from the beachfront.

We paid minimal attention to whatever instructions we were given, and as we headed out to sea, we tied the lifejackets to the mast so we wouldn't lose them. We were pretty far out when the boat tipped over. No problem, we quickly moved to right it before the sail got too soaked. I have to say we were pretty deft at standing on the pontoon and using our body weight to right the vessel, but the moment both pontoons hit the water a gust of wind caught the sail and whoosh, the boat started to sail away.

"I forgot to hold the line! I'll get it!" I shouted and started swimming. He said no you can't catch it, and within that moment's hesitation, the boat was too far gone. I was twenty-five, and sure my dad was going to die young: possibly in a boating accident. We were so far from the beach, no one would see our heads bobbing out there.

"Don't worry," Dad said, pointing downwind at our flailing craft. "They'll see the boat and then come find us." We treaded water for so long he got winded, and I started to worry.

"Dad, come on. I can totally swim to shore. I'll drag you."

"No sweetie don't be silly. You'd never make it."

"Yes I would," I insisted, and starting waving my arms.

"No, no, don't do that. Save your strength." That didn't sound good.

The whole experience could have been 20 minutes or an hour, but at a certain point I started thinking about the sickly poetic nature of my dad drowning out here and at some point I swear I heard him say *save yourself.*

We kept our eye on the boat, waiting for someone to notice it, and finally watched as a big cruising sailboat slowly approached it, saw it was unmanned, and set sail directly towards us. Thank God! At first it looked like they must have seen us, but then they started tacking back and forth, clearly searching for lost souls. I started waving my arms again. Dad told me not to again. I was fine, but he did not sound good. I really wasn't sure they would find us in time, then I had a brainstorm.

"Dad give me your shorts!" I shouted. He was wearing neon orange swimming trunks and a royal blue tee-shirt. He handed me the shorts, and I started waving them like mad in the air. We watched and we watched and suddenly, like magic, the sailboat saw us, and headed straight toward to us. We were rescued, not by pirates, but by straggly sunbaked old salts. They tried to get Dad aboard, but he was so tired, he asked them if he could just hold onto the dinghy for a few minutes, which turned into ten. That's when I knew how close we had come.

I shook my head at the memory. Imani was standing in my office doorway talking. Something about extra credit, her soliloquy.

"You know how you said I'm a deep thinker?" she asked.

"Mmmm…"

"How come you can see that, and they can't see it at home?"

"Good question." These days pausing before answering a question came naturally because my brain was so overcast. "First of all, it's my job to notice that."

"Yeah, but, I mean—"

"Imani," I chose my words carefully, as I always do when talking to a kid about a parent. "Maybe it's about perspective. Sometimes you can't see something when you're too close to it. You know what I mean?"

"Hmmm. Yeah. Maybe. You may have a point there, Miss Erica," she said, smiling now. She shuffled in place.

"Anyway, what's up?"

"I want to recite my soliloquy for extra credit, but I don't want to do it in front of everyone."

"That's fine. You've seen your average right?" She nodded. "You have an 89."

"I know, I know, but there's the test…."

"Good thinking. Anyway, I'd like to hear it again. You want to do it now?"

"Yes, I think so, but I'm not looking at you. And don't you be looking at me either," she said, smiling.

"Don't worry, I won't." She recited it smoothly, with more emotion and evidence of understanding than before.

'Tis now the very witching time of night,
When churchyards yawn and hell itself breathes out
Contagion to this world. Now could I drink hot
blood
And do such bitter business as the day
Would quake to look on. Soft, now to my mother.

O heart, lose not thy nature; let not ever
The soul of Nero enter this firm bosom.
Let me be cruel, not unnatural.
I will speak daggers to her, but use none.
My tongue and soul in this be hypocrites:
How in my words somever she be shent,
To give them seals never, my soul, consent.
                    (3.2.419-432)

"No mistakes! Woo-woo!! You got it girl!! Now make sure you never forget it!" She was smiling and practically sashayed out the door.

I walked into the classroom, thinking how far Imani had come this year and hoping she'd go on to college, write poetry, and eventually become a teacher.

My head was down scanning the lesson plan when students arrived, and I sensed a small mountain had pulled up alongside the podium.

"Miss Erica, I uhhh... forgot to do the homework," said Gino. Pause, pause.

"C'est la vie, Gino Angelino," I said, shrugging my shoulders. At least he told me.

"But could I still do it and get credit for it?"

"The reading response, yes. And try to take the quiz—who knows, you might get a point or two. You could talk to your classmates now to find out what happened."

The kids were dropping their bags, getting settled, and confirming details about the reading. I shuffled my papers and wondered why there were so few students here today. The bell rang.

"We have so much to do!" I cried. "Pick up your returns! Why is everyone late today? Yeesh."

"Hey Miss Erica, Miss Erica, I've got something for you," said Bradley.

"Oh yeah, what?"

"What is the past tense of Will-I-am Shakespeare?"

"Hmmm...I have no idea."

"Would I were Shookspeare!" he said, with a satisfied smile.

"Ha! That's great!" Before I could confirm he found that online somewhere (he was looking up Shakespeare stuff!), Jerome came in with a furrowed brow in place of his usual wide smile. He dropped his backpack on his desk and came toward me. He did not look good, and it struck me he had never looked anything but lighthearted and fine up until that moment.

"Hi Jerome, what's...up?" I said.

"Albert won't be here today. I have his reading response, though."

"Is everything okay?" I asked quietly, hoping it was just a cold.

"Well," he said, "it will be. It's ...well...it's happened before. He went off his meds so.... Hopefully he won't lose more than a day."

"Yes, agreed. And thank you," I said, looking straight into his eyes.

"Yup." He turned and went back to his desk.

"Hey Miss Erica," said Jimmy, seeming genuinely curious, "is Claudius worried about Hamlet?"

"Can someone explain the two different ways in which the question 'Is Claudius worried about Hamlet?' could be interpreted? Catherine?"

"Well, it could be worried if he's okay, how is he doing... concerned for his wellbeing, or worried about him as a threat."

"Exactly, thank you. Good question, Jimmy. Let's come back to that." I looked around the still empty desks.

"No Duncan again? No Feona here either?" They were both absent yesterday.

"No, she's here, her stuff is here," said Meredith.

"Her stuff's here? Good." I started going through the attendance. "Mei-Mei's here. Diane and Sage are here. The Peanut Gallery is full!" I pretended not to hear their giggles. "Gino is kinda here, Vincent, probably also kinda here...Jerome is here, and Jimmy is here. Meredith, Catherine, Luis, Bradley, and Coleman are here. Great. Everybody up!" They rose with varying degrees of alacrity. "Good morning everyone!"

"Good morning, Miss Erica!" a chorus responded.

"Look what's happening!" I exclaimed, pointing up to the homework, "you're almost done *Hamlet*! Act 5: scene 1 tonight." Feona slipped in, draping her tie-dye fleece blanket over her lap and legs. "What was I going to say next? By the mass, I forgot what I was saying. I'm like Polonius! Did I say good morning already?"

"Yeah," said about a third of the voices.

"There are two scenes in Act 5. In my opinion there should be three because 5:2 is so long—cover your mouth when you yawn—" Vincent smiled and belatedly put his hand to his mouth. "—and it's two different settings. I don't know why Shakespeare did it that way, but I'm not in charge, so there's just two scenes left of the greatest play in the English language. 5:1 is the famous gravedigger scene," I recited:

> *Alas, poor Yorick! I knew him, Horatio—a fellow of infinite*
> *jest, of most excellent fancy. He hath bore me on his*
> *back a thousand times...*
> (5.1.190-193)

Lately I couldn't get to the end of *bore me on his back* before my eyes squeezed up against the pressure of rising tears.

"Yorick," I pronounced. The name reverberates with the ages. "He's the king's jester and this is a famous moment. Think about who you would cast as gravediggers and why."

"You mean in this class?" Bradley asked.

"Up to you," I responded. "Could be someone here, could be a famous person—or both! But think about the why."

"It's supposed to be someone famous?" Imani asked.

"Well, it could be someone you know, if you're producing it locally, or someone from Hollywood if you have a big budget production, okay? Also, in preparation for reading this famous scene—"

The door opened, Duncan walked in, pulled out the blue upholstered office chair behind his desk, and let his backpack slump to the ground. I stopped mid-sentence, looked him in the face and said:

"Greetings," with a formal nod.

"Greetings," he said.

"We were talking about Yorick and I was saying that while *To be or not to be* is the most famous line and speech, the gravedigger scene is, in a lot of ways, the most iconic scene. It takes place at the grave that's being dug for Ophelia."

"Wait, who's Yorick?" Duncan asked.

"You'll see, you'll see."

I didn't want the play to end. I liked existing in a world where the only dead dads were literary. When this class started, my dad was still alive.

"While you're reading notice what the gravedigger says about the privileges of greatness. He refers to what *great ones* get away with."

> *And the more*
> *pity that great folk should have count'nance in this*
> *world to drown or hang themselves more than*
> *their even-Christian.*
>
> (5.1.27-30)

"The gravediggers in Act 5 are similar to the watchmen in Act 1. This play is set in a monarchal world and is about royalty, greatness, supremacy, and obedience. We looked at the power structure: king over queen, monarch over subject, parent over child. Yet, the play starts with blue collar workers—regular guys—and the final act begins with ditchdiggers."

"Miss Erica, do people still do that? Dig out graves by hand?" Meredith asked. "Don't they have machines now? Seems like it would take forever."

"I don't know, it's a good question."

"Extra credit to find out?" asked Coleman.

"Sure!" I said.

"Awww," said Bradley.

"The main gravedigger suggests the ditchdiggers of society hold the *oldest profession* because Death is the oldest business! Because everyone dies. There will always be hospitals and midwives to bring human beings into the world, and there will always be funeral homes, gravediggers, preachers and crematoriums to usher them off this mortal coil. Gravediggers know firsthand that everyone—rich or poor, powerful or puny—becomes wormfood in the end."

"#wormfood!" said Meredith.

"Ha! Yes! Good one! Think about Greatness vs. Goodness. If we're all going to die, all going to be wormfood, what does it mean to be human? What is the role of ambition? What should we try to do? When you read 5:1 tonight, keep your eyes peeled for another reference to the idea of #wormfood and the circle of life." I took a deep breath. "That's the set-up for tonight. We have so much to do today, maybe we won't have a quiz, okay? But quiz tomorrow definitely." Gino looked stunned, which is how I had been feeling.

Yesterday I started seeing things on the periphery of my vision. I felt like I was navigating the spirit world and the natural world simultaneously. Spirit energy came, caught my attention, and flittered away. Unexpected movements edged into my sight line like a flutter, a flash of light, or a mouse skittering into a corner. I saw the shadows as spirits. A cardinal kept crossing the road in front of me on the way to and from work, blazing crimson in the barren brown landscape. I just knew it was my dad saying hi.

"It's funny how Ophelia is now in on calling Claudius a girl. She's like, *Good night, ladies,*" Coleman said.

"Yes! I never noticed how this develops into a motif before. I learn something every day from you folks! Let's do this scene starting from line 4.5.42, when Ophelia starts singing. Remember Gertrude refused to see Ophelia but Horatio convinced her it would be unwise not to. Who wants to be Ophelia? You have to be crazy and singing. Meredith? Go for it! Be goofy, weird and wild! Move a lot."

"Who's going to be the Queen? Be freaked out—not a lot of lines but you need to pantomime reactions: shocked, horrified, scared reactions should be visible in your face and body language. Mei-Mei? Perfect. Okay, the King?" Jimmy's hand was up before I got the word out. "Same thing Jimmy, you have a few key lines but it's about your expression and body language. Everyone else—put your books down and watch the players." They did it well, with feeling.

> *QUEEN: Alas, look here, my lord.*
> *OPHELIA: [sings]*
> *Larded all with sweet flowers;*
> *Which bewept to the ground did not go*
> *With true-love showers.*

KING: How do you, pretty lady?
OPHELIA: Well, God dild you. They say the owl was a
baker's daughter. Lord, we know what we are but
know not what we may be. God be at your table.
KING: Conceit upon her father.
OPHELIA: Pray let's have no words of this, but when
they ask you what it means, say you this:

"Do I have to sing?" Meredith asked.

"Yes, but it can sound really bad," I said.

[Sings.]
Tomorrow is Saint Valentine's day,
All in the morning betime,
And I a maid at your window,
To be your Valentine.
Then up he rose and donned his clothes
And dupped the chamber door,
Let in the maid, that out a maid
Never departed more.
KING: Pretty Ophelia—
OPHELIA: Indeed, without an oath, I'll make an end on 't:
[Sings.]
By Gis and by Saint Charity,
Alack and fie for shame,
Young men will do 't, if they come to 't;
By Cock, they are to blame.

Suppressed giggles. "Yes," I said, "She's talking about sex."

Quoth she "Before you tumbled me,
You promised me to wed."

He answers:
"So would I 'a done, by yonder sun,
An thou hadst not come to my bed."
KING: How long hath she been thus?
OPHELIA: I hope all will be well. We must be patient,
but I cannot choose but weep to think they would
lay him i' th' cold ground.
                    (4.5.42-75)

My shoulders tremored. Dad's in the ground. The *cold ground.*
Except it's Costa Rica so it's probably not that cold. Yesterday
I talked to Maureen and she told me more about the burial. I
could see the images flowing out of her mouth, but I couldn't
hold on to the words.

"The funeral home told me they would bring the casket
to the cemetery at 2PM." She sounded manic and yet weighed
down by an unbearable load. "Walter and I were planning on
leaving here at 1:30—the cemetery is only one minute away.
Caesar—you know Caesar, you met him, that young man who
lives down the road, he's only 19...and a dear friend of David.
Caesar called at 1:15 and said that David was already there, so
we rushed down. Paul, who coordinated everything, was there,
and the casket was closed." She described details like a movie
playing right before her eyes.

"His grave is up on a hill, you know. Erica, it was incredible.
Incredible. It was on a hill so everyone couldn't fit. It was standing
room only and so they came up to the casket, touched it, left a
flower, then walked along so others could come up. Everyone
came, Erica. Ticos and expats and the ladies from my reading
group. There must have been 80 people. Did Walter tell you?"
she asked, not really slowing down for an answer.

"He said there was singing."

"A little girl started singing, can't have been more than six. She loved David. He brought her candy. 'Confeeti, confeeti,' he'd always say. I haven't slept for at least 60 hours. The voice of the child was beautiful. I'm not sure what song."

"Ave Maria?" I asked.

"Church songs. It was all in Spanish, I couldn't understand any of the words. The voice of that child. Singing all alone. The most beautiful songs. She sang the first one alone, then other ladies joined in. They sounded like angels."

I could hear the awe in Maureen's voice. "That little girl would come up to our gate and ring the bell when she knew David had gotten back from America. He brought her chocolate. The kids all loved your Dad. They wanted that candy, too. It made them so happy."

"That sounds amazing," I said, wanting to get her back to the burial. The details of her story were so ethereal I felt compelled to get as many of them as possible before they started evaporating.

I heard Meredith continue.

> *My brother shall know of*
> *it. And so I thank you for your good counsel. Come,*
> *my coach! Good night, ladies, good night, sweet*
> *ladies, good night, good night. [She exits.]*
> (4.5.75-78)

I wanted to stop there, but Jimmy was on such a roll I hated to steal his monologue. I gave him my full attention and he gave it maximum animation, pacing around, grabbing Mei-Mei as Gertrude by the shoulders, angrily pleading at the sky and ground for sympathy.

KING: *Follow her close; give her good watch, I pray you.*
[Horatio exits.]
O, this is the poison of deep grief. It springs
All from her father's death, and now behold!
O Gertrude, Gertrude,
When sorrows come, they come not single spies,
But in battalions: first, her father slain;
Next, your son gone, and he most violent author
Of his own just remove; the people muddied,
Thick, and unwholesome in their thoughts and
whispers
For good Polonius' death, and we have done but
greenly
In hugger-mugger to inter him; poor Ophelia
Divided from herself and her fair judgment,
Without the which we are pictures or mere beasts;
Last, and as much containing as all these,
Her brother is in secret come from France,
Feeds on his wonder, keeps himself in clouds,
And wants not buzzers to infect his ear
With pestilent speeches of his father's death,
Wherein necessity, of matter beggared,
Will nothing stick our person to arraign
In ear and ear. O, my dear Gertrude, this,
Like to a murd'ring piece, in many places
Gives me superfluous death.
                    (4.5.79-103)

We all clapped. With Albert out today, Jimmy had the chance to shine.

"Claudius is losing it," Gino said.

"Why?"

"Because he said, *like to a murd'ring piece*. Doesn't that give it away? His guilty conscience is getting to him."

"Good point. I honestly don't know why he says this—and then *superfluous death*. What else in these last lines seems like a Freudian slip? See it? Anyone?" Niente. "Look, anything else here remind you of Claudius's crime, and how he did it?"

"Ear, ear!" shouted Feona.

"Exactly. Luis, what's significant about Claudius saying *ear and ear* when he's so upset about Polonius' murder?" He looked down at the book. "Gino said he thought Claudius was losing it—saying stuff that might reveal his crime. What is Claudius's crime again, Coleman?" I asked, trying to light a fire.

"Murdered his brother for gain."

"Yes. And specifically how? Luis, do you remember how Claudius killed King Hamlet?" He should be able to get this. Everyone knows this.

"He poured poison in his ear!" Luis said with a smile. "I get it."

"You know how when you are trying to keep a secret or cover a lie, things keep seeping out? That's Nature in Disorder. Truth will out. Every reference to 'ear'—like when the Ghost tells Hamlet *the ear of Denmark* was *rankly abused*— echoes Claudius's unnatural act. Anything else? We didn't talk about the pirates! Vincent?"

"That's what I was wondering. Were there pirates back then?"

"Pirates have been around as long as man has sailed the seas." It's fun to see them surprised at pirates in Shakespeare. "Who thinks they understand what happened to Hamlet at sea?" Meredith was waving her hand. She did a good job explaining how Hamlet escaped the boat taking him to England by jumping onto an attacking pirate ship.

"But why would he go with pirates?" asked Jerome. "Why would they help him?"

"Good question. Anyone? Catherine?"

"It says they dealt with him like *thieves of mercy, but they knew what they did: I am to do a good turn for them,*" she read with finger tracing the lines.

"What does it mean?" I asked.

"He's going to do something for them," boomed Duncan.

"Yes, exactly. You can imagine Hamlet told them, 'Look, I'm a prince, if you help me, I'll give you serious treasure."

"Go Hamlet, dealing with pirates," Jerome nodded. I smiled and nodded back.

"So," I said, changing the subject, "I think the characters at Elsinore are under pressure; they probably need someone to talk to. Let's send them to a therapist!" The girls were smiling; we've done this before with other books.

"You know the language of therapy? What happens at the therapist's office? You've seen it on TV if you haven't gone yourself." I instructed them to get into groups of two, and one group of three. "One will be the character and the other the shrink. Review the basics of your character, figure out where their 'head's at'. How will they behave in therapy? Consider: do they come willingly, or did someone make the appointment for them? Are they sarcastic, cynical or serious? Remember, use body language and tone of voice to convey feeling. Questions?"

"Can we make stuff up?" asked Gino.

"You can make stuff up but stay in character and don't change what did happen. Make sense? Get with your partner." It is so satisfying to hear students working together and the room filling with overlapping conversations, ideas and laughs.

I headed across the hall. There was another email from Kirstin. She saw Dad several times after he died, and she came to know and love him. What she saw explained things, like why he wouldn't talk about dying. "Saying goodbye was too terribly sad," she told me in our last session. It doesn't sound like much, but it made perfect sense to me. I got up and went to the window and looked out into the dark gray sky.

Sometimes I felt my dad was closer than ever. Sometimes I felt HE. IS. GONE. Gone, gone, gone. Fresh realities caught me off guard. Now when I looked around a movie theater or grocery store, I thought about how half the people there had already lost their parents, and for the other half, it was only a matter of time. I'd drive by churches and funeral homes and realize that every day someone somewhere was planning a funeral or writing an obituary. He is survived by....

Survived by. Surviving. The verbiage in obituaries struck me. Surviving are.... Exactly. Because that's what we are doing: Surviving. Barely. Who knew such a deep truth about life and death was hidden in plain sight? Turns out Shakespeare's most popular play is a great place to deal with *the thousand natural shocks that flesh is heir to.* Teaching *Hamlet* this time around was like taking a graduate course on grief. Delving deep into the play's universal truths distracted me from the personal horror of losing my dad.

I used to make myself cry imagining how awful it would feel to lose my dad. Now I welcome any effective distraction to avoid feeling the pain. Work, food, drink, gardening, home improvements, reading, binge watching crime shows. Surely God didn't give us the capability to numb our painful thoughts and emotions *to fust in us unus'd.* I'll take any respite I can get from the waves of grief's reality that keep catching me off guard, crashing over me, and leaving me gasping for breath and drowning with tears.

"Okay come on back! Before we get started with therapy, make sure your reading responses are on the desk. This week, we are finishing the play." I heard surprised energized murmurings. "Monday is the review, Tuesday the test. You do not want to miss the review. It helps a lot."

"Are we getting a study guide?" asked Sage.

"I'll have that for you tomorrow. Who's first?" No one volunteered.

"Let's have Claudius and Gertrude. Some couples therapy!" I rubbed my hands together gleefully.

Claudius and Gertrude were played by Coleman and Bradley in crowns, rocking back and forth in red plastic chairs. It was visually comedic since they chose Bradley, six inches taller than Coleman, to be Gertrude.

"Wait," I interrupted. "Gertrude, could you put the wig on under your crown? Make sure you sound like a woman." There were giggles.

"We got this," Bradley added in a surprisingly high voice, with a flourish. He took the hair piece, settled it under his crown and poofed it up on each side. More giggles.

"Glad you guys came here for couples therapy," said Feona the Therapist, her hair pulled up in a large auburn topknot and Vincent's glasses sliding down her nose. My clipboard served as her notes. "You married under unique circumstances. Your relationship is very new. You were previously brother and sister-in-law. How are you handling your relationship?

Coleman looked over at Bradley with folded hands and eyes fluttering. "It's going great," he said, rubbing his hands together like someone who scored. Everyone laughed. Bradley fake smiled and shrugged his, I mean her, shoulders.

"What brings you here?" Feona continued.

Coleman's Claudius was surprisingly peacocky, with his purple velvet crown, and a sword through a belt loop on each side, hands resting on the hilts like they were pistols. "Hamlet's acting mad lately and I don't know how to deal with it," said Gertrude/Bradley, continuing in a laugh-evoking falsetto.

"He's crazy," said Claudius/Coleman, waving it off, "he's out of his mind."

"What makes you think he's crazy?" asked Feona.

"Uhh, he's crazy?!" Coleman said as if it was the question and the answer.

"Just because his dad died and…and I married his uncle…." she looked away from her husband, clearly more on her mind.

"He's mad in love with Ophelia," stated Claudius.

"Gertrude, are you happy you got married?" Feona asked.

"Of course she's happy," said the king.

"Well," Bradley shifted uncomfortably in his, I mean her, chair, "I felt like the people wanted me to marry Claudius, and it was my duty." Coleman looked at Bradley's Gertrude and turned his body towards her, chewing gum, hands up, no longer the confident monarch.

"Baby! Baby?"

"Did people tell you they wanted you to marry Claudius?" Therapist Feona prodded.

"Did they?" Claudius squeaked.

"Half and half," Gertrude said, tilting her hand side to side to huge laughs. Claudius was agape.

"How do you feel about this, Claudius?"

"I feel upset and shocked," his voice wavered. Fabulous! I almost felt sorry for Claudius.

"So," continued Feona, "knowing this information do you regret marrying her?"

He looked Gertrude up and down with a slight leer, checked his swords then adjusted his crown. "Naaaah."

"Why not?" asked Feona, furiously taking notes.

"'Cause I'm the king.'"

Queen Bradley turned to Coleman's Claudius, with his hands on his hips and high squeaky voice, "Wait, did you marry me to become the king?"

Coleman laid back in his chair and stretched his legs out and said, "You married me cause the people wanted you to! Don't even give me your crap!"

Everyone was laughing so hard. Then there was an awkward silence. Totally appropriate considering what just happened.

Feona switched tacks. She might have a real future as a therapist. Or an actress, certainly. "What's the most difficult part of your relationship?"

"The stepson," blurted Claudius.

"I thought you considered him your son?"

"Stepson."

Perfect. They were getting somewhere raw. It felt so real.

"Hamlet should consider Claudius as his father," said Gertrude "but he's having trouble with it. That upsets me. I am his mother after all."

We were coming down from the hilarity before, and this part seemed boring in comparison.

"Has Hamlet told you how he feels about you marrying his uncle, and so quickly?" Feona asked.

"Mm hmm," said Bradley. His campy delivery was reminding me of Jack Lemmon playing a woman in *Some Like It Hot.* "One time, and then...it resulted in an accident."

Huge laughs. Of course they were alluding to when Hamlet killed Polonius in Gertrude's chamber. It was so satisfying to see them make those connections and so hilariously. I wished I taped it.

"Great, guys," I said, when I caught my breath. "Thank you."

Next up were Diane as Ophelia and Duncan as her shrink. I felt sorry for them following that show, but it juiced them up. Diane entered from the wings (meaning, from in front of the closed classroom door) shrouded in strips of plastic bag as a ghost. I swear the air crackled with theatrical energy.

"Hate, hate, only hate," she chanted. Whoa.

"Why are you angry?" Duncan, the therapist, asked.

Her voice was wobbly and numinous. "Hamlet. He lied."

"Hmmm," Duncan said. "Lied. About what?"

"He said he loved me!" she wailed. "Then he said he didn't." She was weaving around the chairs, waving her arms through wispy pieces of clear plastic trash bag.

"Please, please, have a seat."

"I can't!" she screamed. "I can't," she whispered. "I need to keep moving. It helps me."

Wow, magnificent! My mouth was agape with a huge smile.

"Ophelia, how are you feeling about Hamlet's affection?" Duncan asked.

"Well, duh…it's a little weird, cause…" she started twirling around slowly "one minute he's yelling at me to go to a nunnery and next he's putting his head in my lap—in front of everyone! I can't take it!" she burst into tears.

"How about Hamlet's outbursts?"

She sounded cogent again and looked the therapist in the face. "That was pretty weird. He started yelling and I'm like, dude, why?"

I loved it when they mixed today's vernacular with Shakespeare's words.

"How are you recovering from your father's death?" Duncan asked, pencil to his lip, clipboard in hand.

"Not so great. I went to visit a little creek…." Here we go. "I sang songs…. like Anne of Green Gables…and next thing you know, I'm wearing this," she said, spreading her plastic shroud. Lots of laughs.

"What about your brother?"

"He's going crazy…" she sang, "like Hamlet. They're the same person. Except Hamlet…I don't know…I thought he loved me and then…. Waaaaah!!!" she started twirling again.

Duncan looked up to see if that was enough. I nodded, smiling.

"Well, Ophelia, that's all the time we have for today."

"Okay," she sang, wafting fairy-like towards the door, "bye!"

Everyone started clapping. "That was fabulous! Diane: what a terrific, terrifying, definitely bipolar Ophelia. Nice! Who's next? Horatio?"

Jerome gave a heartfelt portrayal of Horatio as a troubled best friend who wasn't sure if he was doing right by his prince or not. Imani as the therapist was a funny foil to him, and she took her job equally seriously, but with less dramatic flair.

"So, Horatio…why are you here?"

"I needed someone to talk to, Doc. I got a lot of stress. I hope I can trust you?"

Imani was unsure at first, then she smiled, seeming to gain confidence.

"Yes, I'm a therapist. It's like confession."

"Here's the thing, Doc. I can't talk to anyone because Hamlet, my buddy, my scholarly schoolmate, my prince…" Jerome gazed off out the window towards the boys' dorm.

Oh. My. Gosh. Love it.

Horatio snapped out of his reverie. "He's going down a dark path and I'm letting him because he insists he knows what he's doing. Anyway, what am I supposed to do?" Jerome cried, plaintive, frazzled and more animated than I had ever seen him before. He picked up speed and continued.

"I don't like it. I don't like it at all. He's got major mommy issues; he's already killed once. I thought I was getting a break when he was sent off to England, but now he's coming back and wants to meet with me. I think he's losing it. He said there were pirates! Pirates! I mean, seriously? This is why I have a lot of stress."

Oh man it felt good to laugh. My whole body felt loose. This exercise always has amusing bits, but it felt extra cathartic this time. As the kids left for lunch, laughing and engaged, I sat at the back of the room thinking, *I love my job.*

ACT FIVE

What ceremony else? What ceremony
else? Must there no more be done?

(5.1.230, 232, 243)

It was Wednesday and I couldn't believe it was already time for Act 5. The graveyard scene, and the end. When we started reading the play, my dad was alive. Now he was in the ground like Polonius, Ophelia, and all those skulls. My father's bones were in the Central American earth. Someone in Costa Rica must have dug his grave. I wonder how many men it took to dig that hole, and how long?

This morning a teacher in the hall asked me, "Are you okay you didn't go back for his burial?"

In the graveyard Hamlet asks the gravedigger, *How long will a man lie i' th' earth ere he rot?* Was my father's a *pocky corpse*, rotting from the cancer long before he died? I tried not to think on it. Which was difficult since Maureen's every phone call and email kept saying she needed to get his gravestone, and she had to stay in Costa Rica to be near him. I wanted to scream he's gone! He's not there! I kept pretending his actual physical being—the silvery forearms, the big white cloud of hair, the sparkling eyes, the voice, the laugh—was somewhere else. Not *i' the cold ground*. But I don't know, maybe he is there.

"Oh yeah, no, I'm fine," I told my colleague. "When I want to visit my father's grave, I'll go to the ocean."

5: 1

How long will a man lie i' th earth ere he rot?

As I crept unwillingly up the hill to school this morning I flashed on how Hamlet smelled the skull in the graveyard. I avoided breathing deeply in fear of dank, ghostly vapors getting stuck in my lungs. I felt dizzy as I reached school.

I got set up for Act 5:1. The main quote at the top of the board was *Alas poor Yorick! I knew him, Horatio*— and centered under that *How long will a man lie i'th' earth ere he rot?* underlined three times. That seemed excessive, so I erased the three yellow lines and sliced in one thick pink one. Today the line *How long will a man lie i'th' earth ere he rot?* took on a new stench. It conjured thoughts I didn't want to think, visions I didn't want to see. Yet now Hamlet's fascination with corpses and (as this year's students started calling it #wormfood) hit me in my gut. My father's body—full of hugs and the greatest comfort a child could know—was decomposing in the dense red clay soil of a hilltop Costa Rican neighborhood where many of the cinderblock houses didn't have four walls.

I couldn't stay focused. The talk of dead fathers, rotting bodies, open graves, depression, and the meaning of life kept pulling me off the lesson plan's script to a memory, or an insight. Hamlet experienced this more than 400 years ago, yet it felt so fresh and new. My face squeezed up in anticipation of the next assault. I shook it off and opened the Act 5:1 file on the podium.

Catherine stuck her head in.

"Hey, how's it going with you-know-who?" I asked.

"Better thanks. I don't like it, but I've felt more free since you said he and I don't need to be friends."

"You were in the same group the other day."

"Yep, and it was fine. Since I stopped getting upset at him for being a jerk, he stopped being a jerk." I noticed one of the male teachers was lurking in the classroom doorway. I gestured him in and Catherine scuttled away.

"I'm Albert's advisor," he said. "I wanted to bring you up to speed."

"What's up?"

"He has a mental health diagnosis. He's got anxiety, and a mild case of bipolar disorder."

That didn't surprise me. He was so focused and intense: tightly coiled and explosive. Never in a scary way, but in a huge, dramatic way. Honestly I was hoping Albert was just quirky, brilliant, and brave enough to express his energetic, untraditional self. The exuberance I admired was being reframed as "issues with boundaries."

"Okay, thanks for letting me know."

Everyone was seated when the bell rang; I walked over to the desk, picked up the skull, stepped into the center of our stage, gazed into its eye sockets, and opened with:

Alas, poor Yorick! I knew him, Horatio—

"The renowned literary critic, Harold Bloom, suggests Yorick, the court jester, may have been the only happy emotional relationship Hamlet had growing up. In the graveyard, when the gravedigger introduces Hamlet to the skull, Hamlet speaks the famous lines:

*Alas, poor
Yorick! I knew him, Horatio— a fellow of infinite
jest, of most excellent fancy: he hath borne me on his
back a thousand times; and now, how abhorred in
my imagination it is! my gorge rises at it. Here hung
those lips that I have kissed I know not how oft.*
(5.1.190-195)

"He's remembering the fun parts of Yorick, his old playmate," I said. "Yorick's been dead since Hamlet was what age?"

"Seven!" said Feona.

"Exactly. How did you know that?"

"It said he had been in the ground three and twenty years and Hamlet is 30."

"Yes—good job with the math."

"Wow," said Imani. "I didn't get that."

"Yeah," said Jimmy, "Hamlet is much older than I thought."

"I thought he was our age," said Vincent. "A student."

"I think it was more like grad school," I said. "Time is not clear in this play. How much time passes, how old the characters are. It's weird."

"Maybe Shakespeare didn't think it was important. Or didn't care," said Catherine.

"Maybe. I have another idea. What if Shakespeare's apparent carelessness, or inaccuracy, with time is actually a reflection of how strange time feels when someone dies?" I looked around for confirmation but only Luis was nodding.

"Anyway, back to Hamlet's reaction to Yorick. Hamlet asks Yorick's skull—could be tauntingly, could be longingly—why Yorick isn't the life of the party anymore, why he can't rescue Hamlet from his unhappy royal family:

Where are your gibes now? your gambols? your
songs? your flashes of merriment that were wont to
set the table on a roar?
                    (5.1.196-198)

"He asks the skull, *Where are your songs?* Hmmm.... When someone dies, do their songs die?"

"Yes!" I heard a few voices say simultaneously.

"Really?" I was surprised. I tried restating the question. "Do someone's songs die when they die?"

"Yes! No one listens to Michael Jackson anymore," Duncan said.

"Oh, come on, now," I complained, rolling my eyes at the ludicrosity. "That is not true."

I thought about dead Michael Jackson and how he'll live forever through his music. Thank God for recordings, photos and videos. In Hamlet's time, it was paintings and books. And memories. Stories.

"Anyway," I continued, "when Hamlet says *Where are your songs?* he's remembering how much Yorick used to lighten the mood. One way of remembering someone is to sing their songs." I looked around and saw some knowing nods.

I decided to pursue it; I had never done this before.

"Let's explore *songs* more. Take a minute to think about a parent, grandparent, or some other person from your childhood. Look back.... Close your eyes if you want. Do they have songs you associate with them?" Pause, pause, pause. "Write the songs on your reading responses."

"The whole song?" asked Gino.

"The title, or some of the words if you want." Catherine and Feona were both in deep and frenzied thought, pencils moving and eyes gazing towards the ceiling. After a minute I asked if they came up with anything; at least half the class said they had.

Before I my dad died I had only noticed *your gibes, your gambols,* and *he hath born me on his back a thousand times.* It had never quite registered that Hamlet is remembering Yorick singing. Yorick was fun. So was my dad. He had inside jokes with each of us, lots of sayings, and he sang a lot.

Not anymore though. Not live and in person. Just in my head. *In my mind's eye, Horatio.* Or ear. *My father, my father...methinks I hear my father.* I see and hear him all the time. Maybe that's where his jokes and songs are, too. A smile turned up the corners of my heart then twisted it into a painful cramp.

My dad loved music and was a happy singer. He would sing around the house and I'm sure that's where I got the habit. He would latch onto some sonorous phrase and sing it (over and over), often without the rest of the song. Usually, it was the first or title line like, "Hit the road Jack," "I can see clearly now," "The first time ever I saw your face," or "She's got a ticket to ride, and she don't care," with his face tilted up, and a smile in his eyes. A lot of our family car memories involve singing.

I was gazing out the classroom window, and then looked around to see half the kids still writing. "How's it going? Are you coming up with songs?"

"Yeah." "Oh yeah." "Not really." "None from my parents, but my grandmother, yes!"

On road trips we'd sing camp songs from my grandparents, and we had two or three cassettes in the glove compartment. Paul Simon's *Greatest Hits* has a lot of great singalongs: "Kodachrome," "Mother and Child Reunion," and "Loves Me Like a Rock." "Me & Julio Down by the Schoolyard" was the best, with its whooping monkey sounds. When that song came on, Dad (driving) would make crazy backbeat whoop noises, my sister and I in the back seat would bounce up and down, thrusting our heads up front between them, going "boop, boop, boop-boop-ba-boop," and Mom would look (at least the back of her head would look) like she thought we were weirdos. Then Dad, laughing with glee, would croon "It's against the la-aw, it was against the law...what the mamma saaaw," (nudging Mom) "it was against the law." Boop, boop, boop-boop-ba-boop. Boop, boop, boop-boop-ba-boop.

Maybe it was my own happy memory, but the mood in the classroom seemed light and nostalgic.

"What were some of the songs?" I asked and was regaled with everything from David Bowie and "Amazing Grace," to John Denver, and Grateful Dead's "Dire Wolf."

Another car game came from my seventh grade science teacher Mr. Stroup. I can't remember the specifics, but he did a sensory experiment where you lightly touch the same spot on someone's arm for a while. They barely discern the touch at first, but after a series of taps it gets annoying. One day I came home from school all excited to show him the experiment. I remember sitting at the breakfast table in Northfield, New Jersey, and ever so slightly tapping his perpetually tan, ashe blonde hair-covered, freckled forearm until he couldn't take it.

"Aaargh!" Dad laughed, giving me the childish satisfaction of driving him crazy. He loved this and would do it up until he died, like when we were playing cards and he wanted to say hello or connect, and he'd always get that smile.

And just like that, the smiling memory turned into a death grip on my throat. My stomach lurched. Oh Dad....

My gorge rises at it.

Another line I scarcely noticed before my dad died. Now it's so obvious Hamlet was talking about the indigestible reality of loss.

The way grief squeezes your gut and makes you feel like you're going to vomit.

"Later in that scene, when Hamlet is contemplating the skull of Yorick, he reflects on the circular nature of existence, how we all return to the dirt, and he says *how abhorred in my imagination—my gorge rises at it.* Anyone know what that means?" Silence. "What is your gorge?"

"Throat!" said Albert.

"Yes! What's he describing?" Nothing. "What's does it feel like when your throat rises? What's happening?" I could see them trying to make it happen, hands at their throats.

"You gag?" said Meredith.

"Exactly. That's the Shakespearean way of saying I am going to throw up. Being face to face with the inevitability of how we all must *pass into oblivion* makes Hamlet feel like he's going to throw up."

I grabbed the podium, leaned forward and looked around the room. I felt woozy and watery. I used to have a strong stomach, and in my younger days neither stress nor heartache ever resulted in weight loss. I've never been too depressed or sad to eat. These days, I can't even taste.

"Now that my dad has died, I've noticed that every once in a while the reality of it washes over me, and I feel like I'm going to vomit." I changed my tone of voice and tried to lighten the mood. "Okay, let's hear something from your reading responses. Questions, comments? Luis?"

"So, Hamlet really did love Ophelia?" he asked.

"Well, that's what he says. How many of you guys have sisters?" I asked, looking around the room. "What would you think if your sister's ex-boyfriend said he loved your sister 20,000 times more than you did?"

"He's a jerk," said Gino.

"Not happening, dog," said Jerome.

"Well," considered Bradley, "it's a different kind of love."

"Yes, yes, that's legit," I said. "Anyway, what does Hamlet do to show how much he loved Ophelia? Did you get that question on the quiz?"

"He gave a big speech," said Meredith, quite self-satisfied. "That's all he does is talk." Ding, ding, I rang the green bell.

"Yes," I said, "exactly. How do we know if we love someone?" I let the question hang. I saw Diane, then Sage, Bradley, and Catherine nod their heads slowly. "Emotions are confusing. Sometimes it's hard to know how we feel about someone. Especially when a lot of other stuff is going on." I looked around and saw a few more nods.

"What else?" I asked,

"More wormfood," said Diane.

"Yes, where?"

"When he talks about Alexander—"

"Could you read that for us?"

Alexander died, Alexander was buried,
Alexander returneth to dust, the dust is earth…
(5.1.216-217)

"Thank you. These references to Alexander speak not just to the idea of greatness and wormfood, but also to the power of story. Alexander the Great. Isn't it cool that you learned about him, and so did Shakespeare? How do we have Alexander or Julius Caesar as shared cultural reference points across the centuries? Because their stories are passed down through the ages. Perhaps the pagans and ancient Romans were onto something in their belief that honor—and the story that goes along with our name—is what lives on."

"In the graveyard with Horatio, Hamlet reflects that even Alexander, the greatest ruler of all, ended his life back in the dirt, and by now, Alexander's corpse was reduced to loam plugging the hole of a beer barrel. Today we might reference Steve Jobs, JFK, Martin Luther King, or even Shakespeare himself. Men who achieved greatness, who, in the end, were just men. Men who lived, accomplished, gained our admiration, and like Alexander, returned to dust. Mei-Mei?"

"It's like that quote…. were you a good king or a good father?"

"Yes! *He was a goodly king. He was a man.* Exactly. You got it."

"Now, Jerome," I said, "question: if you're rich, does it matter what kind of a person you are?"

I saw the wheels turning. "When I'm rich I'm still gonna be a good guy," Jerome said. "But…no," he continued, "if you're rich, it doesn't matter what kind of a person you are…you get away with anything."

"Is that true?" I asked. "Do rich people get away with more than average folks?"

A few mutters…maybe they're too young to know this, unless their parents complain about it."

"Of course they do. It's the law of the jungle," Jerome said. This was exciting. There were a few rumbles and mutters, but mostly impressed sounds from his classmates.

"Good. And you're right, Jerome. Whether we like it or not, it's the law of the jungle. And it seems 'twas ever thus according to Shakespeare. In the Yorick scene, the Gravedigger is digging Ophelia's grave, and he's talking about something not being fair. Did anyone pick up on that?"

"If she hadn't been a noblewoman, she wouldn't have gotten a Christian burial."

"Yes, Feona, yes! *Why there thou sayest! And the more pity that great folk should have count'nance in this world to drown or hang themselves more than their even Christian.* This is exactly what Jerome was referring to. Rich people have different rules."

"Even at the end, at burial, the rich use their influence. But after you're dead, when you go to the other side, what really matters?"

"What kind of a person you are!" Catherine said.

"Again, back to the text, what's the best illustration that power and influence don't smooth over problems when you get to the other side? Anyone?"

"Anyone?" I flashed to my dad laughing with his head tossed back. "Come on, what dead person is reporting from the other side?"

"The ghost," said Duncan.

"Yes, the ghost. And why does he have problems?"

"Because he was killed before he got to repent," Feona shouted out. That girl is getting the English award.

"That's it! He wasn't ready. *No reckoning made... In the blossom of his sin...with all his imperfections on his head....*"

"The ghost's point was, he wasn't ready. He's in purgatory, on his way to hell it seems, because he didn't have time to get ready before he died. No death bed repentance for King Hamlet because he was murdered. He didn't see death coming."

"You can't see death coming," I heard Imani mumble.

"Back to Ophelia. Laertes is upset because they aren't doing enough for her. The coroner says her death was *doubtful.* Raise your hand if you've been to a funeral." Only four or five hands didn't go up.

"Has anyone been to a memorial service, or a celebration of life, held a short time after a death?" Only three hands. "Well, as horrible as it is when someone dies, one of the good things is you see friends and family you haven't seen in a while and reminisce." I saw confirming nods. "Putting on a funeral or memorial is work. Sad and exhausting work that's an important step of grieving. If death is unexpected, the family is in shock and they focus their shock by gathering, telling stories, collecting pictures and preparing the service."

My experience with my father's death was different. When I was in Costa Rica for our final visit one item on my "to talk about" list was what would be done after Dad died. He and Maureen decided he would be buried in the colorful cinderblock cemetery at the end of their clay dirt road. Dad believed in cremation, but in Costa Rica it's the costliest way, and would have required shipping his body four hours north to the capital of San José to the country's only crematorium.

"The good thing about funerals and obsequies is they give you something to do, and people to be with. What stinks is at the end of a funeral, you say goodbye forever to the dead person. Closing the chapter. If it's a burial versus a cremation, the casket with the body is lowered into the ground." An involuntary shudder spread goosebumps over my flesh. Dad.

Yesterday I talked to Maureen. I wanted to hear about the burial again. To get more details. I could see the picture she described. "Can you tell me about the burial again? The flowers? You said something like everyone was carrying a flower. Did they drop them down into the grave? Or put them on the coffin?"

"Remember I told you about the little girl that was singing? I told you about that didn't I?"

"Yes, yes."

"They all came up and put flowers on his grave, did I tell you? It was incredible, Erica. These people have nothing, but they each had a flower. When the songs were over, David was carried to the grave. Lowered to his final resting place, and I kissed the first dirt that was to go on top of him."

"I think Dad was in his final resting place about 3:20PM. Erica, I did not stay to watch the men with shovels." She started crying again. "There were six shovels, to cover my husband. I sent my final kiss when I kissed the first dirt. I did not want to see them cover him in so much dirt. Is that bad? Oh David, my David. I hope that wasn't bad."

Of course it wasn't bad, I told her.

"The casket was closed. Paul said to keep it closed. Everyone wanted me to open it. But Paul pulled me aside, and said, 'Maureen, don't open it, I don't want you to see him this way.' I said I did not understand. He gently told me, there was blood oozing from his mouth. This was later confirmed by Pat and two other close friends at different times." It was evident she was right back in the moment and describing it as it unfolded. "Naturally, I was upset. Erica, we had him embalmed. At least we asked for that and paid for that…."

"The last time I saw him was at the funeral home, when I gave him the slippers Callie had brought down for him. I also gave him his glasses because he loves to read. I kissed his fore-head. That is the last time I saw my man," she wailed, "8AM on the morning of his burial. They put flowers on top of the casket, and again in the grave. The priest asked me to put in the first handful of dirt. I picked up some dirt and I kissed it, and I dropped it on top of my husband. I had never hurt in my heart so much, until that moment."

"What else?" I asked. "Then what happened?"

"They don't have a system like the USA for lowering the casket. The men who carried the casket had three straps waiting for them at the grave. At the grave, they put those straps under the casket and lifted my husband with those and moved him above the grave. They lowered him with those, and on one side kept collecting the length of strap, to use again," she was speaking slower with each sentence and I felt she was losing her thoughts.

"I never wanted to remember or tell you and Paige," she then continued, "but about two feet from the bottom, one man lost his grip, and the casket tilted and opened, and Dad rolled. I screamed. But it was for a few seconds, and it was ok."

My mouth hung open as I held the phone suspended next to my ear. I was *so attired in wonder* I couldn't speak. My dad came out of the box? Is that what she was saying? I don't know what I would have done had I been there.

"Dude, Hamlet and Laertes jump into her grave," smirked Coleman. "Uncool."

"Actually, no," I said, my eyes still wide from the real-life graveyard scene I was remembering. "There's no textual evidence that Hamlet jumps in—though we often imagine he did. Would someone read this starting at *Hold off the earth awhile*? Coleman?"

> *Hold off the earth awhile,*
> *Till I have caught her once more in mine arms.*
> *Now pile your dust upon the quick and dead,*
> *Till of this flat a mountain you have made*
> *T' o'ertop old Pelion or the skyish head*
> *Of blue Olympus.*
>   (5.1.258-266)

"Let's see who you picked to play the Gravedigger," I said, shuffling through the quizzes. "'Will Ferrell because the Gravedigger is a clown, he's funny and so is Will.' 'Albert, because I imagine the Gravedigger as quick and sly with his words,' 'the actor Filch from

Harry Potter? Because he's creepy but can be darkly funny, too.'
'Heath Ledger if he was alive.'" I flipped through a few more.
"Interesting," I said as I read Meredith's answer. "Do you mind
if I read yours?" I asked her.

"Sure," she said with a pregnant smile.

"Meredith said herself, because she's 'sarcastic, funny, a
little rude, and good at punning.' Somebody else said you, too.
'Because she's dark and can come up with witty, clever comebacks.' Looks like you have a just self-estimate." She was smiling
wide as I flipped through the rest of the quizzes "Here's another
one. 'I would cast Meredith because she has a good sense of
humor—comic relief!'"

"Jeremy Irons," shouted Bradley, arm in the air. "He was
Scar in the Lion King."

I kept reading. "'Coleman because he acts matter-of-factly
but with humor. Morbid humor works well.' This is one of the
most iconic scenes in the play. Each production handles it, and
its humor, differently. Does the Gravedigger know he's speaking
to Prince Hamlet or not? Clearly, this gravedigger knows a lot
about the recent history of Denmark and is up to date on local
gossip. So how does he not recognize Prince Hamlet? If he does
recognize Hamlet, why does he act like he doesn't? Let's watch
this scene from Kenneth Branagh's version; see if you think this
gravedigger knows it's Hamlet or not, and what in his demeanor
gives you that impression."

I started the video. The blackout shades were down, and
the projector cast a blue hue. The kids were at their desks, and I
sat on the floor, remote in hand, my back to everyone. I settled
down and let the scene wash over me. I love this version and I
hadn't seen it for almost a year. The scene begins at a misty, gray
gravesite in the woods.

"Do you know who the gravedigger is?" I asked as he started talking and his face came into view. "Who's the actor? No one? Seriously? You guys have a problem. You really need me. That's Billy Crystal! Yeesh! Have you seen the movie *Analyze This* with Billy Crystal and Robert DeNiro? No? It's hilarious," I told them. *Harry Met Sally? City Slickers?* Nope. I can't believe what these kids don't know.

Going to the movies was one of our main family activities. The second-to-last night in Costa Rica was the Oscars—*there's a divinity that shapes our ends*—and Dad must have been saving his energy because he watched the entire show with us. Even the Red Carpet special beforehand. At that point, I didn't know when he would die, but I knew he wouldn't live to see another Academy Awards. I wonder if the thought crossed his mind, "this is my last Academy Awards"? My dad loved the movies. Old ones, new ones: from *The Godfather* and *Once Upon a Time in America*, to those *Twilight* and *Hunger Games* movies. He introduced me to my first favorite movie, *Guys and Dolls*.

"Frank Sinatra and Marlon Brando in a musical," he had said, grabbing the VHS tape off a low shelf in the aisle of Shore Video, the first video store of my life. "Can you believe it?"

During the Oscars, it occurred to me how uncomfortable their couch was. All my life, Dad sat in the corner of the couch. Now he was separate from us on a reclining island of taupe faux suede. It looked lonely and unnatural. He didn't want to talk about dying, and I tried my best all week not to be maudlin. But when I realized that Dad was all alone over there, when he always watched TV with his arm around one of us, I moved over and sat on the hard, cool tile floor next to his chair, my head about level with his arm on the armrest.

Tears had been quietly streaming down my face throughout the Memoriam. When the screen with big photos of Hollywood immortals split, the tinkling opening notes of "Wind Beneath My Wings" began to play, and Bette Midler came on stage. Within the first few bars my stomach and eyes squeezed tight. A heavy chill sank around me. My arms and hands went numb. I could feel the cold of the tile through my shorts. I was weeping by my father's side. Not silently anymore. When she sang "I would be nothing without you" I squeezed his arm. He patted my hand while keeping his eyes fixed straight ahead.

"Why did I get to be so lucky?" he asked, gazing past the screen in wonder. "Why did I get to have so much fun?"

Dad made a practice of contentment and appreciation. Every morsel of goodness was a bonus and he'd never been ripped off or gypped by life no matter how much he'd lost. Through the years I sometimes saw this quality as apathetic, unambitious, or even weak. Now I see it as incredible inner strength and grace. More than anything, _Grace._

My father's journey on this planet was from high to low. From country club, house at the shore, Ivy League; to selling his boat and all his fishing rods and moving to a third-world country where he could live off his Social Security when he could no longer afford life and hurricane insurance in Florida. Even when that meant seeing his kids less frequently.

I used to think "How could you not want more?" Look around, Erica. He did want more. He wanted more life for as long as he could have it. He wanted more time with Maureen. He wanted that house in Costa Rica. And in those final days he told Larry he was okay, he'd had a good, full life, and he was ready. "I'm just worried about Maureen."

Grace. Ready to go when it's time. Grateful for visits from family, but never embittered or resentful there weren't more.

Lucky. He felt lucky.

So did I.

Quiet tears were spreading down my face while the scene I'd watched at least 20 times played out before me.

> *HAMLET: How long will a man lie i' th' earth ere he rot?*
> *GRAVEDIGGER: Faith, if he be not rotten before he die*
> *(as we have many pocky corpses nowadays that will*
> *scarce hold the laying in), he will last you some*
> *eight year or nine year. A tanner will last you nine*
> *year.*
> *HAMLET: Why he more than another?*
> *GRAVEDIGGER: Why, sir, his hide is so tanned with his*
> *trade that he will keep out water a great while; and*
> *your water is a sore decayer of your whoreson dead*
> *body.*
>
> (5.1.168-178)

"Shakespeare's father was a tanner," I croaked out in the dark, the words catching in my throat. The music was building and when we got to the Yorick scene I felt something in Branagh's sighs and groans that cut straight through my gut.

Ah…*where are your gibes now? Your gambols? Your songs?*

Where are my dad's jokes and songs now? In the ground?

I used the ends of my sleeves to wipe my eyes and dry my cheeks, not knowing or caring if the kids knew I was crying. Tears spread across my face again during Hamlet and Laertes' fight over who loved Ophelia more. My timing of the video was perfect, and the bell rang just after Branagh's Hamlet said *The cat will mew and dog will have his day*. I pressed pause so the screen would stay on and the room dark. I sat frozen and numb on the floor looking up at the grave as the students shuffled out to lunch.

5: 2

There's a special providence
in the fall of a sparrow

(5.2.233-234)

Once the classroom was empty, I wrote key quotes on the board for the next class. Top center in caps was: *THE REST IS SILENCE*

Followed by:

> *Good night, sweet prince, and flights of angels sing thee to thy rest*
>
> ~ ~ ~
>
> *There was a fighting that would not let me sleep*
> *There's a special providence in the fall of a sparrow*
> *There's a divinity that shapes our ends*
> *The readiness is all*

Tears spread to my cheekbones as I wrote the word "sparrow." I stepped back and a wave of surrealness washed over me. I am an English teacher. I teach *Hamlet*. *Hamlet*. And my dear old Dad is dead. Dead, dead, dead.

The next morning Vincent and Jimmy Wong were sword fighting and Albert was in a choreographed duel with an imaginary rival.

"Eeeeyah—touché! Take that!" he said with alternating thrusts and parries. Vincent and Jimmy were using the foam swords and bending them into each other's guts.

"Miss Erica are we acting out the sword fight?" Albert asked.

"Of course we are! Are you getting warmed up?"

"Yep," he said, with an impish grin.

"Good. Yes, Catherine?"

"Can you explain what happened with the pirates? I can't picture it."

"Yes, good place to start. Can anyone explain what happened? How did Hamlet get on the pirate boat? Duncan?"

"Pirates attacked Hamlet's ship and he jumped onto their boat to escape Rosencrantz and Guildenstern."

"Why would he do that?" I prodded.

"Because they were going to kill him," said Gino.

"Right. It's important you understand what happens to Rosencrantz and Guildenstern and that you have an opinion about it. It's a question on the test."

"Wait," said Bradley, pen in hand, "can you say that again?"

"Yes. First can someone explain what happened to R & G so we all understand? Feona? Do you want to just read it starting at 5.2.15?"

Up from my cabin,
My sea-gown scarfed about me, in the dark
Groped I to find out them; had my desire,
Fingered their packet, and in fine withdrew
To mine own room again, making so bold
(My fears forgetting manners) to unfold
Their grand commission; where I found, Horatio,
A royal knavery—an exact command,
Larded with many several sorts of reasons
Importing Denmark's health and England's too,
With—ho!—such bugs and goblins in my life,
That on the supervise, no leisure bated,
No, not to stay the grinding of the ax,
My head should be struck off.

> *HORATIO: Is't possible?*
> *HAMLET: Here's the commission. Read it at more leisure.*
> *[Handing him a paper.]*
>   (5.2.15-31)

"Isn't it interesting he kept the original order?" I said. "Why would he do that? Jimmy?"

"To use as evidence against the king. To prove he tried to have him killed."

"Yes, exactly! Hmmm...I wonder why he hasn't used it yet? So then what happened? Sage?"

"He wrote a new commission."

> *I sat me down,*
> *Devised a new commission, wrote it fair—*
> *I once did hold it, as our statists do,*
> *A baseness to write fair, and labored much*
> *How to forget that learning; but, sir, now*
> *It did me yeoman's service.*
>   (5.2.35-40)

"Yes. He says he knows how to write like a clerk so the new order looked official. Next look at line 43 for what Hamlet said he wrote. Victor would you read it?"

> *An earnest conjuration from the King,*
> *As England was his faithful tributary,*
> *As love between them like the palm might flourish,*
> *As peace should still her wheaten garland wear*
> *And stand a comma 'tween their amities,*
> *And many suchlike ases of great charge,*
> *That, on the view and knowing of these contents,*

Without debatement further, more or less,
He should those bearers put to sudden death,
Not shriving time allowed.
    (5.2.43-52)

"Review: who are the bearers of the order?"

"Rosencrantz and Guilden-whosits," said Coleman.

"Right. So Hamlet stole the order that was supposed to…"

"Have him killed," said Meredith.

"And he rewrote it to say…"

"Kill Rosencrantz and Guildenbutt!" cried Coleman. He got some laughs.

"Let's look at Horatio's reaction. Coleman, would you read from line 63?"

HORATIO: So Guildenstern and Rosencrantz go to 't.
HAMLET: Why, man, they did make love to this employment.
They are not near my conscience.
    (5.2.63-65)

"Okay, thanks, stop there. This is how Hamlet feels about sending R & G to their deaths—for the test you need to explain what happened and tell me how you feel about what he's done."

"Wait, did Rosie and Guildy know what the letter said?" asked Feona.

"What do you think?"

She took a moment. "It was sealed, so probably not."

"Hamlet tells Horatio he doesn't feel guilty about sending them to their deaths: *why man, they did make love to this employment, they are not near my conscience*, meaning that they were happy to do this errand for the king, even if they didn't know what would happen to Hamlet in England."

"But he didn't have to have them killed," said Luis.

"Let's think about this. Was it harsh? Vengeful?" Silence. It looked like they were thinking.

"I'm not sure, but he didn't have to have them killed," said Luis.

"Fair enough. Hamlet didn't have to have R & G killed. Or did he?" I was thinking about it myself. I was trying to do what I tell them to do. Take it backwards. What is the logic behind what happened and what didn't happen? "What would have happened if he didn't write their death warrant? When they got to England?"

"It wouldn't matter," Sage said, "because Hamlet would be back in Denmark by then. Or with the pirates."

Ding ding, I hit the green bell. "Ha! That's it! When Hamlet rewrote the order he didn't know he'd be rescued by pirates. He had to assume they would all make it to England together."

"Oooo," said Albert, stroking his chin. "Good point."

"Miss Erica, what is this *no shriving time allowed*?" asked Diane.

"Ahh, good eye. If you look on the left-hand page you'll see that means 'time for confession', meaning what?"

"Like with Claudius?" asked Mei-Mei.

"Yes, exactly. He doesn't want them to have time to pray and save their souls. He wants to send them straight to Hell!"

"Hammy's getting harsh," said Gino.

"Yep. What else did you guys notice?"

"He mentions Providence!" Imani called with a smile.

"Good! What else?"

"Divinity?" said Catherine.

"Absolutely!" I took the Sword of Truth off the chalk tray and banged on the line *The readiness is all*. "What does Hamlet mean? What is he saying?"

Pause, pause, pause. Remember count to ten. Give them a chance. "Yes, Jerome?"

"He means you got to be ready to revenge. He's been waiting too long." No, dammit.

"Okay, possible, but are they talking about revenge?"

"He has to be ready to fight Laertes!" said Luis.

"That's true but look at this: *There's a divinity that shapes our ends, rough hew them how we will.* Who knows what 'rough hew' means?"

"Does it have to do with carving wood? My grandfather's really into woodcarving," said Imani.

"Yes—"

"He has to be ready to die in order to get revenge!" said Gino. They weren't getting it.

"The point here is, we have hopes and dreams and goals. We start off life as a block of wood, if you will. We watch, we learn, and we whittle off pieces here and there to shape our lives in the direction we want them to go. We get summer jobs, do volunteer work, apply to schools, save or spend our money, make certain friends. We like to think we can direct where and how our lives will go. The fact is, we can cross the pike on our way home from school today and get hit by a car. Everything changes. So, what Hamlet's saying here is, yes, we do have to be active participants in our lives, we do have to try to make things happen, but in the end, it's not just us—there's another force in control. Who?"

Whoops—gave that one away.

"God!" a few voices said in unison.

"Yes, God! There's a *divinity*. A higher power that has a say in how our life goes, no matter how hard we try to control it."

I walked into the semi-circle of desks and slowly tapped my sword on the surface of one desk then another.

"If you don't die now," tap, "you're going to die later," tap. "If you die later," tap, "you're not going to die now. *The readiness is all.*"

Silence. Count one, two, three. It's seemed all the more quiet because I had been getting louder and louder, emphasizing *readiness* with all the meaning, tone and force I could.

"Why does this start with a sparrow, by the way? What kind of a bird is a sparrow? What do they look like?"

"Little." "Brown." "Not sure." "Good question."

"You're right. Sparrows are cheerful, dutiful, plain little brown birds who go about their business. There are a lot of them. So many they go unnoticed. They are the antithesis of special or notable. Sparrows symbolize the common man. When it comes to dying, even the greatest among us is a sparrow." I let that sink in and tried my best to appear contemplative.

He was a man, take him for all and all....

My dad was not common. Not to me. Not to Paige. The longer I live, the more dads I hear about, the more I see he was not common compared to a whole world of dads. My stomach curled. I started thinking about how Dad was a sparrow. Is a sparrow. The more ghosts and messages that swirled around my own life, the more I started to feel this play was haunted. Not in a bad, scary, way. In a magical, all-knowing way. *There's a special providence in the fall of a sparrow.*

The little guy. The common man. My dad was a bird of quiet nobility if you paid attention.

My father never—at least not in my lifetime, at least not as far as I know—aspired to be an eagle instead of a sparrow. Unlike me, he was humble. Never envious. From what I can tell, he lived a charmed life when young: rich, popular, privileged, spoiled. A few years ago, I had asked him about the summer he spent traveling in Europe after he graduated from college.

"I was such a jerk back then," he said.

"Why? What makes you say that?" I asked.

He shook his head and said "I was so spoiled and selfish. I was traveling with two other guys—my roommates—and when we were in a city with a fancy restaurant they couldn't afford, I would go by myself." He half-laughed and shook his head like he couldn't believe it. I could see him. My dad. College graduate and bon vivant on the road. I thought of that guy on my own first gastronomic tour of Europe. I wish I knew which fancy restaurants he went to. One in San Sebastian, I knew that. I wish I had been on that trip.

"By Act 5: scene 2, Hamlet has changed," I began. "He's gone from *To be or not to be*, to *Let be*. Hamlet has always been a thinker, now he's philosophical. We see this in Act 5: scene 1 in the graveyard when he ponders the human race's ancient progression from man, to corpse, to worm food. He asks Horatio if he thought Alexander looked at the world like this. In other words, did Alexander the Great contemplate his own mortality?"

I have to pause here and take a deep breath. Don't rush to the next step—let it sink in. Let them think.

"Sometimes in life," I told them, "things happen to us, and suddenly we see the world differently. Here, with the help of the Gravedigger's laissez-faire attitude toward tossing skulls and bones about, Hamlet, at age 30, with a dead father and a totally messed up family, beholds a simple yet profound truth: everyone dies. There is only one thing guaranteed in this life: You're going to die. I'm going to die. Even the strongest, richest, most famous and influential among us are going to die."

Pause, pause, pause for effect. "We all gonna die!" I waved my arms to encompass all. "If we know we're going to die—what's the point?" I continue. "Why are we here?"

"To make a heaven from the human race!" said Meredith, knowing she had the right answer.

"Yeah, to become angels!" said Bradley. These two had been in church schools all their lives; they knew their doctrine.

"To help each other," said Sage.

"To learn how to be a good person," added Mei-Mei.

"Good, good," I said. "Here you are, Seniors, on the brink of having to Make Something of Your Lives. What are your hopes and dreams? What do you want out of this life?"

"I want a family," said Luis.

"Kids," said Catherine.

"Play in the NBA," said Jerome.

"Get a good job and make major bank," said Jimmy Wong.

"Good! What are you going to do with that major bank?" I made sure my tone was smiling and curious.

"I don't know, buy stuff. A cool car. Help out my friends… my Mom, my sister…be the man," said this small, beefy, dorm boy from Korea whose thick bangs hit the top his black plastic Wayfarer frames.

"That's great," I smiled. "You can do that."

I started to pace from one side of the room to the other, head down like I was thinking.

"You know what?" I looked up at them. "Today is a good day to die." Silence. A few quizzical looks. "Today is a perfectly fine day for me to die. I can say that to you honestly. Why? Not because I'm depressed. Not because I'm done with life. Are you kidding me? I just bought a house and the tulips are coming up. The whole summer is ahead. If I'm going to die, couldn't it be in September? After my birthday? Nonetheless, I can stand here and say, in all honesty, if today is the day, I'm ready. I'm not Claudius who can't repent my sins; I'm not King Hamlet who didn't know it was coming and hadn't started being good yet. I've been the best person I can be. Yes, my room is a bit of a mess, but basically, I'm good. I'm ready to meet my maker. That's the point. *The readiness is all.*"

I've given some version of that speech for years now; I inherited it from Mrs. Esther. But, this year, with my dad dying, and now dead, being ready to die took on deeper meaning. I anticipated and second guessed the timing of my father's death for so long. I wanted to be ready. I maintained solid flesh through it all by not breathing too deeply, moving slowly through time and space, and treating the whole thing like a tragic play I couldn't stop reading but knew would eventually end.

"Let's act out the final scene!" I said.

"Can we go outside?" asked Sage.

"Yeah!" "Yeah!" "Can we?"

"Great idea. Where should we go?" Within less than a minute we decided to go to the front of the school where a large staircase led to the big brass front doors. It was a great stage. I assigned roles and set up the blocking. The main action —the duel— took place on the sidewalk at the bottom. The old stone facade and flagstone steps provided an appropriately dignified backdrop. Sage came into her own as Gertrude rolling on the ground:

No, no, the drink, the drink! O, my dear Hamlet!
The drink, the drink! I am poisoned.
(5.2.340-341)

"*I am poisoned, I am slain*, what's with the theme of obvious death statements," muttered Feona. I nodded. Great point. *I die Horatio....*

As usual, most lines were recited haltingly; it is legitimately challenging to read and act at the same time. Nonetheless the words came alive.

Double I was lying on the sidewalk laughing through her reading of Laertes' confession:

It is here, Hamlet. Hamlet, thou art slain.
No med'cine in the world can do thee good.
In thee there is not half an hour's life.
The treacherous instrument is in thy hand,
Unbated and envenomed. The foul practice
Hath turned itself on me. Lo, here I lie,
Never to rise again. Thy mother's poisoned.
I can no more. The King, the King's to blame.
(5.2.344-351)

I think Jerome surprised everyone by roaring:

The point envenomed too! Then, venom, to thy
Work. Yaaaaaaaah!
(5.2.352-353)

He lunged across the step to Coleman who was playing Claudius and machete-chopped him in the neck. Then Jerome moved forward with the black plastic wine glass someone had given me for extra credit.

Drink off this potion!
(5.2.357)

Jerome said, holding the cup in the air.

"Force him to drink!" I shouted.

"Oh no," Coleman said ironically, rolling his eyes, but smiling, "don't make me drink," his arms stiffly in the air in mock surrender as Jerome put the cup to his lips and lifted it. "Oh, I am dying," Coleman deadpanned as he lowered himself to the ground.

Hamlet, at the bottom of the steps, on his knees, with the corpses of Gertrude, Laertes and Claudius at his feet, his book in one hand and the other arm in the air, shouted, *O, God, Horatio!* seemingly out of the blue, laughed at his own outburst, and then delivered the rest of the lines at normal volume, finally folding himself dramatically down to the ground in death.

Jimmy Wong, as Horatio, stood waiting patiently while Jerome got through Hamlet's final words, then he gently lowered himself to one knee and said:

> *Never believe it.*
> *I am more an antique Roman than a Dane.*
> *Here's yet some liquor left.*
> (5.2.373-375)

like he was confessing, I've always secretly loved you, bro. Then Jimmy turned his head around, scanning the steps for the little bit of poison liquid left.

"*O, O, O, O!*" Jerome cried at the end, punctuating each syllable with a full body spasm.

The sun-covered stone staircase was strewn with bodies, swords and tossed aside copies of the play. Gino as Fortinbras and Duncan as the Ambassador to England loomed large at the top of the stairs. Raising a sword, Gino announced:

> *This quarry cries on havoc. O proud Death,*
> *What feast is toward in thine eternal cell*
> *That thou so many princes at a shot*
> *So bloodily hast struck?*
> *AMBASSADOR: The sight is dismal,*
> *And our affairs from England come too late.*
> *The ears are senseless that should give us hearing*
> *To tell him his commandment is fulfilled,*

*That Rosencrantz and Guildenstein—*ha ha*—are dead.*
Where should we have our thanks?
     (5.2.403-411)

It looked so cool, I wished that a big donor had driven by at that moment, or someone from Admissions had come out. I don't know why I had never thought to do it out there before.

5:2.2

Now cracks a noble heart

(5.2.397)

The following day was review for the test. Our class was the period after lunch and students had been trickling in for the last five minutes. I saw Albert coming down the hall by himself, so I asked him if everything was okay. He glared intensely into my eyes.

"I went off my meds. I was doing fine."

"Yes, you were. You've always been great here."

"Thanks. Well...I'm baaack!"

"And just in the nick of time," I said.

Sage and Diane were playing with the wooden swords, clack-clack-clacking and smiling.

"Miss Erica, can I use your sword?" asked Coleman, turning the Sword of Truth over in his hand.

"Only for good." He smiled, jabbing the air.

"You know you can take stage-fighting classes in college?" I said.

"Really?" Albert and Coleman asked simultaneously.

"Yep."

"Cool." I didn't know there was such a thing as stage fighting classes at their age. I didn't even know film was a legitimate field of study. As Mrs. Esther always said, you don't know what you don't know.

"We have a few more things to cover from yesterday then the rest of the class will be review. I'm not talking about anything today that doesn't pertain to the test, so fasten your seat belts and open your ears. And take notes! Unless you've got an audiographic memory."

"Is that a word?" asked Duncan. "Audiographic?"

"I don't know!" I confessed. "What's the word for photographic memory but with stuff you hear? Anyway, I'm allowed to make up words. Shakespeare did! Keeps things fresh, don't you think?"

"When we do, we get in trouble," said Coleman. Seriously? I wondered how often he made-up words.

"Yeah, teachers are like, *that's not a word*," Jerome boomed.

"Here you can make up words. Especially if they make sense."

"Wait, wait," said Coleman, waving. "We can use made-up words on the test and you won't count it off?"

"If I understand what you're trying to say. But that's the risk you take."

"What about spelling?" asked Jimmy. "Does spelling count?"

"Yeah," said Bradley, taking notes, "does it? Do we need to know how to spell Rosencrantz and Guilden...Guildenberg?"

"Stern. Guildenstern," laughed Catherine. I thought she wasn't going to talk to him. But he laughed back.

"Can we abbreviate?"

"For the test tomorrow, as long as I can understand what you mean, if you make a spelling mistake I will not charge you. For the quote identification part, you may abbreviate the names. Make sure you write it clearly."

"What if you write R&G because you're not sure which said it?" asked Gino.

"You can only get a maximum of half a point."

"Awww."

"Anyway, we need to look at Horatio and Hamlet's final words to each other, and Fortinbras's arrival. Let's start here" I pointed to *The rest is silence* on the board. "These are Hamlet's last words—"

"He says, *O, O, O, O,*" Sage said. Peanut Gallery.

"True," I said, "but those aren't words. Huh, think about that. Our last words aren't words at all but sounds. Anyway, those are Hamlet's last words. What were his first words? Who remembers?"

"A little more than kin and less than kind," Feona called out.

"Right. The test is 60 percent quote identification. Some you identify the speaker, and others will ask for the significance. For example, part of the significance of *A little more than kin and less than kind* is it's Hamlet's first line. But what else? What does he mean? Mei-Mei?"

"Now they are double-related, and he's not nice."

"Who's not nice?" I asked, just to make sure everyone was tracking.

"Claudius," she said.

"Yes, Imani?"

"It says *Good night, sweet prince.* I've definitely heard that before," said Imani. Okay, good.

"Yes! A lot of you have probably heard the phrase *Good night, sweet prince, and flights of angels sing thee to thy rest*: now you know the context. Horatio is talking about the sleep of death. He also says *Now cracks a noble heart*—whose heart is he talking about? Coleman?"

"His own."

"Exactly."

Now cracks a noble heart.

His heart. My heart. Corazón.

I didn't know it at the time, but when I said goodbye to my dad, my heart broke in ways I have not yet begun to comprehend.

Tuesday could barely be called our last "day" in Costa Rica; it was the briefest of mornings. Our bus out of San Isidro del Generale left at 8 AM. Dad, weak as he was, hadn't left the house the entire week I was there. But he rode with us to the terminal. Can you imagine driving your kids to their bus, knowing you will never see them again? It felt like walking through a memory. Like this was another of a hundred sad but not forever goodbyes at the end of a visit. This could not really be the last goodbye. The end.

I stood on the sidewalk next to the open passenger side window, Dad's arm resting on the car window frame, the bus getting ready to leave, and me holding his arm. I ran my hand across the silvery hairs on his forearm as if committing the image to memory one more time. I remember standing next to the car, taking a few deep breaths, looking over to the bus, then back to Dad's face, then away again, knowing for certain this would be the last time we breathed the same air. It seemed unfathomable that Paige and I would get on that bus and never see him again, though that's what was happening. We had to go to our jobs. We couldn't take over their house and lives for what would turn out to be three more weeks. We had a good visit. "His last good week," Maureen kept saying. He was lucky. We were lucky. It was enough.

I can't quite remember what I said or how I said it. I'm sure he was trying to make it okay, even though it was the worst thing ever. My eyes were hot with tears that gave me chills as they streamed down my face. I guess I croaked out, "Bye, Dad." He probably said "Bye, sweetheart." I'd do anything to go back to that moment and never leave. Stay there and not let him die.

But we said goodbye to our father and left him to die alone. No, not alone. Not alone at all. With his much loved and much appreciated wife. She was his day to day. It was their walk to the end. We got his last good week. Good old Dad living for his kids 'til the end. It was enough.

When Paige and I got on the bus, I was wailing. For some reason I had to put it into words:

"We are never going to see our dad again!"

"Don't say that!" she started weeping, too.

"It's true, it's true," I said, shaking my head. I had to make sure I knew the significance of the moment.

But did I really? I had worked hard to be as prepared as possible. To have as few regrets as possible. But in the end, as much as I hate to admit it, Maureen may have known more than I did. Where I was obsessed with accepting my dad was going to die, she refused to think on it. I knew it was the natural course of events, and I was lucky I had him as long as I did. She knew he was her person and wanted fifty years.

Maureen and I did not have a ton in common, and it's safe to say we got on each other's nerves, especially in the beginning. But Maureen was my father's best friend; she loved him. She didn't pick on him or criticize him or think less of him for smoking, eating crappy food or not reaching his career potential. They had fun. They had a good fifteen years together while I was busy living my own life. She may not have started out as my kind of person, and God knows she put us through hell about insurance money, gravestones, and the mortgages in Florida, but thanks to her, my dad ended his life deeply cherished and appreciated. She was so grateful to have found a good man who was kind to her. Of course she wanted fifty years. Who can blame her?

On that northbound bus, through the misty twisting high mountain turns, was the first of many times I would cry so hard I coughed and gasped for air.

"So, Horatio is a good friend. On the test you have to compare Horatio and Rosencrantz & Guildenstern as friends to Hamlet, and you need to cite specifics. Anyway, back to Hamlet's last line.

It's ironic because besides Jesus Christ, there is no other character who has more written about him than Hamlet. The rest is not silence. We are still talking about Hamlet, and at any given moment, somewhere in the world, you can find a version of the play in production." I took a breath. "And yes, Jesus Christ can be seen as a literary character. The Bible is a classic literary text from which Chaucer, Shakespeare and many others have drawn. It's not just a religious text, but a cultural one." Something I didn't discover until I got to university in my 30s.

"Look at Hamlet's last words to Horatio. What does Hamlet ask Horatio to do for him? Would someone read Hamlet and Horatio? Starting at 5.2.370? Do it from your desks." Albert's hand shot up before I said the word 'read.' "Okay, Albert, are you Hamlet, or Horatio?"

"Hamlet!"

"Who's your Horatio? Jerome, how about you?" Aww. The roommate. I couldn't resist.

Albert laid his body across his desk with head facing across the room, book in the air, his other arm outstretched toward his Horatio.

> *HAMLET: Horatio, I am dead.*
> *Thou livest; report me and my cause aright*
> *To the unsatisfied.*
> *HORATIO: Never believe it.*
> *I am more an antique Roman than a Dane.*
> *Here's yet some liquor left. He picks up the cup.*
> *HAMLET: As thou 'rt a man,*
> *Give me the cup. Let go! By heaven, I'll ha 't.*
> *O God, Horatio, what a wounded name,*
>   (5.2.370-378)

Wounded name, I thought, as the kids continued to read. What's in a name? Family name, history, reputation, honor.

Two years before my father died, we hosted Easter and a family reunion at the big mansion we rented outside of Bryn Athyn. That's when Dad went to visit "Daddy's window" at the church in Jenkintown. How do you live three miles away from a church with a stained-glass window dedicated to your father and never tell your children about it? Never take them to see it? And it wasn't just Dad. My uncles never mentioned the window to their children, either. Turns out parents don't share every key piece of their life stories with their kids. Who knows what wounds are *sicklied o'er* with time? He hadn't seen that window for fifty years, but towards the end of his life he went to see it and told us about it.

It's sad the way things last and parents don't. My grandfather didn't last long enough to meet any of his grandchildren. Barring demolition of the building, his window will outlive us all. A few weeks ago I found a birthday card my father mailed me in 2007. His writing on the page. A piece of paper he chose, held, touched, wrote upon. His words written in sharp boxed caps leaning slightly to the right. I ran my finger over each one.

The joy with which you have always (and still do) filled my life knows no bounds.

There is no more blessed Dad.
Love you, Dad

The other day I found a picture. Dad was sleeping on the glassed-in porch at the mansion during the Easter reunion. It was the last time he was in PA. We still have the white wicker chaise he was lying on. The thick-striped Hudson Bay blanket he had over his legs was the one he took to college in 1955. High quality blankets last longer than people. But blankets do not last longer than stories. Neither do stained glass windows. Maybe that's why it is so important to Hamlet that Horatio tell his story. It's his final request of the one person he knew he could trust.

Whoops. I missed my cue. Awkward. I took my three lines and tried to focus on the scene. I repeated *what a wounded name*; it didn't seem right without it.

> *what a wounded name*
> *Things standing thus unknown, shall I leave behind*
> *me!*
> *If thou didst ever hold me in thy heart,*
> *Absent thee from felicity awhile*
> *And in this harsh world draw thy breath in pain*
> *To tell my story.*
> *[A march afar off and shot within.]*
> *What warlike noise is this?*
> *[Enter Osric.]*
> *OSRIC: Young Fortinbras, with conquest come from Poland,*
> *To th' ambassadors of England gives*
> *This warlike volley.*
> *HAMLET: O, I die, Horatio!*
> *The potent poison quite o'ercrows my spirit.*
> *I cannot live to hear the news from England.*
> *But I do prophesy th' election lights*
> *On Fortinbras; he has my dying voice.*
> *So tell him, with th' occurrents, more and less,*
> *Which have solicited—the rest is silence.*
> *O, O, O, O!*
> (5.2.378-396)

"What does Hamlet mean when he says *wounded name*? Whose name will be wounded?"

"His," said Catherine.

"Yes, why?"

"Well…I'm not sure," she said.

"Let's look at how you knew. Line 378. It's confusing because he interrupts his own thought with a qualifier:

> *what a wounded name,*
> *standing thus unknown, shall I leave behind*
> *me!*

"Shakespeare's proclivity for injecting qualifying phrases into his characters' speech can throw us off track. Forget, for a minute, *standing thus unknown*, and you have *what a wounded name shall I leave behind me*. It makes more sense. He's worried about his family's name, how it will go down in history, if the kingdom of Denmark never hears how and why these corpses got strewn across the castle floor. He's dying. The only thing left is his family name, honor, and the stories told after he's gone."

"Cool," muttered Coleman.

"Let's list the things Hamlet asks Horatio to do for him. His dying wishes, if you will. Hamlet says:"

> *—Horatio, I am dead.*
> *Thou livest; report me and my cause aright*
> *To the unsatisfied.*
> (5.2.370-372)

"He asks Horatio to tell everyone what really happened here, and why. What's the next thing he asks Horatio to do? Or not to do, as the case may be?"

"Don't kill himself," said Bradley.

"Yes. And please notice the way he says that:"

Absent thee from felicity awhile
And in this harsh world draw thy breath in pain
To tell my story.
                    (5.2.382-384)

"What Hamlet's suggesting here is that he knows death might seem like happiness to Horatio right now, but he wants him to hold off on the relief of death at least long enough to set the record straight. There's one other thing Hamlet asks Horatio to do. What is it? Anyone?" Niente. Hmmm. "It has to do with Fortinbras. Look at line 392." Nothing. "Sage could you read that for us?"

But I do prophesy th' election lights
On Fortinbras; he has my dying voice.
So tell him, with th' occurrents, more and less,
Which have solicited—the rest is silence.
O, O, O, O!
                    (5.2.392-396)

"Thank you. So, in other words?" No one. "Sage what does Hamlet want Horatio to do regarding Fortinbras?"

"Tell him he approves of him as the next king."

"Yes, exactly. So, you'll know the answer to the question what are Hamlet's dying requests to Horatio?" Some affirmative sounding mumbles.

"Wait," said Meredith, listing off the points. "It's tell my story, tell why this happened, and tell Fortinbras he has my approval to be king of Denmark?"

"Yep. Cousin Vinnie?"

"Horatio started the story the same way he ended it—as a messenger!"

I gave a slow nod, "I never thought of that."

"Star?" he asked.

"But of course," I said, dinging the green buzzer and peeling off a big one.

That afternoon Mei-Mei came by to recite *To be or not to be.* I had never seen her so animated. She jumped up and down and was prancing around the room before she started.

"I'm so nervous!" she bounced.

"Don't worry, just jump right in. If you mess up, you can start again."

She stopped, took a few deep breaths, and then began slowly pacing back and forth, reciting the lines perfectly.

"Oh. My. Gosh. That was fabulous!"

"Thank you," she said smiling and pacing. I suggested she do it one more time so I could record it and send it to her father. She messed up several times, but we finally got a good rendition, and I emailed the video to the address she gave me in China.

Tuesday after the long Easter weekend we were back in the classroom, and it felt like a new season. Maybe, finally, it was spring. I was proud to surprise the students with graded tests, and after we went over the few problem areas, we spent the rest of the period watching YouTube videos I'd collected over the years. Some were different productions of the play, some referenced *Hamlet*, like scenes from *Gilligan's Island, The Simpsons,* and *Sassy Gay Friend.* My point is to have fun, and show Shakespeare is alive and well in today's culture.

On our last day together, I stood at the door when the bell rang and shook each student's hand, thanked them, and bid them adieu: another ritual I picked up from Mrs. Esther. Each of them looked me in the eye and thanked me. Duncan and the Bermuda Triangle were first, and the handshakes were cordial, the thank yous mutual. Then Meredith and Catherine hugged me. Maybe following their lead, maybe of his own naturally sweet accord, smiling Luis hugged me, too. I stepped back, looked into his warm brown eyes and nodded "You did a great job." Jimmy Wong smiled up through his glasses, nodded his head and shook my hand in vigorous unison, "Thank you, Miss Erica."

Jerome tried to give me one of those handshakes that have two, maybe three, parts, and I faked my way through. Shaking hands and saying goodbye to 16 teenagers who are on their way to lunch is rushed at best, but I tried to draw it out as much as possible with personal bits for each.

"Thank you, Coleman. Sleeper Award! You were great."

"Diane, best and longest reading responses ever!"

"Albert," I said shaking my head, looking up at him. "You were awesome."

"You too, Miss Erica," he said, shaking my hand earnestly then lurching into a gangly teenage boy's version of a don't-let-our-bodies-actually-touch hug.

I noticed Diane lingering in hall as I was saying goodbye to the last students. I turned and stepped across the threshold.

"Hey Diane, what's up?"

"Ummm, Miss Erica, I was wondering...can I come after school and recite *To be or not to be*? I think I've got the whole thing. Can I come at 2 pm?"

"Two is good," I said. If she still had the whole thing memorized, she was better than me. I always get muddled in *the proud man's contumely, the law's delay, the insolence of office, and the spurns* part. I was looking forward to it, then I remembered I was supposed to fly to Florida for my father's second funeral. This needed to be fast.

"Miss Erica?" Diane poked her head in at 1:56PM.

"Come in, come in! I'm excited. And jealous! I can't believe you have the whole thing memorized— fabulous!"

"I had to relearn some of it. It's been months." I nodded and smiled in sympathy. "I did it a couple of times for my parents and today in the lounge before chapel, but I hope I don't mess it up now."

"You won't, you won't!" I assured her. "Don't worry, you can have as many starts as you need," I said, hoping, believing, it wouldn't drag out so that I'd miss my train to the airport.

"Give me a second, okay?" she said, looking at the book and pacing side to side.

"Take your time. Tell me when you're ready, and don't worry, I won't look at you. You do your thing and I'll watch the speech. Whenever you're ready." Not a jot of her strawberry blonde shyness showed as she spoke to the chalkboard behind me, to the walls, and even straight to my face for a few lines. Gone was the demure one, and unleashed was every bit of mystery, sorrow and mischief that lay behind that knowing smile and those black-dot eyes of hers. Boom. First try. All the way through. The further she got, the wider my eyes, and the more solemn and apprehensive my affirming nods. How do they do this? I don't think I ever would have or could have done this at their age.

"Woo hooooooooooooooo!" I cheered when she finished. I stepped out in front of the podium, raised my arms in the air and bent over at the waist several times, bowing to her accomplishment. "Amazing! A-may-zing! You are my hero! Great job, Diane!" She was beaming. "One-hundred percent! Not one mistake! Of course, you don't really need the extra credit."

"I know, but I really wanted to do it."

"And I'm so glad you did. Now, Diane…."

"Yes?"

"You've got to remember this for the rest of your life!! All that hard work. Just every month or year make sure you still know it, okay?"

"Yes," she said, her head bowed a little. "I'll try."

"You do it—and you come back in a year or two and check on me—I will try to have it memorized by then too. You've inspired me!" We said our goodbyes, she hugged me, and before I knew it I was on my way to Florida, exactly six weeks after my father's burial, to help create his second funeral.

When I talked to Maureen in Costa Rica about Dad's funeral, I told her I wanted to have a service for him in the States. It was a relief when she heartily agreed, and then my heart sank when she said, "In Florida."

"Okay, yes, but I'd also like to do something in PA. I was thinking at his family church in Jenkintown."

"That would be nice, too. But we have to have something for the kids in Florida." For her kids. Dad's step-kids, though "David always insisted they were his kids, and never wanted to use the word 'step.'"

When I arrived at PBI for the gathering I stood on the sidewalk, silent tears pricking my eyes and tightening my chest. Waves of sorrow and loss crashed over me. PBI always meant a Dad pick-up. Now I'd never see that full head of beautiful silver hair smiling through the car window again. My sister pulled up without him, and she and I began a series of harried errands to organize the service for the next day.

We had the Celebration of Life at my stepsister's house, rearranging the furniture in the kitchen/dining room to create an altar and a gathering area. Mom and Ray came. Dad's first and best childhood friend, Jerry, came with his wife and gave a touching tribute.

I prepared an opening speech; I guess you can call it a eulogy. I started with how my father knew that "Life was better than the best movie," and "all that really matters is what kind of a person you are."

I could have gone on and on, summing him up forever. He was a source of patient, unconditional love, who left us in freedom. He knew not to sweat the small stuff way before it was a thing. He was deeply affected by all he lost when his dad died so young. He knew nothing was more important than your kids. He said "Dads pay," for as long as he could manage to pick up the check. He knew how to tell a story; he was a master of the pregnant pause, only seeming to, but never actually losing, his train of thought. He knew we would someday regret not having gone out fishing with him every chance we got. In his final years, he'd shake his head in dismay and say, "My father would have put aside anything to play golf with his sons, but we always had something we'd rather do."

He never gave a guilt trip. He always managed to get us what we asked for at Christmas, long after he could afford the expensive gifts I had the audacity, or cluelessness, to request. He said, "you can order whatever you want and you don't have to finish it," at restaurants with us kids. He was the best pancake maker.

He always showed up. For years he'd meet me at the gate. He rescued me so many times. He loved to hear the details of my day and my life. He quoted me back to myself whenever he heard I was doing something particularly interesting, saying: "It's a once in a lifetime chance!" with delight and wonder in his voice. He kept track of who my friends were, and it delighted me every time he'd ask me, by name, about a friend he met only once but felt like he knew.

It's sad he never spent much time with my friends. When I was growing up, my parents weren't those kind of parents. In Northfield, they were the strict uncool parents who did not spend bonding time with my friends. Then I went away to school and made friends who my parents saw from time to time (and heard about *all the time*) but who only hung out at our house once or twice. Then Boston and New York, and my friends—my life's blood—were just stories and pictures, the backdrop of my adult life. It must be painful when your child goes and makes their own life, somewhere else. How do parents not have their heart broken every day? Maybe they do.

"What can I do for you Dad? I wish there was something I could do," I asked him one of the last days in Costa Rica.

"Just have a good life."

Talk about grace. How did I get so lucky?

My father didn't have a mean bone in his body. He joked around a lot, but never belittled me.

"What do you mean? Your father was the biggest teaser out there," Tom said the other day.

Maybe so. I never thought of him that way. I guess the difference was that I was in on the joke. There was never anything but pure affection radiating from my father's funny comebacks and gibes. Thanks to him I find myself a perennial source of amusement. "It's good you can entertain yourself," was another one of his sayings. He had such a good laugh and there was a special version, brimming with delight, when something amazing or lucky happened to someone he loved. I would call him and say "Guess where I am?"

"Paris?! NYC?"

"Nope," I'd say with satisfaction, "Boston, Mass," and you could hear him throw back his head and laugh.

I ended his eulogy with a version of what I had said at my friend Charlie's funeral, little less than a year earlier.

I embrace the idea that time in Heaven is very different from what we experience here on earth. Even though each of us who loves

David may live decades aching his loss, David himself won't
experience that lengthy waiting and longing to see us.
For Dad, who I truly believe is at peace, it will be but a short
time while he gets healthy, builds his house, works on his boat, and
prepares to welcome each of us he loved into the life of Eternity.

It was a special day and felt right to send my father off with everyone together remembering him.

I saw him once. He was a goodly king.
He was a man. Take him for all and all,
I shall not look upon his like again.

So many talked about what a big, warm heart he had.

His heart, his heart, corazón….

My father was all love. Losing people you love is incredibly painful. Losing someone who loves you so completely is devastating.

The day I came home from the memorial service in Florida, I sat on the porch with Tom and our friend Rich, both men who had long since lost their fathers.

"I figured something out," I told them.

"What's that?"

"Dads don't die."

They both agreed, nodding wistfully.

Dads don't die.

How do you get someone back? Or keep them here while accepting the fact they are dead and gone? Forever. My Mom says she dealt with her father's death by "just pretending he went somewhere else." I could mostly do that. Pretend the latest tropical storm knocked out the lines on their mountain top paradise and Skype can't get through. That mostly worked. Except when

Maureen called from the number he always called from, their Skype address, still with "David Cantley" and his picture on it. Not only would my heart jump and sink simultaneously, I had to listen to how much she missed him.

> *Why, she would hang on him*
> *As if increase of appetite had grown*
> *By what it fed on.*

She cried all the time.

> *Like Niobe, all tears—*
>   (1.2.147-149, 153)

I knew she suffered, and I tried to be there for her, but sometimes I wanted to say, "There's a big difference between 15 years and 47." I came to realize there's also a big difference between being someone's daughter thousands of miles away, and someone's companion, best friend, and helpmeet every single day, especially while he battled cancer.

Since I hadn't lived with him, I could keep a delicate hold on Dad's presence in my life.

My father—methinks I see my father.

I can't think about him too hard, or too specifically, or for too long a moment. I can glance at the different pictures around the house, but I can't let myself sink into them. Accepting death requires a healthy amount of denial. It's the opposite of "suspension of disbelief." It's a tacit decision to slip reality and believe in magic. There are all sorts of good reasons he can't come to the phone right now. He's not dead, he's fishing. Or at another expat's house playing cards. Or at the beach.

About, my brains!
Let me not think on 't!
Remember thee?
Ay, thou poor ghost, whiles memory holds a seat
in this distracted globe. Remember thee?

Is it bad if many of my most precious relationships take place primarily in my own head? I love traveling alone because I can be with whomever I want in my mind. I can't imagine going on trips in the future and not having Dad there to tell stuff to. Maybe this is the way to survive until we see each other again. It helps to believe we will all see each other again.

And until then, my dad will be right there when I need him. *In my mind's eye Horatio.*

EPILOGUE

Absent thee from felicity awhile and draw
thy breath in pain to tell my story

(5.2.382-384)

In retrospect I treated my father's death like any story to analyze and make sense of. I took notes and made connections with the text of the play, constantly looking for and finding parallels. One day in May I came into the stuffy, dark classroom, pulled up the shades, opened the windows to let in the cool damp air, and wrote on the board, LOVE → GRIEF → GRATITUDE.

After we took the quiz, this second round of students stood up and read the *too, too sullied flesh* speech and looked for the references to death being a common part of life.

"Are they right? Is death common?" Grumbles. "I mean, it is, right? You know, we're all gonna die?" Maybe that was harsh. "As some of you know, my dad died a few weeks ago." Wows, murmurs, hushes. "While I was teaching *Hamlet!*" I raised my hands in the air like a resident of an Italian neighborhood who can't believe you took his parking spot. "It's intense, let me tell you. I've seen way more in this play since my dad died. I'm going to share everything I've gleaned so far. Because I'm here in it. Now."

"First off: Death has in it everything we need to know about life. Death is about Love. And memory. And how time changes in the face of eternity."

I pointed to the board to each word in succession: LOVE → GRIEF → GRATITUDE.

"I know it's cliché, but true. Death and loss make you appreciate what you have."

Later that day, I reconsidered my theory. It's not Death that teaches us, but Grief. Death is the reaper; Grief is the knower. First Death comes knocking (or bursts through the kitchen door) and then Grief moves in. Don't try to second guess Grief. As painful as it is, I suggest letting Grief be in charge, at least for the first weeks.

Grief has a life of its own; it clarifies and teaches. Grief prioritizes with violent precision. *Death be not proud* the John Donne sonnet begins. Death and Grief have taught me there's nothing in this world to be overly proud of, because, #wormfood, we are all going to die. The question is, how do we want to live?

Two Days before graduation, I found a card on my desk with "Miss Erica" written on it. The "i"s had circles for dots, and there was a smiley face as well. Inside the envelope was a cheery card complete with circles dotting every single "i".

Dear Miss Erica,
Thank you for being a teacher. :)
Thank you for sharing your knowledge with such zest and enthusiasm!
You led me to cherish every page of "Hamlet," and to appreciate writing in a new way.

If at the beginning of the year anyone had predicted that I would deliberately and independently memorize Hamlet's entire TO BE OR NOT TO BE soliloquy, I would have thought they were crazy. But you've done the impossible, and made teenagers appreciate Shakespeare, as it deserves to be appreciated.

Out of all of the wisdom, tips, advice and guidance that you gave us Senior girls, the first idea that spurred my interest was when you said that notes, highlights and written conversations in books increase the value of them. Then it was suddenly fun to be interested in the literature, because you cared about our ideas and wanted our feedback. You were the first teacher who made me feel intelligent and I could see other students opening up in the warmth of the same appreciation, and being able to express themselves, and that's just awesome. You taught me creative thinking that can make anything interesting. I hope to remember TO BE OR NOT TO BE for the rest of my life, Thank you

<3 Diane

Graduation Day is the completion of another school year; it's always a huge deal. Time for a victory lap. Teachers, parents, students: we all survived. Each year we cheer another group of kids across the finish line as summer spreads before us. It's a moment I stand in gratitude for my position here. It's also an annual connection to my own graduation day, which took place on this same campus, in the same building, same double gym, on the same parquet floors with the same creamy-white painted cinder block walls lined with the same banners from graduating classes dating back more than 130 years.

My graduation was June 6, 1984. Dad was there. Alive and well. And younger than I am today. His ugly coppery-orange Cadillac Eldorado was parked in the same parking lot we all still egress to after the ceremony. If I squint out towards the thick green lacrosse field I can still see it. He tossed me the keys to the car—much to my mother's dismay—so I could drive myself to the 7-Eleven to buy a pack of Newports, or whatever I smoked at the time. I was barely allowed to graduate due to a disciplinary infraction a few days earlier. I was dormed the night before graduation, missed the graduation dance and banquet, and broke the pearls my mother lent me to wear with the graduation dress she worked on in the basement for months, pinning, cutting, sizing, and sewing with more love and care than I ever gave her credit for. I lost about a quarter of those pearls outside on the ground somewhere.

I was officially a Bad Kid on the day of my high school graduation. Mom could barely look at me, she was so disappointed; Dad tried to smooth things over. All I could think about was whether my boyfriend was mad at me and what me and my friends were going to do that night. I thought I knew everything that day. It all boiled down to one thing. Adults were idiots, knew nothing about real life, and were just getting in our way.

Now there I stood, outside graduation, thirty years later, a teacher at the school that barely let me graduate, hiding behind my giant black sunglasses, sweat trickling down my legs beneath my Harry Potter robe. I looked around at the tearfully smiling, also-sunglassed parents, snapping pictures, and holding bags and cards. I think kids have changed since the 80s. They can't possibly be as self-absorbed as I was back then.

I wasn't in the mood to press the flesh, but there were a few students I wanted to congratulate. Starting with Mei-Mei who was in a stylish, off-white, form-fitting Chinese style button-up dress, which I had to compliment. Standing next to her was a thin, faded man with wire-rimmed glasses. As I approached them, I heard her tell him something I assumed meant "This is my English teacher," and I heard "Hamlet" in there somewhere. He bowed and I bowed back. She gave me a fine paper gift bag with a shiny, thick cardboard box containing a silk scarf. "Thank you, Miss Erica," she bowed slightly.

"Thank you, Mei-Mei. Stay in touch." I guess her dad came after all.

Next I saw Albert, who came bounding over. We shook hands, and I looked up at him.

"Miss Erica," he said, formally, with an unlit cigar in his left hand. "I want to tell you I really liked the way you taught *Hamlet*." Albert Einstein. The kid who was so smart I was scared to teach him. He was still shaking my hand. "No, really, I like the way you do it. It was really good. I got a lot more out of it than I thought. Thank you."

"Thank you, Albert," I said, still shaking his hand. "That means a lot to me. Really. And you were great."

"Okay, bye!" he said, turning away, "have a great summer!"

Then I saw Bradley, puffing on a cigar. I took a few steps towards him. His face was sunburned, and his tux crisper and more buttoned-up than his compatriots.

"Miss Erica," puff, "I liked really liked *Hamlet*." Puff. "Don't tell anyone. It's too embarrassing. But I really liked it."

"I'm glad Bradley, I'm glad. Congratulations."

And then, on my way to leave, who did I come face to face with but Jimmy Wong, who I hadn't seen in at least a month. He was smiling so big, also carrying a cigar, not yet lit. Someone must have been passing them out.

"Miss Erica!" he said and opened up his arms.

"Congratulations Jimmy! You made it." He just kept nodding and smiling and playing with his cigar. "And nice tie-cummer-bund combo!"

"Miss Erica, I just want you to know I enjoyed your class. It's one my of best memories."

I floated up the hill from the Field House and across back campus. I had survived. I went to my office and classroom to double check that everything was left in decent shape. I had no intention of showing up again until at least mid-July. As I walked down the hall I saw an envelope leaning up against my office door. Inside was a white lined piece of paper with a handwritten sonnet from Imani. She always did have an ear for iambic pentameter.

> *I learned to be or not to be in class*
> *I had no clue the people'd die so fast*
> *It's sad to know that Hamlet's not alive*
> *Unfortunately everyone has died*
> *Turns out Hamlet turns up in lots of shows*
> *There's not too many friends but mostly foes*
> *It was in Elmo and My Gay Best Friend*
> *And Monty Python too, that's not the end.*
> *Our Senior class learned lots, and acted out,*
> *The Kings and Queens and Hamlet, don't you doubt.*
> *Also we learned it through the Lion King*

In Gilligan's Island we saw them sing.
It makes me sad to see English class end.
It be ephemeral, no time to tend.

I slumped down into my chair and let my head fall onto my arms on the desk. After a few minutes I walked home, rereading the sonnet along the way.

The weather was finally warm. I loaded up my surfboard, hopped into the van and headed down to Ocean City, NJ. It would be the first time I saw the ocean since Dad died; the first time I visited what I considered his final resting spot. I had a plan; I wanted to do something ceremonial. I bought three dozen roses, white, red and yellow, and sat on the beach, plucking petals off and packing them into a Ziplock bag I then stuffed into my wetsuit. It was a calm, flat day and I paddled out past the jetty. Then I sat there for a while and thought about Dad.

My father called the ocean "the healer" and throughout my life, I heard him say "Gotta get into the healer." I gazed into the past and saw the royal blue whale-shaped kiddie pool he used as a boat to bob us up through the waves. I saw him catching sand sharks and giving them to me to scare the boys on the beach. I remembered him saying that visiting us in Ocean City and being in the sea every day "gave him another five years." That was 2009. Five years ago.

As I bobbed around far past the jetty, I sent out messages to him. Then I opened the baggie and tossed a few handfuls of petals out onto the water. The rest I placed in a pile on the board and let the water lap over the thin velvet bits and carry them away. Slowly they began to disperse. I didn't stay out too long because I wanted to take pictures of the petals on the water, so I paddled back, left my board on the shore, got my phone, and waded into the water. I wanted to send photos to my uncles, cousins, Paige and Mom. And I wanted to put them on Facebook. After a while I backed up onto the shore—eyes still fixed on the petals, as I knew they'd be gone soon. A graying, grizzled, long-haired surfer guy walked past me in the ankle-deep water.

"Did you do this?" he asked.

"Yeah," I said, for a quick moment concerned he might accuse me of ocean pollution.

"It's beautiful, man."

"Thanks." I said. "My dad died. It's for him."

"Beautiful. Great idea."

It was beautiful, but it wasn't as impressive an effect as I had hoped for, since they spread too quickly and you couldn't see the yellow ones in the water. I wanted to send photos to my family, but they wouldn't be able to tell what the petals were. Oh well. It was a private moment.

Then something astounding happened. I turned around to walk back to my chair, and all along the hard, wet sand for almost a block was a band of red, yellow and white petals, tracing the shape of the waves that had brought them ashore. It was spectral. It made me think of the sea change in Ariel's song in *The Tempest*.

> *Full fathom five thy father lies.*
> *Of his bones are coral made.*
> *Those are pearls that were his eyes.*
> *Nothing of him that doth fade*
> *But doth suffer a sea change*
> *Into something rich and strange.*
> *Sea nymphs hourly ring his knell.*
> (1.2.474-480)

I thought of a "sea change" as what happened to a person after a long period at sea. Since my father's death, this passage means much more. It suggests magic, that what's good and true about a person will be recycled into something new and precious once they're gone.

We had the last of my father's three funerals at the church of his boyhood on Father's Day weekend. Everything seemed to come together in the most providential way. My parents had met each other 55 years earlier at the stables of a mutual friend, who was now a minister. She agreed to do the service. The church welcomed us, parishioners they had never met before, and let us act like The Church of Our Savior was our church. As if, like Fortinbras says when he takes over the crown of Denmark at the end of the play, we had *some rights of memory* in that place. My uncles did have rights of memory there, but my sister and I did not. Once again, I stood in awe of the unsung work that goes on behind the scenes in the business of death. It felt like an incredible blessing to have the trinity of my father's home church, my heart and home religion, and a wise and loving eulogist who not only knew my father and his family, but also had her own acute understanding of the magic between love and loss.

The service was beautiful. The address perfectly captured Dad and how much he was loved. Paige and I sat together in the front center pew, Tom right behind me, reaching to hold my hand over my shoulder a few times, and Mom and Ray to his left, behind Paige. I'm sure both Paige and I cried the entire time, an experience so viscerally liberating I felt as if my body was going to melt and wash away. It was a strange sensation.

> *Oh that this too, too sullied flesh would melt*
> *Thaw and resolve itself into a dew!*
> (1.2.133-134)

In addition to the hymns we selected, we played two songs at the end as a sendoff. The first one was Jimmy Buffett's "The Captain and the Kid." The second was the Soggy Bottom Boys' version of "I'll Fly Away," during the middle of which Paige and I got up and left the building. The last verse of "The Captain and the Kid" was the perfect closing message and I cried so hard.

> *He died about a month ago, as winter filled the air*
> *And though I cried I was so proud, to love a man so rare.*
> *He's somewhere on the ocean now, the place he oughta be,*
> *One hand on the starboard rail he is waving back at me.*

I can't play those lines enough; they hit the exact right spot.

> *...I was so proud to love a man so rare.*
> *...he is waving back at me.*

By the time we got back to the house I must have been all cried out, because once the service was over, it was one of the best family reunions we ever had. It was the most perfectly warm, dry, clear mid-June day, and our backyard was green, expansive, and felt like a portal to heaven. Dad was there.

"Did your dad ever get to see this place?" my cousin Kelly's husband Kevin asked that evening as we sat playing cards on the porch.

"No, he didn't. The last time he was up here was that Easter weekend we all had," I said.

"When was that again?" Chris asked.

"That was 2012," I said. "Thank God we did that, huh?"

"Yes, that was great," said Kelly.

As much drama as there was dealing with Maureen and her problems after my dad died, and as much sadness as we had bidding goodbye to an era, all the phone calls, plans (even the misunderstandings and triangulations) were in a way wonderful, because they gave us cousins and our uncles something focused and energized to talk about. Planning the flights, coordinating airport pickups, managing meals and finances and getting in touch with extended family members I knew in name only. It felt good to have something to do, something concrete to talk about, a project to work on together. You don't want to look forward to the next death but dealing with death does bring people together. Everyone was there to say goodbye to my dad.

He had three funerals, two without a grave. If I want to visit my father's spirit, I'll go to the ocean. He's not in Costa Rica. He'll be wherever I think of him. *In my mind's eye, Horatio.* He's still in the house in Northfield; he still has his boat—whichever one, it doesn't matter. He still has the brown Raleigh three speed he fell off trying to copy me riding no-handed. I can see him riding that bike under the shady patch of Putting Green Avenue, to the left, just beyond our driveway. I can still tell him about my latest once-in-a-lifetime chance; he's still on the other end of the phone.

There's nothing either good or bad but thinking makes it so. The problem with having a good childhood is how much you miss it when it's gone. The problem with being so deeply, fully, accepted, loved, and cherished by a parent is how spoiled you get. And how much you ache for them when they're gone.

Don't say gone.

Maybe the clichés are true. Maybe the dead are never really gone. Maybe the reason Dad never talked about how I would manage to live without him was because he knew I would never have to. That he would always be with me. *Of course* I can still call him and hear his laugh as he tries to guess where in the world I am this time. *Of course* I can.

I can go through most of my days suspending belief, refusing to think, much less really believe, that he's dead. I mean, really, there's no point forcing the issue in my head, is there?

He's still on the other end of the line.

As long as I don't dial the number.

As long as I don't look too closely.

Or try to hug him.

Or try to prove to anyone he's there.

If I do, I'll be like Hamlet with Gertrude in the bedroom scene:

> *QUEEN: Alas, how is 't with you,*
> *That you do bend your eye on vacancy*
> *And with th' incorporal air do hold discourse?*
> *Whereon do you look?*
> *HAMLET: On him, on him!*
> *QUEEN: To whom do you speak this?*
> *HAMLET: Do you see nothing there?*
> *QUEEN: Nothing at all; yet all that is I see.*
> *HAMLET: Nor did you nothing hear?*
> *QUEEN: No, nothing but ourselves.*
> *HAMLET: Why, look you there, look how it steals away!*
> *My father, in his habit as he lived!*
> *Look where he goes even now out at the portal!*
> *QUEEN: This is the very coinage of your brain.*
> (3.4.133-157)

If I tell them I still see and hear my father, they'll just think I'm mad.

THANKS, AND THANKS, AND EVER THANKS

This book has taken years to bring to fruition, and I owe debts of gratitude to many people who have encouraged me along the way. First, Professor Elizabeth Vogel, at Arcadia University, who embraced the project as my thesis advisor, counselor, and fan; and second, Professors Richard Wertime and the late William Meiers, also from Arcadia. Each of these teachers made me a better writer by being wonderful teachers themselves.

By th' luckiest stars in heaven I was scooped up by my publishers Lisa Hagan and Beth Wareham at Lisa Hagan Books. Having two such fine professionals and human beings as my agent, editor, and champions from the beginning gave me confidence & perseverance. Beth Wareham read and improved every version of my manuscript: her editorial vision is that of a hawk and the shape of this book is as much hers as mine.

Great fortune gave me amazing students and colleagues at the Academy of the New Church, especially in the English Department. Those blessings were precipitated by the good fortune of landing in the classroom of the great James Shapiro at Columbia University, where I fell in love with Shakespeare; then by being hired by principal Margaret Gladish, and embraced as a teacher by the iconic Esther Yardumian-Smyth.

A thousand thanks go to Tom Brecht for making a place in our beautiful home for my family as we mourned, for giving me the space I needed to grieve and write, for being an early reader, a proponent of believing in yourself & your dream, a devoted partner, and a source of motivation.

Dues of gratitude to these compassionate friends and early readers: Anders Alfelt, Bethany Creed Asplundh, Betsy Asplundh, Jenn Asplundh, Susan Asplundh, Professor Suzanne Bernhardt, Donna Bostock, Karen Bussen, Christopher Cantley, Herbert L. Cantley, Kelly Cantley, Mark Carlson, Robin Childs, Mickey Dean, Ali Durand, Marion Fisher, Laura Gladish, Sarah Gladish, Deborah Grayson & Jonathan Russo, Carolyn Heilman, Karen Heilman, Leann Hill, Eileen Holland, LynnEllen King, Reverend Emily Jane Lemole, Brooklyn roommates Rachel Lindsay & Steph Rose, Tracy McNeil, writing buddy Michele Mitchell, London Shakespeare advisor Lara Muth, Laura Nash, Mary Odhner, Laura Orthwein, Kris Pitcairn, Martha Pitcairn, Jerry Pyle, Yvon Ros, Michelle Rose, Christine Roth, writing coach Victoria C. Rowan, Kira Schadegg, Gwenda Sheedy, Dalia Stoddard, Professor Aram Yardumian, and Esther Yardumian-Smyth.

Kingly thanks to Yvon Ros, for enthusiastically reading multiple versions and picking out errors; and to Ian Smedley for the painstaking precision of his proofreading and copyediting.

I'm doubled with thanks to Brett Traussi, who believed in me and my dream, and who with gentle kindness and genuine pleasure cheered me across the finish line multiple times.

Thanks to Maureen Cantley who ended up teaching me so much about love, and who made sure that a very good, kind, simple man felt deeply loved until the end.

In the end this is a love story, and I'm grateful to my Finkeldey, Cantley, and Ballard family members who have given me so much love and forgiveness throughout my life, especially my sister Paige Nicole Cantley, and my parents Emily & Ray Ballard.

About the Author

Erica W. Cantley has two degrees in Literature and Writing, and one in Culinary/Restaurant Management.

In addition to her careers in teaching and the restaurant business, she has worked as a bike tour guide, a private cook, tutor, menu translator, caterer, event planner, camp counselor, creative writing workshop leader, restaurant consultant, recipe tester, copywriter, founding editor of *The Gourmet Garage Gazette*, freelance writer for *The Beard House Magazine, Time Out New York, Food Arts, Restaurant Business, Chefs Magazine* and *The Philadelphia Inquirer.*

She managed restaurants in Atlantic City and Boston before moving to New York, where she worked her way up from reservationist to the first female maitre d' in Daniel Boulud's empire.

Cantley did her junior year abroad in Paris, working a part time job at the Ritz, and after graduation moved home to Pennsylvania to teach high school English at her alma mater, The Academy of the New Church, for sixteen years.

She continues to study and write about Shakespeare, and is involved in opening restaurants in New York City.

This is her first book.

22873603R00176